BOOKS BY JEFFREY MEYERS

Biography

A Fever at the Core: The Idealist in Politics
Married to Genius
Katherine Mansfield
The Enemy: A Biography of Wyndham Lewis
Hemingway
Manic Power: Robert Lowell and His Circle
D. H. Lawrence
Joseph Conrad
Edgar Allan Poe: His Life and Legacy
Scott Fitzgerald
Edmund Wilson
Robert Frost
Bogart: A Life in Hollywood
Gary Cooper: American Hero
Privileged Moments: Encounters with Writers
Wintry Conscience: A Biography of George Orwell
Inherited Risk: Errol and Sean Flynn in Hollywood and Vietnam
Somerset Maugham
Impressionist Quartet: The Intimate Genius of Manet and Morisot,
Degas and Cassatt
Modigliani
Samuel Johnson: The Struggle
The Genius and the Goddess: Arthur Miller and Marilyn Monroe
John Huston: Courage and Art

Criticism

Fiction and the Colonial Experience
The Wounded Spirit: T. E. Lawrence's Seven Pillars of Wisdom
A Reader's Guide to George Orwell
Painting and the Novel

Homosexuality and Literature
D. H. Lawrence and the Experience of Italy
Disease and the Novel
The Spirit of Biography
Hemingway: Life into Art
Orwell: Life and Art
Thomas Mann's Artist-Heroes

Bibliography
T. E. Lawrence: A Bibliography
Catalogue of the Library of the Late Siegfried Sassoon
George Orwell: An Annotated Bibliography of Criticism

Edited Collections
George Orwell: The Critical Heritage
Hemingway: The Critical Heritage
Robert Lowell: Interviews and Memoirs
The Sir Arthur Conan Doyle Reader
The W. Somerset Maugham Reader
Remembering Iris Murdoch: Letters and Interviews
The Mystery of the Real: Correspondence with Alex Colville

Edited Original Essays
Wyndham Lewis: A Revaluation
Wyndham Lewis by Roy Campbell
D. H. Lawrence and Tradition
The Legacy of D. H. Lawrence
The Craft of Literary Biography
The Biographer's Art
T. E. Lawrence: Soldier, Writer, Legend
Graham Greene: A Revaluation

RESURRECTIONS

RESURRECTIONS

authors, heroes—and a spy

JEFFREY MEYERS

University of Virginia Press

CHARLOTTESVILLE AND LONDON

University of Virginia Press

© 2018 by the Rector and Visitors of the University of Virginia

All rights reserved

Printed in the United States of America on acid-free paper

ISBN 978-0-8139-4168-4 (cloth)

ISBN 978-0-8139-4169-1 (ebook)

First published 2018

9 8 7 6 5 4 3 2 1

Library of Congress Cataloging-in-Publication Data is available for this title.

Cover art: Detail from *Resurrection of the Flesh,* Luca Signorelli, 1499–1502. (Art Collection 2/Alamy Stock Photo)

CONTENTS

PREFACE

As virtuous men pass mildly away
And whisper to their souls to go,
Memory wishes for a stay
To keep them for a time below.

The force of a gifted and imaginative personality is compelling and seductive, and writers are enchanters. Once under an author's spell, I wanted to learn every thing about his life. My biographical investigations into writers and artists led to the friendships that are the subject of this intellectual autobiography and personal memoir. I record what they looked like, how they lived and what they said. In our conversations and correspondence I was most curious about the relation between their lives and art, the public image and the real self. They provided many insights into their profession: how sensitive they were to criticism, how they advanced their careers and achieved fame, how feuds and quarrels started and ended, how reviews were written and prizes awarded, how they struggled financially and went on writing despite illnesses and mental problems, difficult marriages or agonizing love affairs. Each chapter of this living literary history—with firsthand knowledge and detailed descriptions of their life, character and opinions—contains an intimate portrait of the artist.

My search for an ideal father, desire to know distinguished scholars, writers and painters, to understand the power of knowledge and the source of art, led me to meet the nine English, American, Canadian and Australian authors described in Part I in roughly the order that I knew them. I'd graduated from college at twenty and taught at UCLA when I was twenty-four, so I was always the youngest among my classmates and colleagues, and searched for older men as father figures. I took college courses from some, sought out others as friends or informants, met them by chance or was introduced by friends. My extensive journeys took me from Berkeley to Spain, London, Los Angeles, Nova Scotia, Long Island, Cape Cod and Greece.

I was attracted to these extremely intelligent men and thought I could learn a great deal from them as I looked for intellectual and artistic guidance. I admired their work and wanted, if possible, to emulate their achievements. Ian Watt, Gerald Brenan, James Salter and Patrick Leigh Fermor were courageous war heroes who risked their lives and whose art was authenticated by action. They were ideal fathers, like the giant race before the Flood, who seem to be disappearing from the mechanized modern world. The men responded to my enthusiasm and shared my literary passions and taste for gossip. They were all lively speakers and, since I liked to talk to a man who liked to talk, I kept a careful account of our conversations. These authors taught me much more than I could learn in libraries and archives, and I was honored by the friendships that enriched my life and (perhaps) my character. We maintained a lively correspondence and, as John Donne wrote in "To Sir Henry Wotton," "More than kisses, letters mingle Soules, / For thus friends absent speake."

All these remarkable friends lived into their eighties and nineties and (except for Paul Theroux) have passed away. Apart from Gerald Brenan, born in the 1890s, these older writers were born between 1905 (the year before my father's birth) and 1929. As my friends died, their memories became more precious. I wanted to resurrect them and keep their memory alive. To paraphrase Erasmus writing to Thomas More, I found almost as much pleasure in thinking of them when we were apart as I did in their company when we were together.

The chapters in this book represent in miniature my career as a life-writer. My biographies have always been driven by fascination with the source of artistic creativity, with people who wrote or painted and with the worlds they inhabited. I established immediate rapport with my mentors, who recognized my potential and took a keen interest in a younger friend. Intensely curious about others, they offered advice and sympathy, encouragement and support. They had no need to swagger and treated me as an equal. I wanted to learn from these literary touchstones, earn their approval and match their quality of mind. Their engaging personalities, intelligence and wit, integrity and high standards, commitment to serious work and intellectual achievement all magically combined to create a noble example and an appealing way of life.

As a biographer I use every source I can find (but don't include all the information I discover): printed books, unpublished material in archives, school and university records, letters from correspondents and, most interesting, personal interviews with people who actually knew my subject—though I always have to be aware of self-serving gossip and unreliable rumor. Using my experience in detection and discovery to create these biographical portraits, I found the military records of Ian Watt and Basil Blackwood in the National Archives at Kew, outside London, as well as unpublished material in several university libraries. I received letters and conducted interviews about Derek Jackson and Nicola Chiaromonte. These chapters provide a valuable record for future biographies of James Salter, Paul Theroux and possibly Blackwood, Chiaromonte and Xan Fielding.

Ian Watt was my teacher at Berkeley. I discovered the records of his experience as a Japanese prisoner of war, which had formed his tough character, and explain how I later established a friendship with the adversary I'd disastrously clashed with in graduate school. His penetrating essays on his years as a POW distinguished between the historical facts and the myths created about the bridge on the River Kwai.

I met Gerald Brenan when I lived near him on the south coast of Spain. A member of the cadet branch of the Bloomsbury Group, he was the first author I ever knew. A rare intellectual on the Costa del Sol, he lent me books and gave me vital encouragement when I started out as a writer. An exemplary man, he led an enviable life, had great friends and never was confined to a regular job.

The crusading journalist and author Phillip Knightley, whom I met in an extraordinary way, also gave me considerable help when I began as a writer and became a loyal tennis partner and lifelong companion. I witnessed his serious marriage problems, and tried to help when he became severely ill and was bedridden for a year.

The learned Donald Greene, the leading eighteenth-century scholar of my time, had a fierce reputation and suffered a series of dramatic heart attacks. An ideal mentor and colleague, he praised my industry and was pleased by my success. He spent his entire productive career preparing to write the life of Samuel Johnson. After his death and with the help of his papers, I wrote that biography.

The charming and hapless Hugh Gordon Porteus was a friend of Wyndham Lewis, Ezra Pound and T. S. Eliot. I saw him frequently when I spent 1978–79 in London. A minor figure in English literary life, he was delighted to be rediscovered by me. He did not get the reputation he deserved because he scattered his talents too widely and never collected his articles or wrote his memoir.

I visited Nova Scotia three times to see Alex Colville, the impressive Canadian realist painter. I saw his studio and his beach house, explored his artistic milieu and discussed the meaning of his work. On a perfect afternoon in his garden, eating lobster and drinking Pouilly-Fuissé, I experienced a rare moment of perfect bliss. In 2016 I published a volume of our correspondence, with my essays about him.

James Salter, fighter pilot and underrated novelist, I visited twice in Bridgehampton, Long Island, and had many lively letters from him. Writing is a lonely profession and we were pleased to strike sparks. In the last decade of his life he had a resurgence of literary power, published widely in America and France, and experienced a gratifying rise in reputation.

Vidia Naipaul introduced me to Paul Theroux, who remains my friend to this day. We'd both quarreled with Vidia, whose provocative antics obsessed us, and were always eager for scandalous news about him. Hardworking and productive writers, we liked each other's work and thrived on stimulating literary talk. I reviewed many of his books and he provided generous blurbs for mine.

Patrick Leigh Fermor—traveler, author and hero—is the transitional figure between the two parts of this book. I spent a long afternoon and evening with him at his home in Greece, and describe how he'd captured a German general when fighting among the guerrillas in wartime Crete. He lived a free life, wrote well and charmed everyone. After his death there was a resurgence of interest in his achievements and work.

I had arranged Marshall McLuhan's notes on Wyndham Lewis for his last published essay, and was later pleased when Donald Greene asked me to revise his essays. I dedicated my books, in homage, to Donald Greene, James Salter and Paul Theroux. As I look up from reading in my living room, my memories are aroused by a portrait of Gerald Brenan and two pictures by Alex Colville.

In retrospect I see that all my friendships involved subtle tests. Could I redeem myself and gain Watt's friendship? Could I identify Carrington's painting in Brenan's house? Could I recognize Knightley on the tennis court in Spain? Could I really, as Greene asked, have read *all* of Johnson's works? Could I convince Porteus that I'd be sympathetic to Wyndham Lewis? Could I write a perceptive book about Colville? Could I match Salter's expectations as a weekend guest? Could I accept Theroux on his own terms? Could I recognize Fermor's mistress and illegitimate son?

The compressed biographies in Part II of this book describe a spy and four more war heroes I wish I had met: Basil Blackwood, Derek Jackson, Nicola Chiaromonte and Xan Fielding. In the course of my reading, their fascinating characters, connected to other writers who interested me, caught my attention. I wanted to interpret their lives and to penetrate the enigmatic aura that surrounded them. Anthony Blunt appealed to my interest in espionage and art; Basil Blackwood was the father of Caroline Blackwood, Robert Lowell's third wife; Derek Jackson, a friend of Patrick Leigh Fermor, married the former wife of Cyril Connolly; Nicola Chiaromonte was a close friend of Mary McCarthy, the third wife of Edmund Wilson; Xan Fielding, the wartime colleague and lifelong friend of Fermor, edited Gerald Brenan's letters.

Anthony Blunt was an eminent art historian and treacherous Russian spy whose scholarly writing—a covert intellectual autobiography—reflected his elusive and duplicitous character. He wrote about kindred artists who echoed his split personality and distorted the facts to fit his dubious thesis. I couldn't help admiring his ability to lead two parallel but contradictory lives and to deceive his closest friends for so many years.

I discovered how Basil Blackwood—handsome aristocrat, grandson of the viceroy of India and highly regarded politician— had died mysteriously while fighting the Japanese during the Burma campaign in 1945. He was killed, tragically and perhaps unnecessarily, by a shrapnel wound in the chest while broadcasting British propaganda on the front lines.

Derek Jackson, a weird genius, had an extraordinary array of talents: Oxford physicist and steeplechase jockey, war hero and inventor, homosexual who had six wives. Serial marriages, for the brilliant and courageous man, were merely short-lived experiments. His homosexuality, I suggest, was an attempt to reunite with his tragically deceased identical twin brother.

Nicola Chiaromonte, an anti-Fascist Italian émigré, was a close friend of Dwight Macdonald and influential member of the *Partisan Review* circle. His profound influence on the New York intellectuals was based on his noble idealism and capacity for friendship, his tragic exile and perilous escapes from death. His love affair with a beautiful young woman nearly wrecked his marriage, but he finally decided to remain with his wife.

Xan Fielding, a Byronic hero and comrade in arms of Patrick Leigh Fermor, fought alongside him in Crete and later became an accomplished translator and editor, travel writer and biographer. His Indian ancestry helps explain his elusive character. Like Gerald Brenan and Fermor, he led an adventurous life and exemplified the delirium of the brave, lived in exotic locales and remained a romantic adventurer.

These remarkable men are linked in subtle and unexpected ways. Patrick Leigh Fermor appears in the chapter on Derek Jackson, Gerald Brenan and Fermor in the chapter on Xan Fielding. Jackson's daughter was a nude model for Caroline Blackwood's first husband, Lucian Freud. My last four subjects are not well known and deserve to be resurrected. By portraying their impressive achievements, social influence and charismatic characters, I have drawn them out of the shadows and into the spotlight.

PART I

1

Ian Watt

(1917–1999)

Prisoner

The sinking by Japanese airplanes of the British battleships *Prince of Wales* and *Repulse* north of Singapore in December 1941, and the devastating British defeat in the Battle of Singapore when the Japanese marched through the jungles of Malaya and attacked the vulnerable Allied army from the rear, destroyed the prestige of the British Empire and the myth of white invincibility. Ian Watt had fought in Malaya, and in Singapore on February 15, 1942, was severely wounded by shrapnel in his back. After the war the doctors thought it was too dangerous to remove the shrapnel, which was close to his spinal cord, and the metal remained in his body. Watt was listed as "missing, presumed killed in action." On July 22, 1942, his mother received an official letter saying he was dead. But he was actually captured, not killed. Five months later the War Office explained the mistake: "It was not until the 17th December 1942 that official information was received from Tokio through the International Red Cross Committee at Geneva stating that he was a prisoner of war, and a telegram was sent to his mother." Later on, Watt became an eminent English professor and author of the influential *Rise of the Novel* (1957) and *Conrad in the Nineteenth Century* (1979).

Recently discovered documents in the National Archives in

Kew, outside London—a Japanese index card with some *kanji* characters and a liberation questionnaire that Watt filled out in the fall of 1945 (WO345/54 and WO344/407/2)—supplemented by new material from his son and daughter, contain vivid biographical details and military information about his three years as a prisoner of war. Though an officer, Watt was forced to work with his men on the infamous River Kwai railroad, eighty miles west of Bangkok, that the Japanese were building to send soldiers and supplies from Rangoon to Thailand. In various prison camps he faced fear and danger, endured starvation and beatings, disease and death marches, and witnessed killings of other prisoners. These documents also describe his attempts to escape (a duty in wartime), his acts of sabotage and the personal courage of his comrades.

For twenty-five years, from 1956 to 1981, Watt continued to think about his experiences as a prisoner of war, and published eight perceptive and poignant essays on the subject: five of them in literary journals, three shorter versions in national magazines. His shifting point of view and varied emphasis show his humane struggle to describe his captivity and come to psychological terms with its devastating effects. He also wanted to distinguish between historical fact and the myth that grew up around the bridge over the Kwai.

Ian Pierre Watt was born in Windermere, Westmoreland, in the lake country of England. He went to the Dover County School for Boys, where his Scottish father was headmaster. In 1938, during the heyday of F. R. Leavis and *Scrutiny,* he earned a First in English at St. John's College, Cambridge. After the war Watt studied at UCLA and Harvard on a Commonwealth Fellowship, and taught for several years at Cambridge. He never got a Ph.D. (who would examine him?) and didn't need one. He then became a distinguished professor at Berkeley (1952–62), Norwich (1962–64) and Stanford (1964–99). In the spring of 1961, as a Berkeley graduate student, I took his seminar on Yeats and Joyce, and clashed disastrously with him. Three decades later, when I'd moved back to Berkeley and he'd moved to Stanford, I met him—now silver-haired—at the home of our mutual friend, the Dostoyevsky biographer Joseph Frank, and finally became reconciled with him.

Watt joined the British army as a private in September 1939 and appeared in the Supplement of the official *London Gazette,* May 10, 1940. On May 28, 1940, he completed the course in an Officer Cadet Training Unit (Artists Rifles). His commander said his military conduct was "very good," called him "able and hardworking" and recommended that he become an officer. His Japanese index card lists his occupation as Student, notes his Cambridge B.A. and gives his mother's address in Swansea, Wales. Her names, Renée Jeanne Gabrielle Watt, reflect his Huguenot ancestors and French middle name. (There's no mention of his father, who died before his wife.) Watt was an infantry lieutenant in the 5th Battalion of the Suffolk Regiment, from the county adjacent to Cambridge, and served from 1939 to 1946.

Watt's confidential liberation questionnaire lists his home address as "Welford," River, Dover, Kent. By contrast, there were eight different prisoner-of-war camps, beginning with the notorious Changi prison in Singapore and others scattered along the railway tracks, from February 1942 to his release in August 1945. That month the American atomic bombs on Hiroshima and Nagasaki ended the war with Japan and saved the lives of thousands of Allied prisoners.

The first substantial question asked Watt to "Give full description and approximate date of each attempt you made to escape, showing how you left the camp, and from which camp each attempt was made." Watt replied in his tiny, difficult-to-read handwriting: "At Chung Kai in July–August [1942] I was in contact with Thai & Chinese bandits or guerrillas; they were to have taken us by barge to Chieng Mai [Thailand] and then to Yunnan [China] on foot for payment there. Escape was planned for full moon in

September; unfortunately I had to leave the camp to go up country; and others were unable to resume the contact." He seems to have recovered from his wound and stoically described himself as "Fairly fit; but a 3 day march in Sept made me go down with Beri Beri."

Watt wrote that Lieutenant Bangs and Lieutenant Ross were also involved in the preparations to escape, but their plans were ruined by disease and sudden transfers. Nicely balancing "down" and "up," he replied: "Lt. Bangs went down in August with severe malaria which renewed his hepataic paralysis; Lt. Ross went up country." Asked about other men who were trying to get out, he said their efforts inevitably ended in capture and death: "I have no direct knowledge of other attempts to escape, although I collected what information I could at Changi, reference the attempt to get General K. E. [surname missing] away by boat, and other abortive and fatal attempts in Thailand." Watt added that essential supplies were theoretically obtainable but impossible to get: "I was aware that money, food, medicine would be made available officially if I could produce a reasonable plan."

The last section of the questionnaire dealt with sabotage. When asked if he was able, as a prisoner, to undermine the Japanese war effort while forced to work for the enemy, he said: "Like all prisoners in Singapore & Thailand I succeeded in small kinds of sabotage—puncturing oil drums we loaded onto trains at Singapore, breaking and losing as many tools as possible, instigating & concealing unsound work on the railway embankment." Watt had "nothing special to report" about courageous acts performed by Allied personnel. But he did comment on the disastrous event at the prison barracks in Singapore in August–September 1942. After the Japanese had recaptured four escaped POWs and the other prisoners refused to sign a promise not to escape, they forced 17,000 men to crowd into a small barracks square with little water and no sanitation, and to witness the execution of their comrades.

Their commanding officer finally gave in to the Japanese demand when, after five days, the men began to die of dysentery: "I consider that Lt.-Col. Holmes—during the Selarang episode; many doctors, notably Captain Churchill IMS [Indian Medical Service]; and many interpreters, notably Captain Draner, showed great courage in resisting the Japanese."

Finally, when asked if he had any additional information, he became rather exasperated by questions that seemed to show a limited understanding of how the prisoners had been fatally weakened and emaciated by the inhuman conditions in the camps. He described the overwhelming problems they faced in trying to escape, including being immediately recognized as Europeans by hostile and bounty-hunting Thais: "owing to the distances involved, the colour difficulty, the language difficulty, & low conditions of help, the advice of my own Lt.-Col., Lt.-Colonel Baker 5 Suffolks, escape, except under very special circumstances, was impossible. This was confirmed by the fate of the few attempts made." Hundreds of prisoners tried to escape, but no one ever succeeded. Watt's military records give a vivid, immediate description of the horrific conditions in the POW camps. Unlike civilian prisoners, POWs had not committed a crime, were starved and beaten, and had an interminable sentence.

John Coast's *Railroad of Death* (1946), slightly mistaking Watt's surname, gave a vivid portrait of his brilliant mind and tough character: "Ian White was one of the brightest young men Cambridge had seen for some years. From the University he had won a double scholarship, one in England and one at the Sorbonne. He was an example of a very good brain in an equally robust body; there was little frail about him." Coast added that to give young officers something to do in prison, headquarters absurdly ordered "three-quarters of an hour's drill before breakfast every day for a fortnight! The troops were as amused and incredulous as we were indignant, and Ian White, Henry and I protested." Watt's son George confirmed that his father was unusually hostile to methodical marching: "The only thing I know about his military service prior to Singapore is a very funny story he told about getting browbeaten and reprimanded by a drill sergeant during some kind of formal military parade."

After the war Watt received pathetically small payments for his wound and his enslavement on the Kwai. The minister of pensions told him that "the Mortar Wound Back on which your claim is based is attributable to war service. The degree of disablement is assessed at less than 20 per cent, and you are accordingly eligible for a gratuity of £150 in final settlement of your case." Nine years later, in February 1955, the Ministry of Pensions paid £46 for his "share of the money allocated to the United Kingdom for the sale of the Burma-Siam Railway." The three-and-a-half years torn out of his life in his late twenties became the subject of Watt's lifelong obsession: his experience on the River Kwai.

Writer

Watt's first essay, "The Liberty of the Prison: Reflections of a Prisoner of War" (*Yale Review*, 1956), was written ten years after he was liberated. It explains how, by retaining their intellectual and spiritual freedom while in captivity, many prisoners managed to survive. In what he called "one of the least-known tragedies of the Second World War," 80,000 men were captured after the fall of Singapore and one-quarter of them died. The prisoners were cut off from all news of the war because the Japanese forbade the Red Cross authorities to visit the camps and they were not allowed to write letters home. They did not know that the tide of war had turned after the victories at Stalingrad and Alamein in the winter of 1942.

Watt describes the horrors of the prisons, which were much worse than the Nazi POW camps. The Japanese, taught that death was preferable to shameful surrender, despised the prisoners and treated them with extreme brutality. Food was meager and the men were starved. Watt himself contracted malaria and beriberi, and eventually lost sixty pounds. Many men suffered from pellagra and flesh-eating ulcers that sometimes forced doctors to amputate their legs. "Sick men," he observes, "delirious with fever, or with jungle ulcers a foot long, would be forced to work till they dropped dead." The "Railroad of Death" cost "a human life for every sleeper laid." As Watt indicated on his questionnaire, escape, though often tried, was impossible: "A thousand miles of mountain and jungle lay between us and the nearest Allied lines in Burma and China." Those who were hospitalized, avoided work and managed to survive felt guilty.

But the prisoners could, at least, take some self-protective measures. Watt explains how they adjusted to the brutal conditions, created an alternate life within the prison and "were, in a queer sort of way, rather happy." They regarded the Japanese as subhuman, "as malign and unpredictable lunatics." They improved their living quarters and grew vegetables, sang songs and told stories, learned languages and listened to educational lectures, and even improvised stage shows that alleviated the intolerable boredom and engendered solidarity. According to one exemplary story, not mentioned in the essay, Watt used pages from Dante's *Divina Commedia* for cigarette papers and memorized each one in Italian before smoking it.

The prisoners' imagination exaggerated the comparative richness of their former lives, and when they finally came home they found ordinary life insupportable. After Watt returned to England in September 1945, he spent most of his time with friends who'd also been prisoners—the only ones who truly understood what he'd suffered. He even had, strangely enough, "a powerful nostalgia for the days when we had not been free" and felt that "being a prisoner in itself had its attractions, because it makes life simpler."

This confirmed Nietzsche's aphorism in *Beyond Good and Evil:* "What does not destroy us makes us stronger." But Watt, trying to be optimistic, does not mention all the darker aspects of his experience. The soldiers' survival, a primitive Darwinian struggle, was not achieved through esprit de corps or liberty of the prison, but on physical courage and psychological strength, on minimal food and medical treatment, on ruthless egoism and good luck.

Between Watt's first and second essay, "Bridges over the Kwai" (*Partisan Review,* 1959), David Lean's brilliant film *The Bridge on the River Kwai* (1957) had appeared to worldwide acclaim. It was based on Pierre Boulle's best-selling French novel *The Bridge over the River Kwai* (1952). Boulle had been a rubber planter in Malaya, a Free French fighter and a POW for two years in Indochina, but he had no direct experience with the railway on or over the River Kwai. Watt knew perfectly well that the film version had to radically change the story to make it more dramatically effective and commercially successful. But his essay on both "Bridges" analyzed the glaring departures in the novel and film from the grim facts of his prison experience.

In the novel, Watt writes, the British Colonel Nicholson builds a symbol of permanence amid the transience of human life, "an incomparably better bridge than the one the Japanese had begun, and on a much more suitable site, even though it would obviously help the enemy's army on the Burma front." In reality, "Colonel T____" (Philip Toosey) was nominally in charge of the British slave-workers. But the Japanese—as their impressive victory in Singapore proved—were perfectly capable of building the bridge and finishing the "three hundred miles of railway in less than a year, over a route which a previous survey by Western engineers had pronounced insuperably difficult." Boulle's novel concludes when Colonel Nicholson, ignoring the advice of the young explosives expert, Lieutenant Joyce, "sabotaged the saboteurs and thus caused both sides [including himself] to be blown up by the mortar shells of Major Warden, their comrade in arms." In the novel, the bridge remains standing. Boulle's theme was "the ridiculous disparity between the West's rational technology and its self-destroying applications."

The film, which inevitably sentimentalized and romanticized the experience, was an even greater departure from reality and from the peculiar horrors of life on the railway. Boulle got screen credit, but Lean wrote most of the script. It was filmed in Ceylon, where the landscape is more lush and tropical than around the River Kwai. The prisoners, wearing boots instead of rough wooden clogs, march into the camp whistling with unbroken spirit. Warden (Jack Hawkins), supposed to be a professor of oriental languages at Cambridge, points to a map of Thailand and calls it Burma. The dashing American hero (William Holden), who does not appear in the novel, has a girlfriend and is miraculously rescued during his daring expedition. The Japanese Colonel Saito is transformed "from the incompetent and sadistic drunkard of the novel to the movie's frustrated artist with an unhappy childhood." Most strikingly, to provide a dramatic climax and satisfy the expectations of the audience, a real bridge that cost $250,000 to build is blown up with a real train crossing it. In the film, Watt concludes, no one "has to pay the full price for cruelty or selfishness or folly." But Watt does not compare the absurdity of the filmmakers "building a fine bridge just to blow it up" and the absurdity of the British soldiers building a fine bridge to help the enemy.

Ten years later, in "Reunion on the Kwai" (*Southern Review*, 1969), Watt recalls his return to the Kwai in 1966 as he tears off the scabs of memory to see if his wounds have healed. He describes the appealing landscape seen from the plane to Bangkok and from the taxi that carries him up-country, stirring up old memories. He visits the war graves of the seven thousand men who'd been buried in rice sacks in the nearby village; the river and bridge that have become tourist sites; and his old Thai friends who'd fed the prisoners in the joyous days after their release. At a companionable but rather awkward dinner, he exchanges gifts, catches up with the news and discusses Thailand's precarious alliance with America during the Vietnam War. This nostalgic account, partly a travel essay, is a rather sad attempt to connect to his old life, a *recherche du temps perdu* that brings both relief and pain. His son George, moving to Thailand a generation later, became a specialist in tropical medicine and practices in Bangkok.

"'The Bridge over the River Kwai' as Myth" (*Berkshire Review*, 1971), which repeats parts of Watt's earlier essays, anticipates the subject of his third book: *Myths of Modern Individualism: Faust, Don Quixote, Don Juan, Robinson Crusoe* (1996). As in his second essay, he contrasts the reality with the novel and the film, and explains how the myth came into being. His theme is how Boulle and Lean "combined to create a world-wide myth, and how that myth is largely the result of those very psychological and political delusions [about European superiority] which the builders of the real bridge had been forced to put aside."

Watt gives a precise account of the daily routine in the camps when they began to work on the Kwai bridge in November 1942: "up at dawn; tea and rice for breakfast; and then on parade for the day's work. We might wait anything from ten minutes to half an hour for the Korean guards [brutalized by and even crueler than the Japanese] to count the whole parade and split it up into work groups. Then we marched to a small bamboo shed where the picks, shovels and so on were kept." The prisoners worked from twelve to fifteen hours a day, and those who could not fulfill their daily quota were severely beaten. Colonel Toosey, whom Watt now identifies by name and greatly admires, first awed the Japanese "with an impressive display of military swagger; and then proceeded to charm them with his apparently immovable assumption that no serious difficulty could arise between honorable soldiers whose only thought was to do the right thing."

The myth began when Boulle "invented the Allied commandos who were sent to blow up the bridge with the same patient technological expertness as had been used by their former comrades in arms who had built it." The bridge was actually destroyed in the summer of 1944 by American bombers, which also killed quite a few nearby prisoners. In this essay Watt expands his answer on the questionnaire by stating that the "sabotage games weren't really very significant; but they expressed a collective need to pretend we were still fighting the enemy." Watt is particularly irritated by Boulle's assumption that "Colonel Nicholson could plausibly get away with his love affair for a Japanese bridge."

After the film was released, the novel became a tremendous success. It was translated into more than twenty languages, sold millions of copies and firmly established the myth, which "seemed to the survivors a gross insult on their intelligence." In the film beautiful maidens were all too eager to help the commandos, and there was no hint of the terrible poverty and disease suffered by the jungle villagers who lived along the river. Both the novel and film reasserted the myth of white superiority, fatally undermined but not entirely destroyed by the defeat of the British in Singapore, the French in postwar Indochina and, in the near future, the Americans in Vietnam. Watt notes that as a myth takes hold, people are persuaded by what they want to believe rather than by what they know to be true.

Watt's fifth major essay, "Humanities on the River Kwai," originated as a public lecture in 1981, after the end of the Vietnam War, and appeared posthumously in Watt's memorial volume, a special issue of the *Stanford Humanities Review* (2000). Recapitulating, sometimes verbatim, his previous essays in a high-minded context, he says he will describe "how the prisoners' lives showed the power of humanistic concerns; and . . . attempt to apply a humanistic approach to what actually happened, and to how it illuminates the issues raised by the novel and the movie."

This essay is enhanced by the drawings of his fellow prisoner Ronald Searle, and by letters to Watt from Pierre Boulle and Colonel Toosey. Boulle wrote that his book was "pure fiction," that "I picked up the name of Kwai on an atlas when I was looking out for a suitable place to locate the story I imagined." Watt notes that Boulle "did in fact intend his novel to raise the issue of collaboration, but not in terms which apply to the bridge or the Japanese.... His Colonel Nicholson was based on two French colonels he had known in Indochina." Watt sharply adds that Boulle made Nicholson "conform to the French stereotype of the English character: an amiable fellow in his way, but egocentric; admirable, but ridiculous; intelligent, but not really grown-up."

The real Colonel Toosey told Watt: "You do describe, as far as I am concerned, exactly what I was trying to do. To put it in other words—which I do not want you to repeat to anyone—I felt I had a mission not only to save as many lives as possible but also to maintain human dignity in those ghastly circumstances, and it is nice to know that at any rate you feel I had a measure of success." The real issue facing Toosey, as all the prisoners knew, was not whether the bridge would be built, but how many prisoners would break down, be beaten and die.

The blacklisted screenwriter Michael Wilson was recruited to deal with the problem of forced collaboration—the prisoners' conflict between duty and workmanship—and to redeem Colonel Nicholson (Alec Guinness) from the accusations of madness and treason. In Wilson's effective but unhistorical compromise, Watt states, "Nicholson both accidentally caused the death of the commandos and then, when he'd discovered what was really going on, blew up the bridge with his own hand as his last act." Watt finally fulfills his own moral imperative by replacing the myth with historical truth and expresses the humanistic theme of all five essays: "The need to record and testify is surely an assertion of the individual's sense that his memory of the past, his historical experience, is an essential part of his sense of self."

Teacher and Friend

I was unaware of Watt's imprisonment when I first met him in Berkeley. Tough and handsome, with a commanding presence and a strange inward gasping laugh, he moved quickly and spoke rapidly. At Cambridge, he'd known E. M. Forster, who liked to cultivate good-looking young men. Still bitter about his wartime imprisonment, he threw away all Japanese applications for graduate school and faculty posts. The Victorian scholar Masao Miyoshi could never have secured a job at Berkeley if Watt had remained there. Fierce and feared, he treated students as if they were in his platoon and took pleasure in ordering them to do petty tasks and erase the blackboard. As he wrote in his unpublished lecture "The Wisdom of Shakespeare," "It's difficult to like someone who runs everything very much as the practised autocrat."

I was twenty-one and had just finished a year of Harvard Law School when I took Watt's Yeats-Joyce seminar. I was then cheeky enough to challenge his ex cathedra pronouncements and to express my own, perhaps naive and ill-informed, opinions. He resented my refusal to defer to his authority when he discussed the crucial questions of *Ulysses:* What is it that all men want? Did Molly Bloom have many lovers before her lusty encounter with Blazes Boylan? Will Molly seduce the young Stephen Dedalus or will Leopold Bloom reassert his marital rights and resume sexual relations with her? I got a poor grade in the course, and learned from Watt's secretary, my girlfriend's close friend, that he'd rejected my application for a teaching assistantship, which came with a vitally needed tuition waiver. But I found other work as a high school tutor and night-school teacher, and since I could take more than two courses each term I moved through graduate school faster than most other students.

Watt left Berkeley to establish an English department at the new University of East Anglia in Norwich, England. But when he returned to America the Berkeley faculty rejected their abrasive and rebarbative former colleague, and he taught instead at Stanford. Though I disliked his imperious attitude, I admired his work and was eager to win his respect. The first step in my redemption occurred when my life of Katherine Mansfield and his book on Conrad were both reviewed on the front page of the *New York Times Book Review* on March 9, 1980. Watt grudgingly indicated that I wasn't quite as dim as I'd seemed to be.

During spring vacation in 1987, when I was writing a biography of Joseph Conrad and wanted to discuss my ideas with a cadre of experts, Thomas Moser kindly arranged an impressive gathering at the Stanford faculty club with himself, Watt, Albert Guerard and Donald Davie. Watt also gave me a copy of his article on the dazzling Jane Anderson, Conrad's mistress, before he published it in *Conradiana* in the spring of 1991. After my Conrad book appeared and I sought his opinion, he generously wrote to me on August 26, 1991: "It is, like everything of yours I've read, very readable; and in the case of Conrad I was fairly hooked most of the time to see your version. . . . It's a book to read; and I expect it will be." Moser later astonished me by writing that "Ian considered you to be among the favored few 'good' literary critics."

When I left academic life and moved back to Berkeley as a full-time writer in 1992, I had congenial meetings with Ian at Joe Frank's house and I was greatly pleased that we'd become, if not equals, at least friends. Ian then was, as he said in his *Southern Review* essay, "a man with rather a bad temper, but who could sometimes be very jolly." His psychological scars were greater than the physical wounds from his war experience. As he observed in "The Wisdom of Shakespeare," "Having known real chaos in the social order, at the fall of Singapore, I recognise the horror of chaos more than [most people]." After his stroke and dementia in the late 1990s the once-strong man and survivor was confined to a wheelchair. Still haunted by his traumatic memories, he thought—by a cruel twist of fate—that his nursing home had become a Japanese prison-camp. His wife Ruth wrote me, "Some days are worse than others and, as you can imagine, it is terribly, unbearably sad."

2

Gerald Brenan

(1894–1987)

Literary pilgrims traveling in Spain forty years ago were drawn to the two distinguished expatriates who shone like beacons at opposite ends of the peninsula. The curly-haired, broken-nosed, cloaked and Córdoba-hatted Robert Graves still granted audiences in the Majorcan village of Deyá. But he demanded adoration, was magisterial and remote, arrogant and austere. When I suggested that his poem "Children of Darkness" had been triggered by T. E. Lawrence's perverse idea that children are responsible for their own conception by inspiring lust in their parents, he vehemently rejected my idea (later substantiated by his unpublished letter that a collector sent to me). Forgetting that as a young man he had once been Lawrence's faithful disciple, he declared: "*I* was never influenced by anyone. I always influenced *other* writers."

The more friendly and forthcoming Gerald Brenan, living amid the fragrance of olive oil, leather and dust in Andalucía, gave much better value. Brenan's books—along with Hemingway's—had aroused my interest in Spain and persuaded me to live and write in that country. Brenan first went there in 1919 to explore the place and to educate himself. He had spent most of his adult life there, and his best books evolved from his personal experience in Spain: *South from Granada,* about his lonely years in the remote mountain fastness of Yegen; *The Literature of the Spanish People,* an overenthusiastic yet authoritative literary survey; *The Spanish Labyrinth,* still one of the most perceptive and reliable eyewitness histories of the Civil War; and *The Face of Spain,* recounting his three-month tour after the war and including an influential chapter on the death of Lorca. Universally regarded as the English expert on the history and culture of Spain, Gerald was the only man I knew who, as an author, was actually doing what I most wanted to do. He had won a Military Cross on the western front in the Great War, had traveled on foot throughout the peninsula and read widely in world literature. Clearly, there was a great deal to learn from him.

I had earned a doctorate at Berkeley, taught in universities in America and Japan, traveled widely and published a number of scholarly articles. I had written my first three books, but none of them had yet appeared in print. My English wife and I had just completed a five-month journey from Frankfurt, through the wilds of eastern Anatolia, to Isfahan and Shiraz, near the Persian Gulf, then back through Europe to England and down to southern Spain. When we arrived in Benalmádena, a village in the hills, twenty miles west of Málaga, we found it decorated with flags and flowers for the procession of images—carried by the men on a huge palanquin—to celebrate All Saints' Day.

The violent contrasts of the Andalucían landscape reminded me of the wilder parts of the American West. The steep road curved up from the sea to the village, through the brown parched hills, creased at the top and gouged down the sides where the sparse rains flowed. Mule tracks wound past the crooked trunks of olive trees, the tops of their flickering silver-green leaves grayed with the dust of the road. The aroma of mint and thyme spiked the air, and mingled with the smells of goats and dried earth. Water splashed through the irrigation ditches to the cultivated terraces whose foundations went back to the Moors. The view from the village, cleared by a fresh breeze blowing in from the coast, revealed the white peaks of the Sierra Nevada rising behind Málaga to the east, and Gibraltar looming up at the Pillars of Hercules to the west. Sometimes, after a violent storm, the coastal range of the Atlas Mountains shimmered across the Mediterranean from Morocco.

I knew Gerald lived nearby but, after many inquiries, was unable to find him. So I wrote to his publisher in London, and in January 1972 he sent us an invitation to tea with directions to his house. When we first met I was thirty-two and he was seventy-seven, but his warmth and responsiveness enabled us to bridge that considerable gap. His late wife, Gamel Woolsey, had come from South Carolina and Gerald (unlike Robert Graves) was well disposed to Americans and respected university professors.

Gerald lived at Cañada de las Palomas ("the path of the doves"), in Alhaurín el Grande, about half an hour inland from the coast. This village lacked the charm and beauty of Benalmádena, had no view of the sea and was dreary in winter. But for Gerald it had the considerable advantage of being untouched by the hideous hotels and apartment blocks that contaminated the coast. It afforded the remoteness and privacy that allowed him to concentrate on his work.

The two-story, whitewashed, red-tile-roofed house—isolated up a steep dirt track—was large and well situated. But, like most Spanish houses, it was bare, cold and uncomfortable, and sudden drafts rustled the thin rugs on the stone floor. As soon as I entered and shook his soft parchment hand, he asked if I recognized a painting hanging on the wall. I could see it was a landscape by his old love Dora Carrington, and this persuaded him that I was worthy of serious conversation. A thin, wiry, remarkably lively man, Gerald was bald, white-haired and pink-skinned. He had a round face, fleshy protruding ears (reddened by the living room fire) and a long upper lip. He dabbed at his thin mouth with a colored handkerchief as saliva slid from its sides. He wore rubber-soled canvas shoes, and his crumpled clothes were spattered with cigarette ash.

A portrait I commissioned by Concha Barreto depicted a three-quarter view of Gerald—wearing heavy glasses, an open-collared white shirt, a grey sleeveless sweater and blue trousers—with an oversized bald dome and a familiar cigarette in his huge right hand. He's standing on the rust-colored tiles of a patio and leaning on a white cinderblock wall, which supports a black cat and is thickly covered with creeping vines and red flowers. The background is a characteristic Andalucían landscape: a blue, slightly clouded sky, whitewashed farmhouses, gentle green hills crossed by narrow mule tracks, groves of olive trees and fields of richly colored flowers. The atmosphere of the painting, like Gerald himself, is calm and contemplative.

As we talked, the intellectually curious and energetic Gerald would suddenly spring out of his hard chair and dash upstairs, two steps at a time, to find a quotation or a reference in a book. He had an excellent English-language library, and would both lend books that I asked for and press others upon me. I eagerly accepted them. Serious reading matter was scarce and I also wanted a reason to keep in touch. Intellectuals were thin on the ground on the Costa del Sol, and life in his peasant village could be quite boring. So he was pleased, I think, to meet someone new who was keen to discuss writers and books. He questioned me closely about my life, education and teaching, my recent travels and knowledge of Spain. Sweet-tempered, enthusiastic and kind, he read what I had written on Conrad, Kipling, Forster, T. E. Lawrence and Orwell, and gave me encouragement and advice.

He deeply regretted, for example, that he had signed away for a flat sum the rights to his early works, and received nothing at all when he was "rediscovered" and reprinted during the Bloomsbury revival. He warned me never to sell my works outright and to have faith in the future of my (yet unpublished) books. He laughed easily, and had no self-importance. He had just been invited to visit the estate of a duke in Granada, but mentioned it in the most casual way. He praised the works of his late wife, but deprecated his own novels and still harbored doubts about the value of his achievement. Responding to his query, my wife told him she'd been an undergraduate at Cambridge. Gerald seemed wistful about this. He expressed regret that he had not been allowed to go to university, and had had to educate himself.

When I encouraged him to reminisce about his own life, he spoke of his military martinet of a father, his experiences in the war, his rough travels in Spain, his tormented and obsessional liaison with that puzzling predator—half nymph, half nymphomaniac— Dora Carrington. I was surprised that Gerald had let Michael Holroyd use the material about Carrington in his biography of Lytton Strachey, instead of first using it himself in his soon-to-be-published autobiography, *A Personal Record*. But this was typical of his generous nature.

Gerald still spoke Spanish with an English accent and had an idiosyncratic way of pronouncing certain words. He would say *peseta* with a short *e,* instead of peh-say-ta. He remembered the Spanish climate being much warmer and dryer than it now was, probably because he felt the cold and damp more intensely in old age. A living source of culture and history, Gerald had witnessed the military rising in Málaga at the beginning of the Civil War. Climbing the tower of his house in Churriana near the airport, he had seen the city bombarded by warships and engulfed in flames.

He told us about unusual places to visit in the distant regions of Estremadura and Galicia, and urged us to cross the Atlas in quest of adventure when we traveled in Morocco. He retained an English prejudice against bullfighting, and could not share my enthusiasm for it. But he could satisfy my curiosity about the massive white-bearded Hemingway, who reminded him of heroic sea captains sailing in Arctic waters. Though Hemingway had praised his books, Gerald was intimidated by his *presence.* He said that when

Hemingway was in the room, there didn't seem to be enough air for anyone else.

Until I met Gerald, authors like Leonard and Virginia Woolf, Bertrand Russell and Lytton Strachey seemed like distant stars in the solar system. But they had been Gerald's personal friends and had journeyed all the way to Spain to see him. He admired their intellect and conversation, yet felt they were snobbish and smug. He told me many deflating stories about them, which later found their way into the biographies by Quentin Bell and P. N. Furbank. By bringing them down to earth and making them come alive, he sent me back to their work with fresh interest and enthusiasm.

The son of an army officer, Gerald had spent much of his early childhood in Malta, South Africa, Ceylon and India. He'd been destined for a career in the Indian police when the war broke out, and was intensely interested in British colonialism. After reading my essay "The Politics of *A Passage to India*," about the novel written by his friend E. M. Forster, he wrote me a persuasive letter in the spring of 1972, defending colonialism and making me see that phase of British history in a more favorable light:

> It's said that the British rule was not resented in India
> till the Suez Canal was built and the Victorian memsahibs
> began to come out. Before that the English had lived with
> Indian girls and been altogether more human. However I
> do think we brought benefits to India in the way of political
> unification, railways (which put an end to the local famines)
> and so forth. Only we ought to have handed over power to the
> Indians far sooner.
>
> What isn't said is that Indian colonialism did great harm
> to the English by making them arrogant, snobbish and stiff
> with racial prejudice. I was in India as a kid and remember
> many of the old type of Anglo Indians. Partly on this account

the Edwardian era was a repulsive one, bloated with money, snobbish (*le vice anglais*) and indifferent to the poverty of the working classes.

I would say that on the contrary European colonialism brought immense benefits to the native Africans, except in Algeria and Rhodesia where there were white settlers. Among other things the Europeans put an end to the Arab slave trade which was horrible beyond words and had depopulated large areas of the country. And the French destroyed the hold of the Saharan nomads on the settled areas. Colonialism did *at first* bring order, peace and prosperity to a very chaotic land. It doesn't deserve to be the dirty word it is today.

When I first met Gerald he was living with a twenty-eight-year-old Englishwoman, Lynda Price. A bit of a lost soul, she had been selling souvenirs in a tourist shop in Toledo when they met. She moved in with him after he had asked her, in a touchingly old-fashioned way, if she would "share his life." Thin, sallow, quiet and rather sickly—plagued by back pains, bronchitis and migraines—Lynda was usually wrapped in several layers of Spanish shawls and seated close to the crackling but not very warm olive-wood fire. We thought it odd when she didn't offer us any of the homemade pie we'd brought for tea, and said she planned to save it for the special guests who were coming that evening.

Lynda moved and spoke slowly and seemed terribly old for her age, while Gerald, always vital and dynamic, seemed decades younger than a man in his late seventies. He still seemed sexually vigorous, though they'd never been lovers, and the half-century difference in their years seemed negligible. As with all his young women, Gerald idealized her, was absorbed by her and looked after her. He also—like Denys Finch-Hatton with Isak Dinesen and Scott Fitzgerald with Sheilah Graham—educated her in his "College of One." He loved instructing, drew up long reading lists and patiently taught his eager, docile pupil to understand the books he loved.

I also met them at the sort of dreary social event that Gerald, withdrawing into old age, rarely attended. They knew a young Swedish artist, Lars Pranger, whose cold geometrical paintings seemed to be produced on a machine by a machine. After the opening of his exhibition at a gallery in Málaga, we all returned to Lars' house for some Spanish champagne. When that was exhausted, the party moved on to the syrupy dessert wine and the fiery brandy (sold in straw-bottomed gallon jugs) of Málaga.

The guests, besides Gerald and Lynda, included a down-at-heels English writer and his miserable, nagging wife; the eccentric Fiona; an arrogant American with artistic pretensions whose family money had backed the art exhibition; and a middle-aged Spanish woman who confessed her besotted love for Lars. When the party ended at three in the morning, I drove Lars' American ex-father-in-law home to his shabby flat in an unfinished apartment block, as rats splashed through the muddy, potholed back streets of Fuengirola. Tired and sad, he feared, like many elderly expatriates, that he would collapse alone in his flat and not be discovered until he was dead.

Lars and Lynda became lovers in 1973. Five years later, he and his small son (his first wife had run off) moved into Gerald's house. Following the pattern of his masochistic relations with Carrington, Gerald first supported a delicate, dependent, passive and poetical woman and then, still deeply in love with her, accepted her affair with another man and finally allowed it to continue in his own home. A true Bloomsbury man, Gerald believed in and practiced free love.

I wasn't able to see Gerald when I returned to the south coast during the summers of the late 1970s. To escape the heat he always retreated to his mountain cottage in the remote Alpujarras, where he had first lived, and I thought I might never meet him again. But when living in London in June 1984, I was distressed to read in the *Times* that Lynda and Lars, now married, were no longer willing to care for the ill and aging Gerald. The article suggested that they had evicted him from his own house and sent him back to England to die in a North London nursing home.

Eager to see him, I rang up the home and arranged a time to visit. The owner warned me that Gerald was terribly frail and asked me not to stay too long with him. But when I reached the large brick house, set back from the road, a Spanish television crew was filming what had become a big news story in their country. After keeping the flame of truth alive when the history of Spain was being written by Fascists, Gerald was now considered a national treasure. Having banned and ignored his books for forty years, the Spanish now eagerly took him up as a patriotic cause. They wanted him to come back to Alhaurín.

Exhausted and somewhat bewildered, he sat on the cramped, glassed-in sunporch and courteously answered the reporter's questions. He expressed his *afición* for Spain and his desire to return home as soon as possible. Watching the interview, I could see how sharply he had declined in the last decade. At ninety he was wrapped in a shawl, his eyes opaque and magnified behind thick lenses, his vision failing. His step was unsteady, his speech halting and he still dabbed the saliva at the side of his mouth. After keeping him for forty-five minutes, the reporter made him walk down the steps so he could be photographed in the scrubby garden. He had broken his leg in 1982, and found this ordeal both difficult and dangerous.

After the crew had departed we talked in the lounge and were closely observed by the other residents, who seemed disturbed by all the fuss. The place looked like a Bournemouth hotel, furnished with typical high-street carpets and chairs, and smelled of boiled vegetables. Gerald had nothing in common with the narrow-minded gossips who lived there.

Though his flight from Spain the previous month had gone smoothly, Gerald was still extremely weary. It took him most of the morning to get dressed, and he still left many buttons undone. He could not find what he needed in the unfamiliar surroundings, disliked the bland English food and kept falling asleep during the day. I nodded sympathetically and tried to encourage him, but felt appalled at his predicament. "All my friends are dead now," he suddenly declared. "I have nothing more to live for. I want only to die." But he still had a tenacious hold on life. He didn't want to burden Lynda, who was fully occupied with her two small children. But he also missed her terribly, felt she didn't love him and was saddened that she'd sent him away.

A few weeks later I learned that publicity had achieved what persuasion could not. The *pueblo* and the provincial government promised to pay for his medical expenses and nursing care, and Gerald went back to Spain, to his village and to his own house, where he died in December 1987. Lars, who had taken Gerald's much-adored companion, also inherited through her Gerald's house, papers, money and royalties.

Apart from this sad interlude, Gerald had an enviable life. He lived as long as Morgan, Bertie and Leonard; he had a good war; he broke away from his father's constraints. Though he was never rich, he enjoyed great freedom and never had to work at a regular job. He had a great many loyal friends in and out of Bloomsbury, traveled extensively and lived mainly in the Mediterranean; had good health and (despite frequent bouts of impotence) his share of attractive women. He developed a clear, engaging style, published several classic books and was still writing in his eighties. As Gerald wrote of his friend David Garnett: "He was not intellectual, but had a great experience of life and one could trust his judgment on everything from literature to politics."

3

Phillip Knightley

(1929–2016)

In the fall of 1971, at Lew Hoad's tennis club on the south coast of Spain, I played a few hours of pickup doubles. Drinking beer after the match, I asked my unknown partner what he did. He said he'd recently published a biography of T. E. Lawrence and I sealed our friendship by exclaiming: "You must be Phillip Knightley!" We continued to play tennis for decades at the Queen's Club in London and on the public courts in Berkeley, California. He was ten years older than me and well established as an author and investigative reporter. I would be impressed to learn that editors had offered him several different designs for the dust wrappers of his books and that he'd been able to ask a *Sunday Times* stringer in Turkey to find and translate some useful information for his Lawrence book. Phil was amused and impressed when, in my hot youth, I went into the office of Quartet Books on Goodge Street and threatened to throw a typewriter out the window if they didn't immediately return my long-kept typescript.

Phil gave me generous help when I was starting out as a writer in the early 1970s. He signed me up with his literary agent, Tessa Sayle, and found a publisher for my own book on T. E. Lawrence in 1973. In the *Sunday Times* archives he discovered a stunning unpublished photograph of the young Wyndham Lewis standing before a lost painting and I used it on the jacket of my biography in 1980. He also contributed a chapter on his life of Lawrence to *The Craft of Literary Biography,* which I edited in 1985. Providing effective blurbs for two of my books, he wrote: "Jeffrey Meyers has uncovered fascinating aspects of Orwell's life that put a new face on one of Britain's most influential authors" and "Meyers brings to life not only Modigliani himself but the exciting, romantic world of Paris in the early years of the twentieth century."

My wife and I came to London in the summer of 1972, and Phil entertained us and helped us to settle. Phil told me the best place to buy tires in London and cheap seats on planes from England to America. He even drilled a baby seat into the back of my Volkswagen bug. After I was hired by the book department at Christie's, he advised me to dig in and immediately secure a desk and phone. When an older colleague, who wrongly thought I was trying to replace him, collapsed and was carried out, I quickly took over his empty desk. An expert in renovation and repairs, Phil had bought and fixed up a decaying townhouse in rapidly gentrifying Notting Hill. After using the extremely narrow, coffin-tight shower he'd installed downstairs, I told him, "I've had sex in a shower, but this is the first time I've ever had sex *with* a shower."

Phil joined me in some biographical expeditions. He came to Kent with me to interview Tim Page, the combat-wounded war photographer and close friend of Sean Flynn, the son of the dashing Errol and an adventurous journalist who had disappeared into the jungles of Cambodia. Phil drove me to see Robert Frost's house in Gloucestershire, and we became so absorbed in conversation that he shot past the highway exit and didn't remember to turn around for ten minutes. Later that day, as I visited Gloucester cathedral, Phil rang London from a red telephone box to hear if he'd missed any news in the last few hours.

We sometimes helped each other financially. When I invited several guests to a restaurant in London, Phil joined us, had to leave early and quietly paid the entire bill. He informed me that the *National Times* in Sydney had reprinted my pioneering article on the FBI's surveillance of Hemingway. The *New York Review of Books,* where it first appeared, had never told me about the reprint and Phil enabled me to collect my overdue share of the royalties. A friend had swindled him out of his investment in a supposedly bankrupt hotel in Torremolinos, Spain. But I inspected the place, reported that it was packed and thriving, and enabled him to recover some of his money.

Kevin Cunningham's brilliant and witty portrait dominated Phil's living room and suggested the ambience of his household. Bald and goateed like Lenin, Phil sits on a brown velvet sofa, beneath an Indian police clock, and wears an amused expression. Framed by an open rear doorway and holding one of his books between piously crossed hands, he sees a lavish display of food and wine on a low table before him and allows a pert white parakeet to perch on his dome. His Indian wife Yvonne, dressed in a white sari, stands behind him on the left; his white-and-brown cocker spaniel sits on a chair on the right.

A genial host, he presided over many lively dinner parties, with leading journalists jockeying for attention and for the Indian cuisine prepared by his wife. At his house I met the cocky Murray Sayle, the dogmatic John Pilger and an "expert" journalist on the *Far East Economic Review* who predicted, just before the collapse of the Soviet Union, that the country was strong and stable. The arrogant and childless Germaine Greer lectured the mothers at the table about how to raise their children. She asked me, "Is there anyone interesting to fuck in Tulsa, Oklahoma?" where she was going to teach. But few potential candidates, I thought, would wish to tangle with that tigress.

After leaving school his son seemed to drift, unable to find a job or a course of study. Against Yvonne's wishes, Phil supported their son, who led a rather meaningless life and spent a lot of time combing his hair until he became prematurely bald. Phil bought him a flat, supposedly to entertain his girlfriends, but the girls never turned up. Instead, they remodeled the flat, his son rented it out for money to live on and moved back into the family home. Phil loyally maintained that his son was a great help to him as an editor. But he made a real mess when correcting the proofs of *Australia* and Phil asked my wife to sort things out and do it properly.

One of Yvonne's friends claimed that he owed a lot of his success to her valuable support. In fact, the opposite was true, and the professional achievements of this kind and tolerant man were undercut by their fierce domestic conflicts. My wife and I had many good times with the Knightleys in the 1970s and 1980s, when all our children were young. In 1976 I dedicated my book *A Fever at the Core* both "To Phillip and Yvonne." But in later years she became Yvon the Terrible: bitter, angry and hostile. Frustrated perhaps in her own career, for which she had no education or expertise, she was jealous of Phil's success, despite all her social and financial benefits. She used old-fashioned Anglo-Indian expressions such as "donkey's years" and was out of her depth in intellectual conversations. Ill at ease after decades in London, she said the English thought she was a Negro, not an Indian, and had called her a "black."

Yvonne cooked and served superb dinners, but remained in the kitchen (Indian style) and did not sit down with her guests. When she finally appeared at the table she mocked Phil's ancestral ties to the Knightleys in England and yelled at him, in front of his friends, "Don't just sit there. Get the soda for drinks!" I quickly jumped up to fetch the bottle and defuse her anger. She insisted that he write his books in a small room crammed with bicycles, old furniture and a mass of unwanted objects, all piled up around him. Given to drama, she declared that she wouldn't drive to dinner at our house with Phil because "I hate him!"

Phil thought she was only happy at their house in Goa. An orphan brought up in an Indian convent, Yvonne worshipped the nuns who'd taught her there, and forced their three children to faithfully attend Mass at the Catholic church. She hung a huge, two-foot, sex-spoiling crucifix over their bed. When Phil admitted that she wasn't keen on sex, I thought he should change his name to Monthly or even Yearly.

Yvonne once asked me about her shy and secretive son, "Do you think he is gay?" "I'm not sure but he's certainly a strange young man and I suspect he might be." "Well, he's not. The mother is always the first to know." "I got news for you. The mother is always the *last* to know." On another occasion, Phil and I were watching soccer on television while waiting to meet friends for dinner. Yvonne suddenly rushed into the room and screamed, "Get out of my house." I calmly answered, "I won't leave till I'm ready" and remained sunk in the sofa until it was time to go. She then banished me from the house, along with all of Phil's friends, and quarreled with most of her own.

Terrified that Yvonne would explode if he invited me to his house, even when he was bedridden, Phil rather desperately said, "We'll have to find a way to meet." When I asked him why he didn't resist her outrageous behavior, he replied, "It wouldn't be worth opposing her. She'd make my life even more miserable than it already is." He offered to buy her a flat, but she didn't want to leave their house. Toward the end of his life she drank a mollifying bottle or two of wine every night. I asked Yvonne if she planned to commit *suttee* on Phil's funeral pyre, but she politely refused incineration.

Born in Australia, Phil was a special correspondent for the *Sunday Times* from 1965 to 1985, and was named journalist of the year in 1980 and 1988. He did not attend a university, but lectured at Lincoln University and received honorary doctorates from City University in London and from Sydney University, where he'd once failed his entrance examination. The newly honored doctor confessed that he and his coauthor had once "borrowed" the T. E.

Lawrence papers from the Bodleian Library, took them home and didn't mail them back to Oxford until they had finished their book.

He coauthored *Philby: The Spy Who Betrayed a Generation* (1968), which had an introduction by John le Carré and was serialized in the *Sunday Times*. Philby, knowing he was close to death, summoned Phil (who grabbed the next plane to Moscow) and gave him revealing interviews that led to *The Master Spy: The Story of Kim Philby* (1988). Phil's most ambitious and best-known works are *The First Casualty [Truth]: From the Crimea to Vietnam: The War Correspondent as Hero, Propagandist, and Myth Maker* (1975) and *The Second Oldest Profession: Spies and Spying in the Twentieth Century* (1986). A versatile writer, he once published an article about being a patient in a catheter ward for a urinary infection. But as an expert in both war reporting and espionage he was greatly in demand at conferences and on television. He was the Australian star of the *Sunday Times*, but left the newspaper when his countryman Rupert Murdoch bought and ruined it.

His most socially significant and influential books are *The Death of Venice*, with Stephen Fay in 1976, which revealed how millions of dollars donated to save the precious city from devastating floods had been stolen by corrupt Italian officials; and *Suffer the Children: The Story of Thalidomide*, with the *Sunday Times* Insight Team in 1979, which finally forced Distillers Biochemicals to accept responsibility for the dangerous drug prescribed for pregnant women and to pay substantial damages to the children who had suffered horrific deformities.

He also experienced some serious setbacks. He lost an expensive libel suit against his book *An Affair of State: The Profumo Case and the Framing of Stephen Ward* (1987) when an Australian cop he'd called corrupt turned out to be alive in his nineties and still litigious. Phil also recklessly put up a £15,000 bond for the WikiLeaks founder Julian Assange and lost it all when his protégé jumped bail and defected to the Ecuadorian Embassy in London.

Phil's success enabled him to buy a country house near Oxford and then a tropical villa in Goa, and he made many annual trips to India and back to Australia. On one of his visits to me in sunny Berkeley he complained of the cold in his friend's house in Connecticut. We appeared together on a literary panel, and after his lecture at nearby Stanford he invaded an upmarket thrift shop and acquired a whole new wardrobe that he hoped would see him out. Phil inscribed *The First Casualty,* "To Jeffrey, to complete your collection of the works (to date) of your old pal and admirer" and *A Hack's Progress,* his autobiography, "To my Yankee mate, Jeffrey, from his rough Aussie colleague, with warmest non-consenting-adult hugs." Yet the rough Aussie sometimes deviated from his democratic principles. He offered to get me a reservation at El Bulli, the posh restaurant near Barcelona, but I didn't want to pay twenty-five euros for a cup of foam. He was uncommonly proud of his daughter's friendship with an "Hon.," the daughter of the Marquess of Queensbury, but I challenged his assumption that aristocrats were superior to other people.

In 2005 he spent almost an entire year in bed with a painful and mysterious back ailment, possibly severe sciatica. I consulted several doctors in America, and constantly urged him in person and by email to get up and regain his normal life. But he remained supine, emaciated and depressed until finally roused by an osteopath and a personal trainer, who mobilized him and enabled him to visit his daughter's house in Ibiza. Slightly drunk in a dark bar in Ibiza, he sat down on a high stool that turned out to be a dwarf. When I traveled to Australia in 2012, he put me in touch with two congenial friends who showed me around Sydney and took me to dinner.

Phil's last two letters to me, grateful for his good fortune and bravely optimistic, were deeply moving. On March 31, 2015, surprised by his own success, he asked: "Who would have thought a boy from Botany Bay would meet the queen three times, a whole posse of politicians, just about every world spymaster and so on. Plus friends like you and Val." On April 26, 2016, just before he was overcome by his terminal disease, he wrote: "Enjoying 3-week-old granddaughter from Marisa, named Devi, and her two-year-old brother Rafael. Spend rest of my time reminiscing as you seem to, too. Spending this summer with all the kids in Ibiza. Life still good."

4

Donald Greene

(1914 – 1997)

At my first interview for a teaching job, while I was writing my doomed thesis on Jonathan Swift and Samuel Johnson, I was asked about Donald Greene's book on Johnson's politics. I knew this work was important, but my thesis director had left me on my own and I was a guided missile without a guide. I was reading the books and articles required for each chapter as I went along and hadn't yet reached Greene. So I fumbled the question, didn't get the job and never finished the dissertation. Ever since then I felt that my fate was obscurely linked with Greene. Supposedly cantankerous, even terrifying, Greene turned out to be warm and personable, and became a close friend.

While teaching at UCLA I began to hear wondrous rumors about Greene: his fabled birth in Moose Jaw, Saskatchewan (he actually had a rather jutting moose-like jaw), with only a strand of barbed wire between himself and the North Pole; and his restless, not to say frenetic movements from high to low latitudes—from the remote fastness of Riverside, California, and the Hebrew hothouse of Brandeis to the desert wastes of New Mexico and the Arctic tundra of Toronto. The elders of all these departments, shocked by his bellicose behavior, had supposedly escorted him to the county line and ordered him to leave town. I heard about his prodigious knowledge, frightening personality and ferocity in scholarly combat; his inflexible antagonism to the honorific "Dr." attached to the name of Samuel Johnson, obsessive hatred of James Boswell and long-nourished but still unpublished biography of the last third of Johnson's life. He later became famous for his spectacular heart attacks at learned gatherings. All this created a colorful legend among the colorless academic drudges.

I first met Greene—a man of wide interests and unusually sanguine about learning something useful from a lecture—when he turned up at my talk on Hemingway at the University of Southern California in April 1981. During question time he grilled me in his formidable fashion, but (since I didn't realize who he was) I just managed to hold my own. Afterward, during drinks, dinner and more drinks with Greene and an old friend, we immediately hit it off. I was outside his field, yet shared his two great interests: eighteenth-century studies and biography. He seemed to like my zest for literary gossip and endless ink spilling, and that evening we began a friendship that was sustained through long letters for the next ten years.

Our correspondence began when I invited Don to write about his biography of Johnson for a collection of original essays, *The Craft of Literary Biography,* which I edited for Macmillan. He jumped at the offer like a trout to a fly. No one seemed to notice that all the other contributors wrote about biographies they had already published while Don discussed a book he hadn't yet written. His unfinished, or not even started, biography became one of the recurrent subjects of our letters.

He later wrote essays for two other collections I edited: on Johnson's *Life of Savage* for *The Biographer's Art,* and on Graham Greene and Evelyn Waugh as Catholic novelists for *Graham Greene: A Revaluation.* Though pleased to get his brilliant essays— always the best and placed first in the book—I realized that I was distracting him with commissions and prompting him to write fascinating letters instead of encouraging him to complete the eagerly awaited biography. He was writing short pieces, and writing to me about his writing, instead of actually writing what he was supposed to be writing about. Since he'd promised to dedicate his life of Johnson to me, I was all the more keen to have him finish it, and felt occasional twinges of conscience about leading him astray.

At the same time, I was amazed to find that I was editing the work of Donald Greene and that he welcomed my criticism: "Very many thanks for the excellent editorial work you did on my Johnson paper," he wrote in March 1983. "You have done a fine job in clearing up some of my long, sloppy sentences. The great majority of your comments I agree with. Please go ahead and make the changes you suggest." Five years later, grateful that I let him run over the word limit, he said: "Your exceptions to my comments on the Greene / Waugh piece are fine with me. It's great to have such a tolerant editor."

When I asked him for a third essay—since we were getting along so well and I was so pleased with his work—he first refused, then agreed: "I had made up my mind that after next month, when I'll have finished various things, I'd turn down every suggestion of a project that would distract me from my long delayed biography of Johnson's later years. But your proposal is very tempting." When I planned a fourth volume, he hinted that he might write another piece: "At the moment I can't think of anything more to say about Waugh. . . . Well, maybe, after a lot of thinking, I could contribute something on Waugh and war." But this never came off. Tired of nagging people to complete the essays they promised and rejecting worthless work pulled out of the bottom drawer, I gave up editing these collections of original essays.

Neither of us was terribly fond of Waugh's son (whom I called "Audubon" because of his owlish expression), but Don was more severe: "I tend to agree with Evelyn's early comments, in his letters and diaries, about Auberon's stupidity. If anyone has ever traveled a long way on his father's reputation, it's certainly Auberon

Waugh. . . . I didn't take to him—never have. He's a sad falling off from his sainted dad."

Don's single-spaced letters—sometimes as long as 1,700 words and little essays in themselves—poured forth a torrent of high-powered erudition. Far from being a narrowly focused specialist, he maintained a lively interest in many contemporary topics: Canadian affairs and military memoirs, psychology and sexual history, movies and popular novels and current fiction from Gore Vidal to John le Carré. The main subjects of his letters were comments on the books and articles I sent him, his quite startling autobiographical revelations, plans for his lecture at my university, medical bulletins about his recurrent heart attacks, attacks on Boswell, explanations about why he was not writing his biography, fascinating research about Johnson's life, discussion of his own character (he quite enjoyed his curmudgeonly reputation) and the sources of his learning: high and low.

Don was the ideal mentor and colleague I lacked in my day-to-day life. I could tell him what I'd been doing and get a frank, authoritative opinion of the work I sent him. He observed, after several decades of teaching in English departments, that "most of my colleagues detest literature, and would rather do anything than deal with it." For all his great learning, he was never dull or fossilized. He was always passionate about literature and ready to discuss any topic that came up.

Don, who never let me get away with anything, sometimes fired a shot, *in terrorem,* across my bows. I once remarked (and instantly regretted my rashness) that when in graduate school in Berkeley I'd read everything that Johnson had written. He immediately challenged me by asking: "Have you read his parliamentary reports, his Vinerian lectures?" And, of course, I hadn't. One of his earliest letters abruptly began: "This is to take you to task for the statement in your *TLS* letter of December 16, 1983, 'Unlike . . . Waugh . . . Hemingway never wrote screenplays for Hollywood.'

Name one screenplay for Hollywood that Waugh ever wrote." And of course, I couldn't. He also caught me out on my assertion that Eliot owed the phrase "a handful of dust" to Conrad: "Surely it's a reference to the instruction in the Anglican Book of Common Prayer's service for the 'Burial of the Dead' (the title of the section of *The Waste Land* where the phrase occurs)."

Unlike many colleagues who resented my publications, Don, no slouch himself, admired my industry and was pleased by my success. He remarked that even his own "commitments don't come close to equalling your amazing productivity"; then added, with considerable exaggeration: "I'm looking forward to reading a few more of your fourteen 1987–88 books."

Like a good teacher, Don could praise as well as censure and often gave me generous encouragement. He was particularly (perhaps overly) impressed when I one-upped him on a fine point of Canadian geography: "You write that Wyndham Lewis 'was born aboard a yacht moored at Amherst, Nova Scotia.' I've passed through Amherst once or twice on the train, and was under the impression that it's not a seaport but an inland town." He later backed down and conceded that "you corrected me by pointing out that in the 1880s and 1890s there had indeed been a seaway leading to Amherst, intended to be part of an abortive project to dig a canal across the Isthmus of Chignecto, but abandoned and the excavation filled in by the time I encountered Amherst. I thought that was one of the most brilliant pieces of biographical research I had ever come across."

My article "The Nobel Prize and Literary Politics" (*Dictionary of Literary Biography Yearbook: 1988*) inspired his incisive two-page essay on this subject: "What a splendid piece about the Nobel prize!" he exclaimed. "Very many thanks for sending it. I've long wished that someone would explode the superstitions about it, and at last you've done it. I wish it would get more publicity. Do please include it in your collected essays. . . . For all that I'm notorious as being cantankerous, I think I agree with about 95% of your Nobel rankings, an unusually high percentage of agreement for me."

He seemed pleased to accept the dedication of my essays *The Spirit of Biography.* When I sent him the book, he wrote: "I can't tell you how gratified I am—overwhelmed would be more accurate—at your kindness in dedicating the volume to me. I'm far from being convinced that I deserve such an honor, when I contemplate your devotion and the immense amount of work you have put in trying to arrive at the truth about the literary figures you deal with." He also commended my "inspired choice of an illustration for the jacket": Luca Signorelli's *Resurrection of the Dead* in Orvieto Cathedral. Just as the fully formed human being, emerging from the ground, has been brought back to life by God, so (the illustration suggested) the biographer also breathes new life into his dead subject.

In more personal letters, Don would reminisce in a revealing way about his own life. A reference to Diana Cooper's autobiography sparked his reference to "a music-hall song of the 1920s that went 'Have a banana! / With Lady Diana'—I heard this from my mother's lips, but I'm sure she wasn't aware of the obscene implication."

My unbuttoned review of a book on homosexual literature for the stodgy *Journal of English and Germanic Philology* (January 1989) prompted a burst of social history and personal memories that undermined his apparently straitlaced background:

> Looking back from my decrepit old age, I like to think of the privilege I had of growing up among western Canadian farm boys who, from the age of thirteen or so, had no inhibitions whatever about ways of getting their rocks off whenever, as was frequently the case, the sensations in their cocks began to be troublesome. They would fuck anything that had a hole in it, including sheep, and certainly each other. . . .

If you visited a neighbor's in the evening and were invited
to stay overnight, you were usually expected to share a bed
with the son of the family nearest in age to you, who, just as
a matter of routine hospitality, would invite you to have sex
with him. So, after a half hour of sucking each other's cocks,
you'd go to sleep peacefully. There was a sort of pastoral inno-
cence about it. I find it somewhat hilarious that Auden, Hart
Crane, Ginsberg, etc. make such a big deal of it.

Don felt that Wyndham Lewis' "characterization of Toronto
as that 'sanctimonious icebox' has always seemed to me the *mot
juste.*" He then rather sadly added, though it's hard to imagine him
nestled in domestic bliss: "I couldn't stand the place myself, partly
because I'm a western Canadian and partly because that's where
my marriage finally broke down."

Many of Don's personal letters tried to explain, or explain away,
the reasons for the recurrent heart attacks that made him such a
spectacular performer at learned meetings. In April 1987 he attributed these attacks to the arch-villains of the academy: literary
theorists and dimwitted deans:

I'd have got back to you sooner if I hadn't spent a week in
the Georgetown University Hospital in Washington. This
happens to me regularly when I give a particularly nasty paper
at a conference. In 1974 I was struck down with a heart attack
in Chicago, preceding an attack on Boswell. This time, at an
"anti-deconstructionist" conference at Georgetown, though I
succeeded in delivering my "keynote address," the deconstruc-
tionists got me two days later. . . .

Your phrase about "my regularly scheduled heart attacks"
encourages me. They seem to take place about every ten to
twelve years, and never seem to last long. Usually they have to
do with some fight with the USC administration.

Two years later, the academic superstar announced that he had just failed his first test: "After being given the most exhaustive physical examination I've ever had (three M.D.s worked me over for two and a half hours), the senior man looked at me sadly and said he thought I might be too healthy to be admitted to the study for a new heart drug."

In February 1990 I invited Don to lecture at my university and darkly joked that I'd have a medical team standing by the podium. Though I had a large house which would have given him complete privacy, Don refused to stay with me. He didn't want his smoking to be restricted. He planned to cut down on long flights, he told me, because "they no longer let you smoke on airplanes. Abstaining for six to twelve hours would make me really keel over." So he stayed in a modest motel and, not wanting to tire him, I drove him the short distance uphill to the campus.

The title of his talk had evolved from "The Lyric Pope" to "A Fresh Look at Alexander Pope" to "'The Constant Muse': Alexander Pope as Lyric Poet," as he searched for an appealing hook to pack them into the lecture hall. Feeling at the thread of argument and crawling along the lines, he spoke rapturously about the beauty of Pope's Pastorals, which I'd never fully appreciated until Don revealed their subtleties. He enhanced his talk by playing an exquisite tape of John McCormick singing, with Handel's setting, "Where'er you walk, cool gales shall fan the glade, / Trees, where you sit, shall crowd into a shade." His lecture, well attended and enthusiastically received, brought a breath of rare scholarship to the playboy university.

Afterward, with the poet Ed Dorn as a fellow guest, we had a small dinner party at my house. The talk was lively, Don puffed away on his ciggies and everything seemed to be going quite well. Suddenly, Don turned florid, gasped and keeled over, and I managed to catch him just before he hit the floor. We all stood up and panicked. He seemed to be swallowing his tongue and I feared he would choke to death—if he weren't dead already. As I held him in a weird *pietà,* I thought: "Donald Greene is going to die in my house—in my arms!" Our fates had indeed become entwined.

The paramedics arrived from a nearby fire station in a few minutes. They were wary of putting their fingers into his mouth and getting bitten, but finally inserted a wedge to hold his mouth open while they extracted some half-chewed meat. I held his hand in the screaming ambulance and he soon regained consciousness. The emergency room was more concerned with the state of his finances than the state of his health, and refused to treat him till I found his insurance card in his wallet. He complained about a sharp pain in his right arm, which turned out to be broken. The hospital exhausted him with a thorough but inconclusive series of tests. Three days later, with his arm in a sling, he was released with no clear explanation of what had actually happened to him.

Since he hadn't had a decent meal for quite a while, I offered to take him out to a good restaurant, but he insisted that he had some nourishing food squirreled away in his motel room. As Don smoked heavily to make up for lost tobacco time, we ate what he called lunch—a small packet of potato chips and half a bottle of Scotch whisky. Considering his diet and habits, it was a miracle that he lived to the age of eighty-two. Strangely enough, Don's apparent heart attack had some positive results. It scared the hell out of Ed Dorn, who swore to give up smoking and kept his vow. Don survived, and the near-fatal experience drew us closer together.

In subsequent letters Don expressed embarrassment about this crisis in our town, and said he was relieved "to infer from your friendly tone that you are not too disgruntled over my performance at your dinner party. I'll try not to do it again." But he still hadn't discovered the cause of his disturbing attacks. In 1990, when preparing for another potentially traumatic conference, he was forced to speculate about it: "At least Tampa, Florida, is at sea level, so I won't suffer from the shortage of oxygen in my blood stream that is one of the theories for my collapse in the Rocky Mountains. (Counter-evidence is that two earlier such occurrences took place in Amsterdam and Washington, D.C. But on those occasions I was suffering from lack of sleep and general exhaustion.)"

Two years later—discounting his alarming illness with a casual "just"—he triumphantly announced: "At last, a cardiologist in Los Angeles has diagnosed it—as half a dozen cardiologists and neurologists around the world, in Amsterdam, Washington, and your town, failed to do—as something called 'Adams-Stokes' syndrome: the heart just stops beating for a few minutes, and if you're standing or sitting, the blood from the brain drains downwards, and you black out (or faint, for that's all it is)." Don's ailment, it seemed, was nothing more than the vapors and fainting fits favored by Augustan heroines.

Don maintained his obsessive onslaughts on Boswell, which won few converts and hurt his reputation, in his letters as well as in his essays. "I've been fighting all my life against the Boswell / Macaulay image of Samuel Johnson 'the man,'" he asserted, and "since I'm trying to slaughter Boswell, I may as well go the whole hog." Refusing, finally, my invitation to lecture where I was visiting at the University of Alabama, he admitted: "I'd love to have the opportunity to hammer a few more nails into Boswell's coffin. But I'm afraid my (at present) precarious health won't permit it."

Not content with his own quixotic battle, Don tried to preempt my choice of who would write the chapter on Boswell in *The Biographer's Art* and strongly urged me to select a hostile critic. When the book appeared with a persuasive essay, Don's dismissal was entirely predictable: "We have my good friend Max Novak, stalwartly upholding the Macaulayan and academic establishment's view of the greatness of Boswell. . . . The trouble is that Max, fine Defoe and Dryden scholar though he may be, doesn't really know a great deal about Johnson."

Though Don (living on borrowed time) continued to publish an impressive number of high-quality articles, he hadn't even
started to write *his* life of Johnson. Though I'd distracted him from
that high purpose, I'd also urged him to reject all proposals and
get to work on that ever-receding book. Quoting, as Johnson did,
tantus labor non sit cassus, I warned him: "the night cometh, when
no man can work." In 1989, he hit on what seemed to be a practical
solution: "Jeffrey, I'm most grateful to you for your insistence that
I get the book written. I'm almost inclined to ask you whether you
would undertake the kind of contract I made with my old teacher
Jim Clifford when I was doing my dissertation at Columbia, that
I would stagger into his office on the first day of each month with
a draft chapter for his perusal. Of course I wouldn't expect any
criticism from you (indeed, I didn't get much from Jim) just that
you would demand to see a chapter on paper."

Playing Hester Thrale to his Johnson, I agreed to be his whip,
but the plan never got off the ground. "When will the biography
get started?" he asked later that year. "Not, I'm afraid, January 1,
1990, as I had hoped. Maybe April 1 if all goes well. I have to go
over to England for a few weeks in March to look at stuff in the
Public Record Office about Johnson's pension. Thanks to your offer to ride herd on it when it really does get started, I may take you
up on this."

Three years later, no closer to beginning the book, he sent
me yet another article and remarked: "I don't know what you'll
make of the enclosed (well, I do know one comment you'll probably make—that instead of wasting my time fooling around with
articles like this, I'd do better to spend three hours a day putting
together my long delayed biography of Johnson's later life)." Don
understood the problem perfectly well but, like a classic neurotic,
couldn't do anything about it. In his very first letter to me of
May 12, 1982, he'd explained:

I'm in the situation which some other biographers have found themselves in—but particularly aggravated in my case—of writing about a subject of whom the "definitive" biography, the "standard" biography, was published long ago, and so will be subjected to the cry, "Just who does he think he is, anyway?"

Clifford never dreamed of tackling the last twenty-two years—the magic years after Boswell had met him and "told us all." After all, Macaulay assured us that Boswell was the first of biographers as Shakespeare was the first of dramatists, Homer the first of epic poets, etc. etc. What nerve on my part!

I'd always thought that Clifford planned to complete his trilogy, but didn't challenge him on this point.

Don loathed the charming and charismatic, pushy and parasitic Jamie Boswell, the most modern of eighteenth-century writers, for spotlighting Johnson's eccentric character and unintentionally shoving his works offstage. But his attempts to demolish Boswell seemed self-defeating, especially when he failed to supplant the *Life* with a book of his own. He also hated Boswell because he knew he could never surpass the man who had known Johnson so intimately and written about him so brilliantly. Don kept delaying the completion, indeed the inception, of the last third of Johnson's life that he had spent his own life preparing to write.

Though blocked in the biography, Don energetically pursued his research—he even went to India—which seemed to justify his regretful procrastination and produced some astonishing discoveries: Johnson as Spy, Johnson as Masturbator, Johnson (almost) as Eunuch:

The Johnson biography is not coming along at all—I get deflected into innumerable other projects. But I hope soon to get down to serious work on it; I've actually been going through a microfilm of Lord Rockingham's papers (Prime Minister, 1765–66), in which are recorded all the payments in his Secret Service accounts of the time, including a number to Johnson. So I hope that in the end the thing will materialize.

I was looking into the business of Johnson and masturbation — after reading numerous 18th and 19th-century medical tracts assuring everyone that masturbation produces blindness and insanity. I'm inclined to believe that this, rather than the sexual perversions described by Krafft-Ebing, was responsible for Johnson's supposed "vile melancholy."

Toward the end of Johnson's life, he suffered from a painful swelling in his scrotum that he first thought a hydrocele, a dropsical accumulation of fluid. . . . But his medical advisers first diagnosed it as a sarcocele, a possible cancerous growth, and were prepared, as Johnson poetically put it, to use "fire and sword" — i.e., to excise surgically his whole genitalia. . . . We biographers obviously have to become our own medical researchers, topographical historians, and quite a few other things to do our job properly.

Like Johnson himself, Don had extraordinary brainpower and eagerness to engage on any subject, moral fervor and a tendency to argue for victory. As Hester Thrale wrote of Johnson, he "displayed so copious, so compendious a knowledge of authors, books, and every branch of learning." But Don also had one of Johnson's radical weaknesses: a "facility of writing, and this dilatoriness ever to write." In the end, he lost the health and will to write his masterpiece and in 1997 was overtaken by death. By a strange yet appropriate twist of fate, which Don would have appreciated, his son allowed me to study his papers and unpublished research. I returned to the subject of my first thesis and wrote my own life of Johnson, which appeared in 2008, the year before the 300th anniversary of his birth.

We met for the last time in the early 1990s, in a Japanese restaurant in downtown Los Angeles. I found Don shrunken with age, slower in speech and slightly distracted. During a congenial lunch, we caught up with literary gossip and news of mutual friends. As embattled biographers, we lamented the decline of English studies in America. Suddenly, Don got up and left the table. We went on talking and paid our bill, thinking he'd hurried away to the bathroom. But he never returned and I never saw him again. I imagined him, like Mr. Magoo on acid, behind the wheel on the freeway—should we have asked the police to issue an all-points bulletin warning motorists that he was on the loose?—and somehow making his erratic way home.

Our modern Joseph Scaliger and Richard Bentley, Don took all human knowledge as his province: the classics and theology as well as philosophy, genealogy, history and European literature. He explained that "most of my low learning comes from having grown up in the company of farm boys in western Canada, reinforced by five years in the Canadian army, largely composed of the same farm boys. . . . Most of the [high] 'learning' I have comes from dipping into the *Encyclopaedia Britannica* when I am bored—the eleventh edition, of course, perhaps the greatest intellectual achievement of the Western mind." Like the Italian scholar Mario Praz, he'd read everything and knew everything, and was the most learned man I ever met. He was also the last of his kind. Our present system of higher education—much less strict, intense and demanding than it was for previous generations—will never again produce such a colossal scholar.

Don looked like Verrocchio's equestrian statue of Colleoni in Venice and had the *terribilità* of that old condottiere. He could boast, with Pope: "Yes, I am proud; I must be proud to see / Men not afraid of God, afraid of me." He enjoyed fierce disputation, engaged at the very end of his life in a controversy about Johnson's politics, and went down like an old battleship, cannons firing from every quarter. Like the poet and critic Geoffrey Grigson and the critic Marvin Mudrick, he had a ferocious reputation, but in person was humane and sympathetic. "Thanks to some outspokenness on my part in articles and reviews," Don observed, "I have the reputation of being hard to get along with. But Stanley Fish, when he was here at USC as a visiting professor, said to me at the end of his year, with some surprise, 'You know, Don, you're a real pussycat.' Well, of course, I am."

5

Hugh Gordon Porteus

(1906–1993)

I do like to listen to people who have been sidelined. . . .
Once they begin to talk, they have things to tell you
that you won't be able to get from anywhere else.
—W. G. Sebald, *The Emergence of Memory*

In 1978–79, while living in London and writing the life of Wyndham Lewis on a Guggenheim fellowship, I frequently saw and formed a close friendship with Lewis' charming, congenial and feckless disciple Hugh Gordon Porteus. A valuable source of information, he was born in 1906, the same year as my father. A minor but significant presence in literary London from the thirties through the sixties, he was delighted to be unearthed and freely reminisced about himself and all his eminent friends, from Lewis and T. S. Eliot to Lawrence Durrell and Dylan Thomas. He made a cameo appearance in all their biographies, but was never fully described. His obituary in the *Independent* of February 8, 1993, called him "a flamboyant figure in London's bohemia." Eight days later in that newspaper Anthony Thwaite described him as "a rather hearty, ruddy-faced, almost tweedy man, with a slightly barking voice."

I dined with him in my flat in Hampstead and the flat off Sloane

Square in Chelsea of his sweet and affectionate companion, Barbara Dunell. She had trained under Roger Fry at the Courtauld Institute, nursed during the war, worked for the Times Book Club, run an art gallery on Mount Street in Mayfair and looked after Porteus when he was ill. When I visited his place in Cheltenham, the once fashionable Gloucestershire spa, I was rather shocked by his poverty and squalor. With the help of the authors Francis King and John Lehmann I wrote to the Royal Literary Fund and we secured a four-figure grant.

Porteus never threw out anything in print. His half century of newspaper clippings was piled three feet high in what he called his *"tel"* (the Arabic word for "hill"), a chaotic but potentially promising elevation, which was difficult to penetrate or excavate. Isolated, lonely and ill, he was keen to talk and correspond with someone intensely interested in his hero. His rambling letters were amusing and entertaining. But I learned most about Lewis from my liveliest and most indiscreet informant in our three formal and focused interviews.

Like Chaucer's Sergeant of the Law, Porteus always "seemed busier then he was." Restless and on the move, he had many different jobs but never settled down to a successful career. Writing in the *TLS* of March 26, 1993, shortly after his death, Julian Symons, who knew him in the thirties when he imitated Lewis in dress and manner, called him secretive and paranoid, and simplistically attributed his disappearance from the English papers to "his inability to write to a required length." When I knew him forty years later, he was not molluscular but open and outspoken, friendly and engaging—perhaps because I was much younger and was not a literary rival. I think he fell into undeserved obscurity because he never put into a book his scattered art reviews, literary articles, poems and translations of Chinese poetry, and never composed (though he planned to write) a memoir. He wrote me, "I've had a £100 advance for an autobiography but—as one of my more realistic girlfriends coldly observed—who on earth would be interested enough to read it?" He was too easily discouraged. His military adventures in the Middle East and friendships with distinguished writers would have been of great interest.

Porteus was short and blue-eyed, impish and good-humored, shabbily dressed in a dark shirt and hairy tie, and unusually animated for a man in his seventies. He was interested in my background, education, writing and teaching year in Japan, and measured his cooperation while he subtly probed to see if I would be hostile or sympathetic to Lewis. As I gained his confidence, he was willing to portray himself in a negative light. He told me about Lewis' keen interest in Porteus' sexual affairs, and how jealous Lewis was of his own attractive and closely guarded young wife. When the young Porteus proudly showed Lewis his artwork, he crumpled up the drawings, threw them straight into the dustbin and exclaimed, "I don't want to look at that rubbish!" The first of their many quarrels occurred when Porteus refused to let Lewis interfere with his early study of the Master and Lewis complained, "When you began to piss against my leg I should have chased you away." During his affair with a Jewish girl whom Lewis knew, Porteus suggestively quoted an ejaculatory passage in *Tarr* and said, "I only go to her occasionally to get milked." Lewis, missing the allusion to his own novel, thought it referred to a more exotic perversion.

In *Self Condemned* (1954) Lewis satirized Porteus as "Rotter" Parkinson, who arouses the wrath of the autobiographical hero René Harding by reading out loud his article in fulsome praise of Harding. As the furious Harding takes his leave, Lewis turns the sexual into an intellectual metaphor: "His critical frenzy had one of its regular spasms. He tore his best friend to pieces and himself as well; so much devotion was embarrassing; how could one really feel at ease with a parasite, and with what ridiculous assiduity he had encouraged this man to feed upon his brain. He went there perhaps once a month, to be milked, as it were." With bitter irony Porteus noted that he, the model for the fictional Parkinson, later contracted Parkinson's disease.

The disease interfered with his self-taught but elegant Chinese calligraphy, of which he was justly proud. After reading Pound's *Cathay,* Porteus taught himself Chinese and drew Chinese characters for the reprint cover of Fenollosa's *The Chinese Written Character as a Medium for Poetry,* edited by Pound. Before publishing his Chinese *Cantos,* Pound asked Porteus to check the ideograms for accuracy. His essay "Ezra Pound and His Chinese Character: A Radical Examination" in Peter Russell's 1950 volume criticized the radical defects of Pound's Chinese but praised the beauty of his imprecise translations. He also accurately predicted, "The significance of China for the future of the world cannot be over-estimated."

As our conversations and correspondence progressed, Porteus gradually revealed his background, multifarious vocations and, to quote D. H. Lawrence, his "absolute necessity to move." He was born in Leeds, the oldest of three sons of an inspector of factories in the Home Office who moved about frequently. "My parents were poor but well educated: and musicians, eldest each of families of seven. . . . My Father began under Socialist and Methodist influences, and joined H.M. Factory Inspectorate initially to ameliorate the lot of the underpaid proletariat. . . . My Papa was a kindly man. As a Civil Servant of a type rare today, he refused bribes, and kept his mouth shut about anything but his work among police and doctors about industrial diseases such as asbestosis (a pioneer there) and other poisons."

Porteus started school at St. Cuthbert's College in Worksop, Nottinghamshire, in 1914, and also attended Reading School, boarded at a school in Huddersfield and studied at Huddersfield Art School. He traveled to France and Italy in 1927 to paint, but got distracted and painted very little. He met his first literary friend, the English Surrealist David Gascoyne, in the late 1920s.

Porteus went to a school for wireless operators in 1928, but got stuck on Morse code and earned only a second-class certificate, which later proved quite useful. He then got a job in advertising, had the Bird's Custard account and invented the catchy slogan "Cheep, Cheap." He also wrote two hundred limericks, some dirty, for Lea & Perrins Worcestershire sauce. He worked at Odhams Press, owner of the *Herald* newspaper, whose literary page was edited by John Betjeman. He first read Lewis' works and met him in the late 1920s, and began regular reviewing for the *New English Weekly* and *Time and Tide* in the 1930s.

After joining Imperial Airways (later BOAC) and drawing route maps, he left secret papers in an unlocked desk and—through his association with Lewis, the author of *Hitler*—was suspected of being a Nazi spy. He was one of seven founding members of the utopian, fuzzy-minded Promethean Society, which advocated eclectic politics, faith in science and pacifism. From 1931 to 1933 he edited and contributed to their short-lived journal *Twentieth Century,* which published Trotsky and Havelock Ellis, Lewis, W. H. Auden and Stephen Spender.

Enlisting in the RAF as a private in 1940, he worked mainly as a wireless operator in the Middle East and learned some Arabic. He wrote, "During the war we were Signallers—Roy Fuller in the Royal Navy in West Africa, I in an R.N. 'Stone Frigate' [a naval establishment on land]—(part of a fascinating spell with the RAF in the M.E., in small units from the Euphrates to Aleppo and Ankara)—in Ras Beirut," an upscale neighborhood in that city. He added, with a gruesome detail, "I was in a hush-hush Signals unit—Sinai, Egypt, Iraq, Libya, Lebanon, Syria (and Turkey with the Egyptologist Walter Bryan Emery).... I planted secret radios on the banks of the Euphrates; meeting only occasional snipers, all caught and publicly hanged in Aleppo."

He'd met his Jewish wife, Zenka Bartek, in 1929 and lived with her in an attic in Pimlico until 1944. She had always been a lesbian, and he found her with a girl when he returned home unexpectedly during the war. But he said, "The decade of my life with her before we married was normal and (as agreed between us) perfect. She wrote to me when I was at the Tel Aviv airport to say—but not why—that she'd decided to leave me. I had a 2- or 3-day blackout at this news."

Durrell had bluntly said that Zenka was ugly, and Geoffrey Grigson had some sharp words about her in his *Recollections:* "Lewis had never met her and never wanted to meet her—admittedly she was an ugly, rather bug-like little body, her dress and look conveyed rather a hint of lesbianism. . . . The little bug-like person chattered on about Spain, in a way all too knowing and too trivial. Lewis treated her with his usual fine courtesy, slightly exaggerated."

The saga of Porteus' marital relations took a strange twist with Derek Stanford's wild assertion in *Inside the Forties* (1977). He was astonished by "the frank open manner in which Porteus could speak of his ruined marriage, his wife having gone off with Geoffrey Grigson. . . . Confronted with our evident sympathy, his verdict on Grigson—'he was the better man'—evinced a magnanimity of mind beyond the average run of humanity." But this scandalous story was not true. The outraged Grigson, repelled by Zenka, sued for libel and settled with the publisher. Zenka became a potter in the Maritime Alps, and Porteus had been living on and off with Barbara Dunell since his wife left him in 1944. He frankly revealed that "Barbara is a nice placid girl for another Old Age Pensioner. I'm not myself queer or given to the contortions of the Kama Sutra. The Missionary position is OK with me."

From 1946 to 1950, sponsored by Eliot, Porteus worked in the Ministry of Information and wrote press summaries. In the 1950s he was employed for a time in the Chinese section of the BBC. While continuing his journalism, he began to do some gardening for four pounds a week. In the 1960s he became art critic for the

Times, the last and best job he ever had, and wrote an article once a fortnight for twenty guineas. But always contentious, he clashed with the prevailing views on art and was paid off with a trip to Tunisia. He left London after the *Times* job ended, and had been stuck in his seedy Cheltenham flat ever since. He self-critically concluded, "I had moved, rather than advanced, from being an unemployed art student to advertising jobs whence I had switched to copywriting and (in the year 1932 of the universal slump) to art criticism and book-reviewing. I was too busily *curious* about everything."

Porteus sent me twenty-eight long, fascinating letters, a total of 140 pages, from October 1977 to August 1985. Mostly handwritten in different colored inks, they contain puns, limericks, unpublished poems, Chinese characters and one haiku. Some are fourteen pages long, others are scribbled around Xeroxes of folio-size newspaper articles and many have extensive marginal notations. He loved sexual gossip, revealed the perverse tastes of a royal duke and the all-too-lively activity in a prominent department store: "The Selfridge lifts were operated by hand-chosen beauties, some tarts, some not. A scandal ensued because the lifts kept stopping between floors. So an order was issued to ensure that in future lift-girls should discard their skirts and wear jodhpurs."

Porteus frequently described, with bitter irony, the cruel physical changes around his disaster-prone flat in Cheltenham: "I am not destitute, but I have such domestic problems that I cannot find time to write. Harassed by landlords, and the din of traffic in what was once a country lane, with the tinkle of a forge where garages now roar, and the meadow opposite my bay window overlooking a sports centre where Rugby is played at night by arc lamps—waal, I guess this is progress, eh?" Six months later he gave a grimly humorous account of the latest cataclysmic events: "The flat here is threatened by Squatters. The mezzanine has the village drab living with the village idiot, whose Romeos climb my kitchen roof over barbed wire, climb over balconies, reproduce keys, leave the front door open to the new riff-raff coming up from Gloster as gate-crashers, and misuse my loo, fouling it up, and come in and out day and night, screaming and playing pop."

In addition to these Job-like trials, Porteus suffered natural catastrophes and personal illness: "I've been in great difficulties. . . . My place here was flooded in my absence . . . and I was so crippled with arthritis that travel, for more than a few hundred yards, was virtually out of the question." The condition of his book on Lewis—with the inscription "For my most devoted and more learned pupil Dr. Jeffrey Meyers, with blessings from Hugh Gordon Porteus"—suggests the state of his library. It has no dust wrapper and badly needs one, and seems to have been carried through combat. It is irrevocably foxed and spotted, stained and smeared, mildewed and moldy—though still precious, for all that, at least to me.

Unduly impressed by my doctorate, Porteus was generous with his praise. "You approached me like a KGB interrogator," he wrote. But "I found you cheerfully stimulating. . . . I enjoyed your company here very much indeed. You are so jolly—a rare trait in academics—together with your brisk efficiency and amazing range of accurate knowledge." When I invited him to write a chapter for *Wyndham Lewis: A Revaluation* (1980), which I edited for Athlone Press to coincide with the publication of my life of Lewis, he thanked me formally "for your kind offer of the honour of contributing to the W.L. collection." As the deadline approached he reported, "I made a list of subjects I wished to broach with you, but it's mislaid under heavy accumulation of unanswered correspondence," which helps to explain why he never wrote the long-awaited essay.

Instead, he enclosed as compensation a delightful irregular haiku, with a pun on the last two words:

The turtle doves their lovey-doves
              their lovey-doves pursue
still on his pine one (turning turtle) flew
out on a limb but now from clouds above
hurtling down a grace note drops for you
         to a p r o l o n g e d
            high COO.

As I was completing my biography he timidly pleaded, "please do spare your punches when you mention me." When the book appeared, he spared his own punches and concluded, "I must salute you for writing a very *true* life of W.L., unlikely to be superseded; and for incidentally doing me proud."

Porteus' own work was significant and, as he justly stated, "I've been an art & lit. critic in all the quality papers—weeklies & sundaes—for over half a century." Besides his book and twelve essays on Lewis, he wrote on Pound, Eliot, Durrell, Auden, George Barker and many others in hundreds of articles in the *New English Weekly, Time and Tide, Twentieth Century Verse, Life and Letters, Nine, Agenda, Criterion, Scrutiny, Listener, Observer, Times* and *Encounter.* Though usually generous, he could also be quite fierce. Reviewing a sympathetic study of Middleton Murry in 1934, he exclaimed, "It is difficult to see how anything of a wide and durable value can emerge from the labours of such an indiscriminate, submissive and parasitic" man. Using a similar phrase, he attacked Herbert Read's Surrealist exhibition in 1936 by declaring, "It is difficult to believe that the author of *Reason and Romanticism* actually is responsible for such an effusion as the prefatory note to the catalogue."

Porteus' *Background to Chinese Art,* a sixty-page Faber pamphlet, was published in 1935 in conjunction with the First International Exhibition of Chinese Art at Burlington House. An expert while still in his twenties, he emphasizes the culture, characters, calligraphy and painting of China. His brief work is studded with insights, such as "Chinese indeed seems to compensate for its poverty as a spoken tongue by providing in its script an intensely expressive miniature drama of gesture."

In a creative surge of 1952 Porteus composed *Dog River,* a dramatic verse-fantasy for radio. The BBC's Kubla Khan-ish description reads: "Dog River—the Nahr el-Kalb of the Arabs—is a Syrian river associated with Tammuz and also with the Egyptian Dog-God, Anubis. It runs for much of its course through underground caverns, in which part of the action of this programme takes place, and which are haunted by the Dog himself." He also contributed "The White Tiger" to *New Poems, 1952: A P.E.N. Anthology,* which included verse by Auden, Day Lewis and Louis MacNeice. Porteus' technically proficient and vividly impressive seven-stanza poem opens with:

> Thud, pad, ripple of Mongol fur;
> Breath, stars, glitter of teeth, spore;
>   Black frost of the tundra.

> Spirits of air and water, fire and earth,
> Open the dark with thunder, and make path
>   Now for the white tiger of the North.

A drinking companion of Dylan Thomas in the thirties, Porteus met the Welshman in a pub (where else?) and was surprised and horrified by the grossness of the poet, who seemed stunned and barely conscious. More significantly, he summoned up remembrance of his friends: Eliot, Durrell, Orwell and especially Lewis. He recalled, "I saw a good deal of Eliot, less of Lewis, after my return from the Middle East. . . . Later I spent much time at the School of Oriental and African Studies, then opposite Faber's, and often dropt in on Eliot for tea."

He then added two tantalizing personal revelations about Eliot's wives: "Eliot's devotion turned gradually to hatred when he found Vivian (as he told my wife and myself at a dinner in our Pimlico attic) head covered with a satin cloth, after midnight, sniffing ether from a bowl. Vivian also paraded with [Oswald] Mosley in a black uniform." After Valerie Eliot had visited Lewis' widow, Froanna, in Torquay, Devon, "ambiguities in Froanna's letters led me to believe that Eliot's widow (Mark 2) was on the point of *marrying* Fred Tomlin!," a distinguished British Council official and disciple of Lewis.

Signing his letters to Durrell "The Wombat" (an Australian burrowing marsupial), Porteus, who had been digging latrines in the Egyptian desert, "was chagrined not to have found any artifacts" and turned his disappointment into verse: "O to toil in Tibet / Where there are no toilets yet." He enthusiastically reviewed Durrell's novel *The Black Book* in 1938 and his poems *Cities, Plains and People* in 1949. When the first volume of *The Alexandria Quartet* appeared in 1957, he encouraged Durrell by measuring him against the gold standard and stating, "You are now doing the best writing since the heyday of poor old Wyndham, and nothing should be allowed to stop the rich heady flow." Durrell gratefully recorded that, apart from Eliot and one other friend, Porteus "was the person whose spirit and sensibility he admired most."

Porteus also offered some intriguing revelations about Orwell. Lewis' follower the colorful poet Roy Campbell falsely boasted that during the Spanish Civil War Orwell "had his vocal chords severed by a bullet from Roy's rifle on the Franco side." When I asked Porteus if he was the model for a similarly named character in Orwell's novel of 1939, he replied, using Orwell's real first name, "Certainly Orwell's 'Porteous' in *Coming Up for Air* was based on Eric's co-tenant Rayner Heppenstall's view of me at that time— conflated with Eric's Etonian contemporary, the Byzantinist Sir Steven Runciman."

In January 1947, when Porteus listened to the radio broadcast of *Animal Farm* in Orwell's flat, the author appreciatively wrote that Porteus, "who had not read the book, grasped what was happening after a few minutes." Orwell also recommended Porteus to David Astor, the owner of the *Observer:* "He was before the war a very interesting critical writer with some rather unusual specialized knowledge, such as, being able to read Chinese."

Another provocative bit of misinformation (similar to Derek Stanford's libel of Geoffrey Grigson) was disseminated when Orwell, absurdly misled when many writers were changing political sides, declared in the summer 1946 *Partisan Review:* "Wyndham Lewis, I am credibly informed, has become a Communist or at least a strong sympathiser, and is writing a book in praise of Stalin to balance his previous books in favor of Hitler." (Only Lewis' first book praised Hitler; his second book was a generally unrecognized recantation.) According to Porteus, the wild rumor that Lewis had become a Communist originated when Lewis said—as a joke—to gossipy Roy Campbell, "Tell them I've changed my views and am now writing a book about Stalin." Campbell repeated this in all seriousness to Porteus, who passed it on to Orwell. Delighted with this sensational gossip, Orwell did not check his source, published it in the prestigious American journal and damaged Lewis' reputation as well as his own.

Porteus recalled that Lewis introduced him to the press baron Lord Rothermere as "my *biographer,*" and he was unduly severe about his awkwardly titled first book, *Wyndham Lewis: A Discursive Exposition* (1932): "It is a very silly book, written by a semi-literate art student over 40 years ago. . . . The book I wrote on W.L. was pretty ridiculous. It was written, or scribbled, as a defence against the only worthy assessment, by Edgell Rickword" in his *Scrutinies,* volume 2 (1931). But he had a daunting task, and it was a creditable achievement to explain for the first time Lewis' difficult works of the late 1920s: *The Art of Being Ruled,*

Time and Western Man and his massive satirical novel *The Apes of God.*

Porteus' unorthodox book attempts to answer three questions: "What is this man trying to do? Does he succeed? . . . Is the result of interest?" He believes that Lewis is "supreme among contemporary filibusters of letters" and in Eliot's words, "the most fascinating personality of our time." The reviews of Porteus' book precisely reflected the views of the editors who published them. F. R. Leavis disliked Lewis, Eliot admired him. In Leavis' *Scrutiny* (March 1933) T. R. Barnes put the knife in: "Mr. Porteus is a disciple . . . and bases his estimate mainly on Lewis' style and his satire. . . . He finds adequate praise difficult: Mr. Lewis' satire is better than Dryden's and his style is as good as Shakespeare's." In Eliot's *Criterion* (July 1933) Michael Roberts recognized the merits of Porteus' book: "His exposition is not only a valuable elucidation of the work of Wyndham Lewis, it is also a shrewd and entertaining comment on contemporary literature and an excellent essay on the place of visual imagery in poetry and prose."

Porteus' letters to me shrewdly analyzed Lewis' complex and abrasive character:

> He was, not without reason, a difficult customer. I found him very hospitable and agreeable whenever we met. . . .
>
> [But] Lewis certainly enjoyed being contentious. So did I! We had magnificent confrontations, always mended quite amicably. Always as poor as myself, he was a most generous host. But "difficult"? Oh yes! You had to sail him like a boat. Lewis, Eliot and Myself were all fair sailors. The worst squabble I had with Lewis was when I rashly observed about something or other that "I know what you are busy thinking!" That really got his goat: though in fact I was quite right. I could almost invariably predict his reactions to my often deliberately teasing remarks. . . .

Lewis had a masochistic wish to pin down his most amiable friends as enemies. Is it ironic that he should marry a masochistic doll? They were absolutely devoted to one another, and thoroughly enjoyed their merely verbal duels or duets. Froanna was a placid devotee, and a superb hostess. I had always supposed that W.L. would be oriental in his intense jealousy if males so much as glanced at Froanna. . . .

I can't say W.L. taught me to write. I may be slipshod as a spontaneous writer. But he did teach me to *see*.

In his anonymous (and unrecorded) profile of Lewis in the *Observer* of August 5, 1956, celebrating the major exhibition of Lewis' work at the Tate Gallery, Porteus was characteristically positive, but now more aware of Lewis' limitations: "It is a perennial fault of Lewis the novelist that his characters and narrative seem to be kept in a semblance of life only by brilliant feats of intellectual manipulation." In his last article on Lewis, a review-essay on Walter Michel's *Wyndham Lewis: Paintings and Drawings* in *Agenda* (Spring 1971), he stated, "It is probably as true now as in his lifetime, I suppose, that Lewis affronts and leaves cold, by his own cool humour and detachment, more people than he attracts by his gifts of uncommon sense and intelligent mockery." He then defends Lewis and explains his formidable achievement.

The versatile Porteus had been an artist, wireless operator, advertising man, journalist, map designer, book reviewer, magazine editor, RAF signalman, précis writer, Sinologist, gardener and art critic, but he never achieved prolonged success in any of these professions. Though he modeled himself on Lewis and was a pale reflection of the Master, the two men had a great deal in common. Both were talented linguists (Porteus also knew some Turkish and Russian), wrote poetry and art criticism, endured long periods of poverty, had unconventional marriages and nourished right-wing political ideas. They also shared many friends, including Eliot, whom Porteus called "sepulchral and lugubrious." He too, as he said of Lewis, had a wide-ranging curiosity and impressive virtuosity. Porteus was not Prince Lewis nor was meant to be, but an attendant lord to provoke a scene or two. But many famous writers valued the friendship of their lively and stimulating, learned and devoted companion. Dedicated to art and literature, he clearly understood and was a passionate advocate of their difficult and provocative work.

6

Alex Colville

(1920–2013)

The work of Alex Colville (awarded the Order of Canada), one of the great modern realist painters, combines the Flemish detail of Andrew Wyeth, the eerie foreboding of George Tooker and the anguished confrontations of Lucian Freud. Behind the North Americans stands their common master, Edward Hopper. Colville's works are in many museums in Canada and Germany—he has affinities with Max Beckmann and appeals to the German "secondary virtues": cleanliness, punctuality, love of order. But he is less well known in England and America. In a long life he resolutely opposed the fashionable currents of abstract and expressionistic art and, as John Bayley noted in *Elegy for Iris,* "No other modern painter is so unconscious of prevailing fashion and so indifferent to what's new in the art world." In contrast to Jackson Pollock's wild action painting, Colville created paintings of contemplation and reflection.

The son of a Scottish-born steelworker and a Canadian milliner, Colville was born in Toronto. "Processed as a Catholic," he later considered himself a lapsed or "ex-semi-Catholic." He grew up in Nova Scotia, graduated from Mount Allison University in Sackville, New Brunswick, and was a war artist with the Canadian army in the northwest Europe campaign and the liberation of the Bergen-Belsen concentration camp. He married Rhoda Wright in 1942, a handsome blue-eyed woman with fine skin and blond hair who had been an art student with him. His wife and muse appears as a calm figure in many of his paintings. They had four children (one son, John, died in 2012). Two of them, Ann and Charles, live in Nova Scotia; his oldest son, Graham, worked for Reuters and now lives in Cyprus.

After the war Colville returned to teach at Mount Allison. He resigned in 1963 to paint full-time and thought he could support himself as an artist, but continued to live in Sackville. He was a visiting artist at the University of California in Santa Cruz in 1967–68 and in Berlin in 1971. Two years later he and Rhoda moved into her childhood home, a large house built by her father in 1920, in Wolfville on the north coast of Nova Scotia. Home of Acadia University, the town has excellent restaurants, wide streets, elegant houses, comfortable inns and a summer theater. In 1984–85 he visited and exhibited in Beijing, Hong Kong and Tokyo.

His daughter, Ann Kitz, thinks Alex was a good father—though withdrawn and always involved with his work. His extremely close bond with Rhoda (they used to take baths together in a special French tub with lion's claw feet) almost excluded the children. He sometimes feared he'd been "feeding on Rhoda's life"—not only by using her as a model in many of his pictures, but also by taking over her house, native town, province and past life. But naked or nude, he always painted his muse with a lover's eye.

Colville's work is filled with visual and verbal allusions that affirm the value of past art and continuity with his own. *Three Girls on a Wharf* echoes the iconography of the Three Graces and the Judgment of Paris. The woman in *Woman and Terrier* holds the dog (their beloved Shasta) in the same tender way that Raphael's Madonna holds the Christ child. *Fête Champêtre,* with its seated woman playing a lute and man snoozing on the bank of a river, echoes Titian and Manet.

I was unaware of Colville's work until the summer of 1998 when, driving to Nova Scotia to see the birthplace of Wyndham Lewis and the childhood home of Elizabeth Bishop, I belatedly discovered his paintings in the Beaverbrook Museum in Fredericton, New Brunswick. In Nova Scotia I saw an exhibition of his work at Acadia University, and bought two of the six books written about him. The bookstore owner gave me his address and suggested I call on him. Though I was eager to meet, I felt unprepared and needed to know more about him. I was immediately struck by the parallels with Wyndham Lewis. Lewis was born in Amherst, where Colville spent his teenage years. Both were Canadian war artists—Lewis in the Great War, Colville in World War II. Lewis, penniless and unknown, lived during the Second World War in Toronto, where Colville was born. Both artists emphasize intellectual content as well as the fine draftsmanship and purity of line that runs from Van Eyck, through Mantegna, Dürer and Holbein, to Ingres.

Alex, I found in the course of our correspondence, read avidly and shared my interest in masculine writers: Joseph Conrad, Ford Madox Ford, T. E. Lawrence, Ernest Hemingway, André Malraux and George Orwell. Many of his works were inspired by literature: by the poems of William Wordsworth and Roy Campbell as well as by the paintings of Piero della Francesca, Edouard Manet and Edgar Degas. Charles Baudelaire, a superb poet and art critic, observed, "One of the characteristic symptoms of the spiritual condition of our age is that the arts aspire to lend one another new powers." Marcel Proust agreed that "painting can pierce to the unchanging reality of things, and so establish itself as a rival of literature." Attracted to works that portray loss and pain, danger and death, Colville transformed verbal into visual images, and revealed how the correspondence between word and picture shaped his vision of the world. He interpreted literature in his own way and, like all artists, used every inspiration he could find to convey the mood and meaning of his pictures.

Alex designed an edition of twelve 14-carat-gold medallions

(1972) based on Isaiah Berlin's famous essay "The Hedgehog and the Fox" about Leo Tolstoy's view of history. The chained medallion has an octagonal frame around an inner circle that's divided in the middle by a thin filament. A strutting long-tailed fox, facing right, stands above; a pointed-nose fat hedgehog, facing left, squeezes into the space below. The inscription in tiny engraved letters around the circle reads: "The fox knows many things, but the hedgehog knows one big thing." Berlin portrayed Tolstoy as a versatile, frisky fox in contrast to the sluggish, single-minded hedgehog. Alex couldn't possibly portray the complex argument of this long essay in his medallion, but he assumed his educated audience would note the source and understand the quotation. He was attracted to the physical contrast of the two animals as well as to the ideas they embodied. Mindful of their symbolic content, he created two charming, golden creatures. He was interested to hear that I'd interviewed the congenial Sir Isaiah when writing my life of Edmund Wilson.

Alex did a picture based on John Berryman's "The Ball Poem" (1948). In this early work a little boy is grief-stricken after losing his ball, which bounces down the street and into the sea. The poem is about "the epistemology of loss"—a major theme in modern literature—and the need to learn early on to face and accept the harsh adversity that defines human life. In Alex's painting (1956) a little boy, seen at a sharp angle from above, wears a tee shirt, short pants and high black-and-white sneakers that project over the tall stone wall above the water. He looks down at his striped football that floats hopelessly out of reach in three concentric circles. With left arm held away from his body and fingers spread, he seems willing to risk a jump into the water, but doesn't see a way to get back up the forbidding wall.

Alex illustrated W. B. Yeats' "The Ballad of the Foxhunter" (1889) with four serigraphs. In his third and most interesting portrayal of the poem, an old, sickly and perhaps dying man, wearing a green jacket, sits in a chair next to three attentive foxhounds and strokes the nose of a brown horse that stands next to him with right leg raised. But the animals can bring only slight comfort. The ghostly hunter, with shadowy white legs, is positioned behind the horse, which blocks out the upper half of his body. Alex prints beneath the serigraph three of Yeats' oneiric, languid and somnolent quatrains:

> His eyelids droop, his head falls low,
> His old eyes cloud with dreams;
> The sun upon all things that grow
> Falls in sleepy streams.
>
> Brown Lollard treads upon the lawn,
> And to the armchair goes,
> And now the old man's dreams are gone,
> He smooths the long brown nose.
>
> And now moves many a pleasant tongue
> Upon his wasted hands,
> For leading aged hounds and young
> The huntsman near him stands.

The Lollards were followers of the fourteenth-century religious teachings of John Wycliffe, a dissident in the Roman Catholic Church and precursor of the Protestant Reformation. He would appeal to the Protestant Yeats and to the lapsed Catholic Colville.

In September 1999 I returned to Nova Scotia and spent three days visiting Alex, Rhoda and their daughter, Ann, seeing his house and studio, exploring his milieu, talking about his artistic career and the meaning of his work. Handsome and elegant, fit and agile at seventy-nine, he wore blue or grey cashmere polo shirts, neatly pressed blue or khaki trousers, high-sided suede or leather shoes.

Slim, five feet eight inches tall, he had blue eyes and a thatch of white hair on his narrow head. He was formal and reserved, with a gentle handshake, yet also generous, lively and enthusiastic. When he found something amusing, he threw his head back and laughed with full-hearted delight. Rhoda, a year younger, was quiet, maternal, perceptive and utterly devoted to her husband.

He meticulously designed his spare, modern and much smaller new house (next-door to his old one) according to the classical idea of the golden mean and the principles expounded in Le Corbusier's *The Modulor* (1948). He carefully calculated the angle of the roof, the height of the windows, the width of the doors, the placement of the light switches and the space between the steps. In his ultramodern dining room he placed two ancient Greek and Etruscan vases in special glassed-in niches. He was pleased when I sent him my research on these vases.

Alex's studio in New Brunswick was in the attic of his house and had a trap door that sealed him off from his family. His new studio was on the ground floor, a few steps away from the sitting room. A striking contrast to Francis Bacon's squalid and chaotic workplace, it was scrupulously clean and neat. It contained a desk, two worktables, two cases for materials, a sink, a mirror, bare white walls and a smooth concrete floor. He drew left-handed and painted with acrylics at a high easel. Reproductions of Nicolas Poussin's *Tancred and Erminia* (1634) and of Max Beckmann's *The Loge* (1928) were pinned above his desk, and a George Stubbs poster decorated his beach cabin. Many of his own works, but none by other artists, hung in his house. He made furniture and all his own frames in a well-equipped carpenter's workshop. The basement also contained a well-organized art storage room—with all his preliminary drawings and serigraphs, a small library, copies of books about him and those reproducing his work—fireproof, double-locked and with its own alarm.

His schedule in those years was as regular as Immanuel Kant's in Königsberg. He rose early, walked the dog and worked from eight to twelve in the morning. After lunch and a nap, he picked up his mail at the local post office and did some shopping, answered letters and made phone calls and let the afternoon "kind of drift away." After dinner at six, he read or watched television, was in bed at nine and asleep soon after.

Rhoda posed for Alex—standing on her head, before and after making love, with her legs apart in the bathtub—all her married life. She found it awfully hard work and didn't like doing it, but was always "a good sport." She'd have much preferred to hide than "model immodestly in the nude" and would never, as in *Refrigerator,* have gone into the kitchen with no clothes on. Alex's children also posed for him. Graham was the model for *Dog, Boy and St. John River;* John for the high jumper in the Mount Allison University mural *Athletes;* Charles for *Road Work.* Ann, unlike her mother, liked posing, which made her "feel special," and considered it a vital part of her life. She appears in many works, from *Child and Dog* in her infancy to *Singer* as an adult. She's posed in *Woman with Skiff* as a woman pulling her boat onto a sand bar.

Remote, isolated, provincial and deliberately cut off from intellectual life (he noted the limitations of the faculty at Acadia University, where he was chancellor for ten years), he preferred to be far away from the art world and didn't need social life or external stimulation. He and Rhoda once seriously thought of becoming lighthouse keepers, but he could also be very social when he was in the right mood. It took him several years to assimilate the experience of World War II and the visual excitement of his first visit to the Louvre in 1945. His great strength and inner peace came from his long happy marriage and close family ties, from being solidly rooted in the Atlantic Maritime Provinces (geographically akin to New England), a haven and refuge that he transformed into the core of his art.

Though deeply nourished by the grey mists and grey seas of

Nova Scotia, his contrasting experiences in the war, Santa Cruz, Berlin and the Orient also profoundly affected his life. The crucial figures in his career, to whom he often referred, were the American Lincoln Kirstein, the first major critic to recognize his work, and the Viennese émigré Harry Fischer, his London dealer at Marlborough and Fischer Fine Art.

We spent two afternoons driving through the riverine landscape that provided the substance of his work, and swam at his beach house on the Minas Basin. At our approach, a crow flew out from under a bridge as if on cue for his *Bridge and Raven*. The blighted trunk and branches of the towering eighteenth-century elm tree at Horton Landing, near the Gaspereau River at Hortonville, has withstood several bolts of lightning. But it continues to flourish and symbolizes, in Colville's painting, the struggle between survival and death. The trestle bridge at Nijmegen, Holland, which Colville painted in 1944, was the archetype of the Nova Scotia trestles that appear in works like *August* and *Dog and Bridge*. The steelworker's son remained fascinated by the rigid geometric structure and high vantage point of the trestles, which connect the distant banks of a river and provide a passage for trains, cars and people. While looking at the elm tree, the trestle and the French Cross at Grand Pré, I was struck by the contrast between their commonplace actuality and the heightened reality in his paintings, achieved through his harmonic composition, angle of vision and intensified details. His absolutely authentic art imposes order on nature, increases our perception of the world and gives universal significance to the particular.

Giorgio Vasari's life of Paolo Uccello recounts how "his wife used to say that Paolo would sit studying perspective all night, and when she called him to come to bed he would answer, 'Oh, what a sweet thing this perspective is!'" Like the Italian Old Masters, Colville saw painting as a form of construction. He made thirty or forty drawings before beginning a major picture, calculated with severe and unyielding perfectionism the geometric definition of space, and drew the viewer's eye to the still center of his work. "His art is meticulous in detail," wrote John Bayley, "as he takes infinite pains over the extreme niceties of composition, and this precision contrasts with the statuesque solidity of his human figures, as massive and mysterious as Piero's and yet wholly absorbed in the commonplace activities of contemporary life."

Colville painted men in relation to women and children, to earth, water and sky, to birds, cats, dogs, cows and horses, to bikes, boats, cars, trains—and guns. His humane, penetrating vision looked far out and in deep, and his monumental figures and unsettling images suggested the metaphysical questions that evolved from his reading Martin Heidegger, Jean-Paul Sartre and the French Existentialists. He saw himself as "a floating observer—curiously detached," and his subjects are often meditative and alone. He believed life is essentially dangerous. There's an element of the contingent and accidental, a feeling of mystery and angst, even in his most idyllic scenes. As Alan Ross perceived, his subjects seem "aware that there was another, more complex and elusive level of living than the merely physical, and that, even among their lakes, snows and woods, they had constantly to be on the alert, both against the elements and against unseen antagonists."

Alex had a fortunate life. His parents supported his decision to become an artist, he was nurtured by a good art teacher at Mount Allison, he became a Canadian war artist, he had a solid family life with four children, his risky departure from a secure teaching position paid off, he received practical help from important patrons, he had an extremely successful career and was frequently honored in Canada. In 1982 the sixty-two-year-old Alex recalled that Titian had painted *The Death of Actaeon* in his nineties and hoped that "I may have another thirty years' work ahead of me." He fulfilled his ambition by living to the age of ninety-two, working until his last few years and creating about two hundred major paintings.

Alex retreated to a remote town so he could concentrate on his work and as he became famous the world came to him. He never lacked inspiration and (like his friend Iris Murdoch) began his next work immediately after completing the previous one. His art portrayed the logic of taut sensations and the delightful deceptions of his invented reality. The hidden features and vivid insubstantiality of his subjects, which suggest people's concealed character and the difficulty of penetrating their inner thoughts, heighten the mystery of the real in his paintings.

I spent several days with Alex on each of three visits from Berkeley to Wolfville. On my second trip, in October 2003, I lectured on Somerset Maugham at Acadia University and joined his family's Thanksgiving celebration. After seeing Alex for the third time, in June 2007, I spent a weekend at Ann's country house in Wallace. Old enough to be my father and an ideal father figure, he was a gracious host. On one occasion, when I planned to take the bus from Wolfville to Ann's house in Halifax, he insisted that his son John drive me there. When he asked what I'd like to have for lunch and I suggested lobster, he bought some fine specimens in the supermarket and complemented them with a bottle of fine wine. That fall day was perfect, the sun dappled the grass and I felt blissfully happy being alone with Alex and Rhoda in their secluded garden. I felt honored by my friendship not only with a brilliant artist but also with a well-read, intelligent and generous man.

7

James Salter

(1925–2015)

James Salter's masterpieces—*A Sport and a Pastime, Light Years* and *Burning the Days*—place him, after Saul Bellow and Vladimir Nabokov, as the best postwar American novelist. His lyrical evocations of people and places, of luxurious decadence and the danger of death, are unsurpassed. I was also struck by how he'd abandoned two successful careers: as a fighter pilot who flew one hundred missions against Russian-piloted MIGs across the Yalu River in North Korea, and as the screenwriter of Robert Redford's *Downhill Racer, The Appointment* and *Threshold.* On July 18, 2005, I wrote to him for the first time, cold, in Bridgehampton, Long Island. I discussed the influence of Hemingway and Fitzgerald on his work, mentioned some places we'd both lived in (Colorado and Japan) and my meetings with his friends: James Dickey, Irwin Shaw, James Jones, Joseph Mankiewicz, Joseph Losey and Patrick Leigh Fermor.

Jim responded on August 6 to what he called my "astonishing letter" and exclaimed: "I was stunned to learn that Dickey was a navigator. He posed as a pilot and one night in Paris, the night we met, told me that if we'd been in the air at the same time he'd have shot my ass down. I see now what with, a sextant. He was a big blowhard, constantly interrupting with imitations of movie actors. But he could write, I agree with you." Jim and I had an immediate temperamental affinity, and could write and talk about subjects of great interest to us. Writing is a lonely profession and we were delighted to have struck sparks.

During the last decade (2005–15) of his long life Jim sent me eighty letters, postcards and emails. He usually typed one-page, single-spaced letters on oversized A4 stationery with letterheads of exotic hotels, sent to him by friends, from Estonia to China, from the sailboat *Olinka* to (disappointingly) Days Inn in Hays, Kansas. His letters discussed writers, reading and readings, family and friends, travels and teaching at Virginia and at Duke (where he earned $20,000 for one week), movies and Hollywood, his books and my books (especially *Hemingway* and *Edmund Wilson*) and his resurgence of literary power and astonishing late success. In his eighties he published *Last Night* (stories, 2005), *There and Then* (travels, 2005), *Life Is Meals* (gastronomy, 2006, coauthored with his wife Kay), *Memorable Days* (correspondence with Robert Phelps, 2010), *All That Is* (novel, 2013) and *Collected Stories* (2013).

He wrote frankly about his early sexual adventures, money and awards, writing schedule and writing problems. I sometimes addressed him as "Tuan Jim," after the hero of Joseph Conrad's Malayan novel. Since my mother's maiden name and his original name was Horowitz, I fancied that we might be distantly related. I also found that in John Huston's film *The Misfits* the 1939 Meyers biplane, which drove the wild mustangs out of the mountains and into captivity, was actually flown by a pilot named Ken Salter.

As our friendship developed, Jim wanted to read everything I wrote. I sent him eight of my books and he generously praised, never criticized, my work. Like my late friend J. F. Powers, it amused Jim to pretend that I was the great author and he the humble drudge. When I asked his advice about selling my screenplays, he replied, "You are dramatically overqualified to write movies. I don't particularly like them. If I go to [work on] one it's with uneasiness. I don't like being in the hands of a director."

Before my first visit he defensively warned me, though he was extremely sophisticated and well read, "I am afraid you're going to find me a little more uncultured than you expected." When I sent him a list of more than sixty errors in the appalling edition of his letters to Robert Phelps, he seemed far less troubled than I was. "Cher Maître," he wrote, "Far from being angry, I am dazzled by your immense and rightfully proud knowledge of all these matters and persons. What you dashed off in an hour or two is far beyond my own knowing."

We strongly disagreed about book editors. He admired and depended upon them, I found them (except for Aaron Asher and Peter Davison) obstructive and incompetent. I was convinced that all the students who got a C– in my English classes had taken revenge by becoming editors. Himself a war hero, he also hero-worshipped others: the astronauts and air aces, the novelist Irwin Shaw and screenwriter Lorenzo Semple, the editors Robert Phelps, Richard Seaver and Robert Ginna. Jim had adopted Phelps' precious Francophilia: his fondness for French phrases and admiration for writers inferior to himself, Paul Léautaud and Colette.

While visiting a friend, I discovered that his father and Jim's father had been in the same class at West Point. I saw a photo of Jim's father in the yearbook and confirmed that he'd been first in his class. Jim recalled: "My own father served only a couple of years in the army after West Point. Careers seemed unpromising for those who had missed the war—he was in the class of 1919 that graduated in 1918 and then returned for a year later on—and the army shrank drastically in size. He was in the reserve and was recommissioned or reactivated in 1940, and then served through WW II, some of it in England."

We mostly discussed literature, and Jim noted the difference between modern poets, such as Robert Lowell and John Berryman, and novelists: "The poets decided to be manic and destroy themselves. The novelists did otherwise, but then a novel requires a lot of organization and persistence, they had to keep their heads." He especially admired and taught Hemingway's "The Short Happy Life of Francis Macomber" and observed, "Hemingway is very affected and can be annoying, but the story, its structure and pace as well as its tone are so good." Edmund Wilson he adored and often referred to as an inspiring literary touchstone: "Wilson seems to represent, both because of when he lived and what he was, a last brave flaring of literature's long eminence. At the same time, reading about him fills one with courage and desire." Wilson's motto from Deuteronomy 31:6, cut in Hebrew letters on his gravestone, was "Be strong and of a good courage."

In a grumpy mood, Jim compared Wilson's apogee to the robotic mindlessness of our own time and declared, "We are swimming in sewage, aren't we? The culture seems to be accelerating and heading, as if towards an irresistible black hole, towards the screen, television, computer, movie house." Jim was violently against George Bush, hated reading about politics and didn't care who won the next election. But he also believed that culture moved in cycles and that there would be a return to a healthier society—though not yet.

Jim was always perceptive about writing. Reading through thousands of pages of his unpublished journals before selling them to the University of Texas, he noted the dominant themes: "I find them filled with the same preoccupations that are in my novels: the sexual life and its paramount presence in life, interesting or clever dialogue, profiles of individuals, occasional incisive observation, self-analysis, and descriptions of incidental women. . . . There are [also] descriptions of other writers and judgments of them and many intensely personal entries about my unhappy first marriage." As he struggled to complete *All That Is,* he remarked on the contrast between ambition and achievement: "You have caught me at the tail end of life. I thought I would snatch the fire from the gods but each time came away with a piece of wood that only smoldered a little."

Using a flight metaphor, he also expressed his cardinal principles as a novelist, which should be carved in stone in all the writers' "workshops": "Don't try to include everything, hold the irony, do not abandon characters—stay with them, persevere, be yourself, the best character with the most wonderful phrases is the author, lift off early." When his exact but distant contemporary William Styron died, Jim took it as a personal blow: "Styron's death, long desired by him according to his son-in-law, and following some terrible final rounds, has hit me more than usual. I've known him since the early 1960s . . . but we were never close. I feel close now."

I wrote two articles and two reviews about Jim's work, for which he was excessively grateful: "The review of [*Life Is Meals*] is *wonderful*, all one hopes, more than one deserves. More than two deserve. . . . Many, *abundant* thanks." He gave me some useful background about his story "Am Strande von Tanger" (On the Beach in Tangier) and wrote that I made him see his work in a new way: "I feel elevated to another level, your perceptive analysis of 'Am Strande' is an adjunct to Literature. Well, I am very grateful. More than that, it made me want to read the story, and it's interesting that you point out connections I was unaware of." Pleased to accept my homage to him with *Samuel Johnson,* he replied (though most of his friends were writers), "I've never had a book dedicated to me before. . . . It's thrilling."

Though I'd caught him "at the tail end of life," he achieved his greatest recognition during his final years. He lived modestly but had, like Scott Fitzgerald, a weakness for the wealth and luxury he'd tasted in Hollywood, and was pleased to be with people who played polo and were rich together. "We were in Egypt in February," he wrote in 2010, "cruising up the Nile with [the English publisher] Christopher and Koukla McLehose, and the Peter Matthiessens. I'm sure you've been there. The legendary tombs and temples were crowded, everything was crowded, Abu Simbel was a 3-hour bus ride each way from Aswan which was crowded, but the days spent sailing up and down the river are what I'll remember, feeling of timelessness."

In 2013, when he won the $150,000 Windham-Campbell Prize administered by Yale, he amusingly remarked that for the eight other winners, "the prize money is meant to enable them to continue writing. For me, it's to enable me to stop." For his *Collected Stories,* which had an introduction by the Irish novelist John Banville, he "got a big English advance (Picador) within a stone's throw of six figures. This is for me *unexampled.*" He proudly related *All That Is* "had tremendous coverage in France. It was, maybe is still, a bestseller. 70,000 copies. I was on the front page of *Le Monde* and the cover of *Lire.* They claim to have discovered me at the very lip of the grave." On June 15, 2015, five days after his birthday and four days before his death, he wryly told me, "I've just had my ninetieth birthday, try to imagine that. . . . [I'm] writing a couple of reviews for the *New York Review of Books,* one on David Mc-Cullough's *The Wright Brothers,* a book I doubt you'd be inclined to read. Bob Silvers has it in his head that I can write about aviation matters."

Jim inscribed twenty-six various editions of his books for me. The three best, signed in three different ways, were:

A Sport and a Pastime: "To Jeffrey. Represents, I think, the *apogee.* Very fondest, Jas."

All That Is: "To Jeffrey, one of its first and certainly most diligent readers. With great affection, James Salter."

Burning the Days: "Dear Jeffrey—you were born just a bit too late to be included—Affectionately, Jim."

I valued his approval more than any other writer's. A friend said the best thing about my *Thomas Mann's Artist-Heroes* (2014) was Jim's comment: "This brilliant and intensely rich book fills one, from the beginning, with the desire to know more—all there is— about Mann and the stories and novels that brought him to preeminence as Germany's greatest modern writer and important moral force. This is a wonderful book written with verve. Thomas Mann, his person, themes, obsessions and art have been of lifelong interest to Jeffrey Meyers, who brings to them the background and breadth that supreme literary art and the tremendous decades from 1900 through the 1940s deserve." This comment really was "an adjunct to Literature."

———

We lived on different coasts of America and managed to meet only twice: for three days each time, in June 2006 and July 2007, at his home in Bridgehampton. But our letters paved the way for stimulating and sympathetic encounters. Jim had short-cropped white hair, high forehead, blue eyes, pointed nose, uneven teeth, a sturdy build and rugged good looks. He was in great shape for a man of eighty-one and tackled a windblown balloon on the beach before his young grandson could catch it. He was an amusing raconteur and attentive host. Greeting me while leaning against the frame of his open front door, he allowed, "You're taller than I expected." Sizing me up, he said he disliked my stagy, professional author's photo, wearing a Córdoba hat, and thought I looked better in person.

All four desks in his house were piled high with papers and left no space to work. The books spilled chaotically out of the narrow shelves, and though he offered to give me a copy with his introduction to Irwin Shaw's *The Young Lions,* we couldn't find it. My wife and I stayed in a bed-and-breakfast place on our first visit. The following year Jim gave us the upstairs master bedroom. His corgi, who was named Paavo after the Finnish runner and slept with Jim and Kay, was recovering from an operation and couldn't climb the narrow circular staircase. Jim let the garden grass grow high and liked "to see the wind blow through it." He also rented a small flat on West 45th Street in Manhattan, which Kay used to write and see plays and films. An attractive woman and worthy consort, she was born in Denver, graduated from the University of Colorado and earned a master's degree in journalism from Columbia. They met during the filming of a television show just after Kay graduated from college and, she affirmed, "he educated me."

Jim withdrew from the summer social life in order to write. But he found the winters in Bridgehampton, where he could work without interruption, were too cold, bleak, boring and depressing to bear. So each year after Christmas they took a week to drive to Aspen. Paavo didn't like flying, and Jim wouldn't trust anyone to drive his dog, papers and possessions to Colorado. He still skied downhill in Aspen, despite the high altitude and his arthritis, and played tennis singles with Matthiessen on "millionaires' courts" in the Hamptons.

Jim had four children from his first marriage, and struggled to educate them all at the University of Colorado. His daughter Allan died at the age of twenty-five in a freak accident when a nail hit a wire in the shower and electrocuted her. His twins, son James and daughter Claude, are "completely unintellectual." James is a builder in Bozeman, Montana; Claude, married to a sculptor, lives in Aspen. Jim's first wife also lives there, but he was "only in touch with her by necessity."

Jim's daughter Nina (with a long *i*) looks like him and was in Bridgehampton when we visited. She lives in Paris and runs her own small publishing company, Les-deux-terres, which translates English-language authors, including Kazuo Ishiguro and Ruth Rendell, and publishes them in French. Briefly married to a Frenchman when she was twenty, she has a well-behaved, bilingual son, Nile, then about ten years old. Pretty but not enticing, Nina was still jealous of Kay's happy marriage and resented us for diverting Jim's interest during our visit. She sulked and was mainly silent during dinner, and sat apart on the beach. Angry and aggressive, hostile and rude, she'd rather be feared than liked. She behaved childishly, was obviously unhappy and seemed to be battling demons. Kay said she'd been that way since childhood, was usually much worse, and she was glad to have us there to ease the tension. Nina demanded more attention than Jim could supply. He seemed apprehensive that she might explode, but was patient and tolerant: a good father. When Jim opened a bottle of Macon, I said the name sounded like an obscene word in French. Nina contradicted me and, tired of tangling with her and thinking she knew more French than I did, I dropped it. I later confirmed that *con* means "cunt" in French and "Ma con" had suggested that to me. Nina either knew this or was far more innocent than she seemed. Jim thought she "just didn't get it."

Theo, Jim's son with Kay, went to Lawrenceville and was a junior at Bowdoin. He spent summers as an intern on Wall Street and with a theater company. Jim had grave doubts about a theatrical career, but wanted to let him have a shot at it. He liked traveling in Europe with Theo and appreciated the liveliness he generated when he was home.

Jim liked to reminisce about his glory days in the air force. But he was not sorry that he'd left to become a writer in 1957 after the successful publication of *The Hunters*. Some of his old comrades had made four stars. Most, retired for thirty years, played golf and ranted against the liberals. He was pleased to be invited by a general, who admired his novel, to fly an F-16 for an hour from an air base in Fort Worth. He hadn't lost his touch—like swimming, he never forgot—and did turns, loops and other tricks. The young airmen were impressed that the old relic had known the astronauts and famous fighter pilots. He remembered the huge air ace Robert Olds—6'2", 230 pounds—who "begged to be a fighter pilot in a small cockpit." But he added, "Heroes are more often made up than true." He described experiencing the effects of oxygen deprivation during training: he started to play cards but quickly passed out. He also explained that if a stowaway tried to hide in the wheel case of a plane he would die of suffocation before he froze to death.

Jim went to a few meetings of the American Academy of Arts and Sciences, but felt like a renegade who didn't belong with all the respectable oldies. "Can you see me with those guys?" he asked. The main advantage of being in the Academy is that "you can say you're in the Academy." He preferred to break a solemn mood and liven things up with some jokes. Gloria, wife of James Jones, asked while dancing next to two gays who were dancing together, "My man has a hard on. Does yours?" A hostess asked Nabokov, who arrived at a Cornell dinner party during a snowstorm, "Did you come in a troika?" "No, a Buicka." At a diplomatic reception the British foreign minister asked an attractively dressed person to dance and was told, "I don't dance. I'm not a woman. I'm the archbishop of Lima."

Jim then ranged through friends in the literary world. Sarah, widow of George Plimpton, could be difficult with biographers. She wanted to protect her young daughters from knowledge of her husband's amorous adventures. Saul Bellow, after hesitating, finally decided to marry a woman (Susan Glassman) with a mustache. His last young wife (Janis Freedman) was a devoted mouse. Jim's closest friends were Peter Matthiessen, living in Bridgehampton and married to an English woman from Tanzania, and Lorenzo Semple in Santa Monica. Jim asked about my meetings in Spain with the writer Gerald Brenan and with the matadors Antonio Ordóñez and Luis-Miguel Dominguín. He liked Dominguín's charmingly formal way of greeting me, "A sus órdenes" (at your orders), and repeated it several times.

Jim was at his best when talking about writing. He used to appear in *Esquire,* but thought the magazine was now garbage and would no longer contribute. He had a new agent who was "big at ICM," went into Vintage paperbacks before signing with Knopf for *Last Night* and *Life Is Meals,* and was annoyed that the publisher wouldn't pay for his plane ticket from Aspen to Berkeley when I invited him to speak. *A Sport and a Pastime* he wittily called "a cross between Henry Miller and Henry James." *Light Years,* with the exotically named heroine Nedra, was not about his first wife but about the conceptual artist Barbara Rosenthal, who had a rather sad and disappointing life. *Life Is Meals* was inspired by a published literary calendar. He and Kay started with notes on their meals, dinner parties and friends, then made their own large, color-coordinated, day-by-day cardboard chart. Showing me his original notes and chart, and noting my appreciative interest, he remarked, "You have a way of gaining one's confidence." Knopf didn't push the book, which sold only 16,000 to 17,000 copies but earned beyond his advance. He's now known as a high-toned foodie writer. He was just starting his new novel, *All That Is,* but didn't like to talk about it in case it didn't work out.

We were supposed to feel honored by an invitation to the first big social event of the Hamptons' summer season: a lavish party thrown by the literary agent Ed Victor. Jim dressed up for the occasion in a dapper white suit and royal blue tie. One friend cattily asked, as if it had been rented, when he had to return it to the store. By contrast to his elegant attire, we drove up the long driveway to the valet parking in Jim's deliberately chosen old wreck of a car, of which he was inordinately proud. He insisted on locking it himself because some of his notes were still floating around inside. The jalopy also provided a notable contrast to Victor's pretentiously parked Rolls Royce, which symbolized the party's vulgar display of wealth and power.

Blythe Danner, actress mother of Gwyneth Paltrow, and Candice Bergen looked delightfully decorative. But there were few intellectual faces. The only other writers I saw amid the swarm of agents and editors were Kurt Vonnegut, who looked ill and died the following year; the journalist Ken Auletta, who seemed to be constantly preening before an invisible mirror; and the biographer Robert Caro. When Caro politely asked what I was working on and I replied, "Johnson," he tensed up and exclaimed, "Wait a minute"—as if to say, "I'm the one who writes about Johnson around here." But he appeared relieved as I added, "Samuel, not Lyndon." I was enraged at the financial exploitation of writers who had earned so little by middlemen who had made so much. Jim, who'd been around longer than me, was resigned to the fact that "authors are nothing." Nina said the party was a "shark feed," but couldn't specify who were the sharks and who the prey.

As we left the next morning both Jim and Kay said they appreciated our considerable effort to get to the end of Long Island and thanked us for coming. Kay, in friendly fashion, kissed me good-bye on the lips. Nina, though glad to see us go, refused to permit Frenchified kisses on both cheeks and saw me off with a stiff, extended handshake. I asked Jim, "Shall we continue to correspond?" and he replied, "Yes, but not so often," and I suggested once a month. The ever-hostile Nina then interrupted with "Wait a minute. I get only two letters a year" and wanted us to cut down to her level. We ignored her injunction and continued to write in our usual way. In Jim's next letter he graciously wrote, "It was such a pleasure to meet you both. I can't say I had no idea—I suspected it would be. After a certain point it's not easy to make friends."

After we'd bought the plane tickets for our second visit, Jim and Kay had a last-minute change of plans and we arrived the day after their exhausting flight from St. Petersburg, Russia. Their nine companions on the trip included Peter and Maria Matthiessen, Jean Kennedy Smith (sister of President Kennedy), Rose Styron, the sculptor Jack Zajac and his wife, Christopher and Koukla McLehose, and a scout from the French publisher Gallimard. Jim had rented a flat with two other couples, a bit far from the city center and from the others in the group. Taxis were difficult to find and, pushed from both sides in a crowded bus, he had his pocket picked. They never met any Russians, but the weather was fine and he especially liked seeing Nabokov's old mansion and Anna Akhmatova's museum at Fountain House. They sat through the entire *Sleeping Beauty* from 7 to 11:30 PM, and then ate scrambled eggs at their flat. Though Petersburg was famed for its beauty, he thought it was ugly and didn't much like it. He thought Moscow, which he didn't visit, must be a horror. Russian food and service were, as always, poor but expensive, especially when traveling with rich, free-spending friends. Though he hated flying and the journey cost a lot, he had a good time and felt it was worth it.

On the first night in Bridgehampton, Kay served a simple summer dinner of cucumber, tomato and onion salad, spaghetti carbonara, watermelon and Blackstone red wine from California. The second night, when the Matthiessens came to dinner, we had stuffed avocado, broiled flounder, creamed potatoes dauphinoise, Spanish flan and Blackstone red. Matthiessen, withdrawn and unresponsive, looked terribly gaunt and seemed to be ill. He said authors now needed an agent who could also edit, but that Jim's agent Binky Urban couldn't edit anything. He praised Becky Saletan as a good editor—though she did absolutely nothing for my two books at Harcourt while dancing attendance on Peter. At dinner Jim gently teased Kay about her pronunciation of *macedoine* and Macedonia, and some aspects of her taste in cooking. When she seemed hurt, he stroked her hand, said he was sorry and promised not to tease her again.

Like Fitzgerald and Faulkner, Jim had swallowed the Hollywood bait and was fond of recalling those lucrative and fantastical years. Omar Sharif, who'd starred in *The Appointment* (1969), told Jim that David Lean used to invite the *Lawrence of Arabia* actors into his tent for tea, while the huge crew waited to start work, and asked for their ideas about the scene to be shot that day.

Lean then deftly maneuvered them into doing precisely what he wanted. Robert Redford had called Jim about a month ago, said he wanted to keep in touch with old friends and invited him to tea at a posh New York hotel. But Redford had broken with several former friends, and Jim was still resentful about having to change the original script of *Downhill Racer* to make Redford look more heroic. Jim contrasted Meryl Streep, who mastered the Danish accent in *Out of Africa,* to Redford, who didn't even try to play an Englishman and was terrible in that film.

Jim had met his great friend the Yale-educated Lorenzo Semple (who died in 2014) in Aspen. Semple immediately propositioned Jim's attractive first wife and suggested they go to a motel, and Semple's wife later found incriminating photos of his longtime mistress. Semple was reluctant to attend a dinner of French aristocrats at Lectoure in southwestern France. But at the end of the elaborate feast and while seated between two beautiful Swedish twins, he made a long speech in French and was applauded by the fifteen guests. Jim rewrote *Avalanche Express* (1978) with Semple. The studio liked their script and flew them to London, but the director rejected it: a great waste of time, but good money.

Jim directed the film *Threshold* (1981), starring Donald Sutherland, about Dr. Christiaan Barnard's pioneering heart transplants. In Hollywood he mostly dealt with people he didn't like and worked long, hard hours, but he was satisfied with the film at the time. His screenplay for *Three* (1969), based on Irwin Shaw's story "Then We Were Three," was laughed at in the Cannes film festival and humiliated him. As an example of the deep corruption in Hollywood, he told the story of the writer who got a $500,000 contract for a script he never had to write. Jim went to a Hollywood party with a girl who said, "There's Brad Pitt. I blew him. Do you think he'd remember me?" Jim couldn't resist remarking that she'd "be easy to spot on her knees."

The next morning Jim apologized for his "drunken ranting"

against the movies. In fact, he wasn't drunk and told amusing stories. To counter his condemnations of all the film producers and directors, I mentioned my meetings with and admiration for Walter Mirisch, Billy Wilder, Fred Zinnemann and Joseph Mankiewicz. Jim agreed that they were all fine men, but exceptions to the rule.

After a few bottles of wine at dinner, Jim had moved on to contemporary writers. He disliked both Salman Rushdie and his work. Though Rushdie had all the qualifications except the ability to write, he thought his recent knighthood would help him snag the Nobel Prize. Asked about the most impressive contemporary writers, he jokingly replied that Joseph Heller had great hair, almost like Einstein's, and that Philip Roth was supposed to be very funny. William Gaddis, who used to live in Bridgehampton, loved movies and was disappointed that none of his novels had ever appeared on the screen. When they went to the movies together, Gaddis would laugh with an appreciative "Heh, heh." Jim had dinner with the recently widowed, eighty-five-year-old Arthur Miller, who turned up with Agnes Barley, a young woman in her twenties. Miller, he said, could be ponderous and boring, and we agreed that Tennessee Williams was a much better playwright. Jim's negative comments were based on his exceptionally high standards and provoked by his belief that until recently he'd never had just recognition and rewards as a writer. Like Edmund Wilson, Anton Chekhov was his literary touchstone, and he quoted the poignant line from the end of *The Cherry Orchard,* "You're going away, leaving me behind?"

He'd read my life of Hemingway, but wanted to know more and asked me for some insider stories about him. He was greatly interested in Kay Morrison, married to a Harvard professor, who had simultaneous affairs with Robert Frost and his hostile biographer Lawrance Thompson. He questioned me about my revealing interview with Kay's daughter Ann and with Ann's ex-husband, on the scene at the time, who didn't understand the sexual complications until he'd read my life of Frost. Jim also questioned me about my friendship and correspondence with the sexually adventurous English novelist, which I later described in *Remembering Iris Murdoch* (2013).

Reading and writing were always favorite subjects. Jim liked to read slowly and aloud, and wondered how I could absorb everything when reading so fast. I quoted Samuel Johnson's belief that no man ever read a book through. I was writing an essay about Jim's work and promised to show it to him when it was accepted, but I wanted to express my own interpretation, not his. Quoting D. H. Lawrence, "Never trust the artist. Trust the tale," he agreed. By chance I heard, while staying with Jim, that my twenty-page piece had been accepted and would appear in the *Kenyon Review* (Spring 2008).

He mentioned Alex Vernon's book *Soldiers Once and Still,* about Hemingway, himself and Tim O'Brien. Vernon discussed Jim's early West Point story "Empty Is the Night," in *Pointer* (October 6, 1944). Jim said the title was not a deliberate allusion to Keats' "Ode to a Nightingale" and Fitzgerald's *Tender Is the Night,* but thought Vernon should have spotted the echo. "Vernon's interested in war," Jim said, "I'm interested in writing." Jim typed and retyped his fiction, labor-intensively, on an old typewriter. He didn't show the work to Kay and another friend until it was finished, and revised again when they'd read it. The phone rang a lot while we were there, perhaps because they'd been away for a few weeks. But he planned to withdraw from social life, as he did the previous summer, and concentrate on his work.

Like Nina in 2006, Paavo caused serious problems in 2007. Thirteen years old, half-blind and very sick, he was having chemotherapy for incurable cancer "to give him one more good year." At breakfast on our third and last day Paavo, after a bad night, had a convulsive fit while his brown eyes gazed desperately at his master.

Jim rushed him to the vet, but he died an hour later. He returned with the dead dog, wrapped him in a blanket, dug his grave in the garden and then worked off his angst at the gym. I felt it was a great release for the poor animal and was glad to escape to the beach. Jim and Kay were both grief-stricken—she cried all afternoon—and could not go out to dine with us that night.

The next morning, regretful about missing our last dinner, Jim was especially kind and attentive. He gave me one of his shirts, wondered how my wife and I had met at UCLA and married while I was teaching in Japan. He also asked for a photo of our daughter, who seemed "to come out of *Vanity Fair.*" We ended bookishly as Jim wrote down the titles of little-known works, including Edmund Gosse's *Father and Son* and L. P. Hartley's *The Go-Between,* that I especially admired. I treasured my friendship with Jim—a heroic man, lively companion and brilliant writer.

8

Paul Theroux

(Born 1941)

In the spring of 1992, when I was a visiting professor at the University of Alabama, Paul Theroux called unexpectedly from Hawaii. He told me that Vidia Naipaul had mentioned my biography of Joseph Conrad and given him my phone number. Paul was writing an introduction to an Everyman edition of *The Secret Agent,* and we had a long and lively talk about Conrad and about Naipaul. I was struck by his Boston accent, his wide reading and sharp memory, as he corrected me on a small detail in George Orwell's *Nineteen Eighty-Four* about an image of a crucifix with a knife in it. He was keen and stimulating whenever we spoke and, as Sidney Greenstreet tells Bogart in *The Maltese Falcon,* "I like talking to a man who likes to talk." Since our first conversation Paul has sent me (so far) more than two hundred letters, postcards and emails as well as an unpublished letter from Conrad and photographs of himself with a solemn Naipaul and with an attentive Dalai Lama.

We first met a year later, in July 1993, when Paul made his seasonal shift from Hawaii to Cape Cod—from the Sandwich Islands to East Sandwich. Since he was seeing his aged mother that day, it took several phone calls to arrange our encounter. Tanned and fit after a seven-mile kayak trip to Martha's Vineyard, he was a striking contrast to the ailing and neurasthenic Naipaul I had recently seen. I browsed through his books while he showered, and we talked and drank through a long afternoon and dinner in a local restaurant. He lived in a grand compound on the crest of a hill, with a fine view of the sea and the main house and guest cottage placed around the swimming pool.

Paul and I found that we had quite a lot in common and a lot of common interests. Exactly two years younger than me, he had grown up in Medford, Massachusetts, where I had taught for four years at Tufts University. His first wife and my only wife were English. Both of us had traveled widely and on six continents, lived abroad for many years and knew several languages. We were both well read and keen on Conrad and Orwell. Hardworking, fluent and productive writers, we appreciated each other's work, and thrived on bookish talk and literary gossip in England and America. He wrote novels and travel books, I wrote biographies and literary criticism, so there was no direct competition between us.

Alluding to the zealous biographer in the story by Henry James, Paul recalled, "On first meeting I felt you might be the narrator of 'The Aspern Papers.' I quickly realized that you are one of the best-read people I know, and we omnivorous readers are a vanishing breed." I asked his opinion of my favorite modern writers: Thomas Mann, D. H. Lawrence, Saul Bellow and J. F. Powers. I was pleased when Paul mentioned that "Mann was the only writer that Vidia unequivocally praised to me." I introduced him to the fiction of James Salter and to the art of the Canadian realist Alex Colville, and Paul responded, "I was much taken by Colville's brilliant paintings and his taste for solitude."

Paul first met Naipaul in 1966 when they were both teaching at Makerere University in Uganda, where Naipaul liked to display his exacting taste and a satiric wit. Judging an African literary contest, he awarded only a third prize because no one deserved a first or second. Driving along with Paul, soon after the Rwanda genocide, he cruelly sang, "Tut, Tut, Tutsi, good-bye." Throughout the years Paul and I spoke obsessively about Naipaul, a powerful presence in both our lives. I'd been anointed his authorized biographer in 1992 and then been rudely dismissed; Paul would have a notoriously bitter quarrel with him in 1996. We both admired and disliked him, fascinated by his genius and his perverse personality.

Paul was half-amused by Naipaul's lordly demeanor and I liked to hear about his Vidiasyncrasies. He was jealous of Paul's luxurious estate and never picked up the check in a restaurant. Paul resented the privileged status Naipaul had with their mutual agent, Gillon Aitken. Though Paul earned much more money than Naipaul, Aitken would get down on his knees and kiss Naipaul's boots, but would not do much (even when standing up) for Paul. Years later, despite Aitken's correct cringe, Naipaul, in search of more money, suddenly dropped him and shifted to a new agent, the authivorous "Jackal" Andrew Wylie. Paul said that Aitken, a terrible guest on the Cape, had expected Paul to wait on him.

Since the arrogant and demanding Naipaul was impossible to please, my London literary friends had strongly urged me to abandon my proposed biography. But for a few months I'd pushed ahead with the project, seeing him and receiving several revealing letters, interviewing people who knew him and learning what I could. But I was inevitably replaced and passed the baton to the next of his several victims. Despite the formidable obstacles—not least Naipaul himself—Paul urged me to write an *un*authorized biography. He offered to introduce me to Margaret Murray in Buenos Aires, Naipaul's long-term mistress and a valuable informant. Very few personal letters existed, he thought, apart from the ones Naipaul had written to him (the André Deutsch archive concerned publishing matters), and the papers at the University of Tulsa would produce few revelations. But having corresponded with Naipaul, visited his homes in Salisbury and London, and met his wife Pat, Paul thought I had the "right understanding" to proceed. He said seeing Naipaul and Pat was the modern equivalent of meeting Conrad and his wife Jessie at their home in Kent.

Conrad's subjects and settings—Africa and colonialism, remote places and the isolation of Europeans in the tropics—were powerful and inspiring influences on both Vidia and Paul, and gave them common ground and an undying rivalry. Paul's incisive comments on the secretive Naipaul extended from 2000 to 2015 and were fueled by the embers of anger. He analyzed Naipaul's complex personality and tried to reconcile his brilliant books and odious character. He explained that Naipaul's habit of asking me faux-naïf questions was "his mode of social behavior, a sort of needling, teasing, mockery set-up. He was curious about your friendship with [the English novelist] Francis King because he is homophobic."

Naipaul, Paul continued, "wanted to sell books by the millions but in fact few people really read him. He was very envious of the fact that my books were not particularly well reviewed but sold well. His were gushed over and fell flat." After reading Naipaul's *A Writer's People* (2007), Paul was pleased to remark that "his amazing ego and pomposity and general unpleasantness are so welcome to me, for now people will better understand my *Sir Vidia's Shadow.*" I reviewed the latter, which had been severely attacked by most critics, in the winter 1999 issue of the *American Scholar.* I praised Paul for describing, as any writer would, his fascinating relationship with Naipaul, which began as he was starting out as a writer: "*Sir Vidia's Shadow* (1998)—as I know from my own experience with Naipaul—provides the most thorough and deadly accurate account of his elusive, intriguing and fascinating character. In Theroux's portrait Naipaul is strange, difficult, unlovable; contradictory, challenging, demanding; fussy, mocking, cruel; self-important, obsessive and vindictive. He hates women and children, music and dogs. But he is also, Paul said, 'brilliant, and passionate in his convictions, and to be with him, as a friend or fellow writer, I had always to be at my best.'"

When interviewed by Patrick French, the biographer of the first half of Naipaul's life, Paul received news bulletins about his former friend, which I was also eager to hear: "Vidia has back problems and is very grumpy, but what else is new? His second wife is ever more tyrannical. He hasn't done anything with his money except salt it away. He makes unbelievable demands on people who invite him to speak. 'I must have $30,000 as a fee. I require six-star treatment for me and my entourage'—direct quote." But he had few takers as his writing declined and his demands increased. Paul added that the biographer had unexpectedly found some sensational revelations: "He took to Patrick French, who told me he genuinely liked Naipaul. Vidia signed some release forms. And in the course of writing French discovered amazing tales, notably Pat's diary, the voice of condemnation from beyond the grave."

Paul's two post-quarrel meetings with Naipaul—at literary festivals in Hay-on-Wye in Wales in 2011 and in Jaipur, India, in 2015—sparked a lot of attention in the press. I asked about Wales, "Was your much publicized handshake with Vidia more a polite gesture than a symbol of forgiveness and resumption of friendship (apparently impossible with him)?" Paul responded: "I had not expected to see him at all. When I did, he looked so frail. I was egged on by Ian McEwan ('Life's too short'). Just a greeting—he was his old self, quite funny. But no friendship resumes after it's ruptured."

Paul wondered if Naipaul would turn up in Jaipur. I guessed that he came because his domineering wife Nadira was bored by his endless complaints while cloistered in their small Wiltshire village and wanted to queen it up as the consort of a great celebrity. Paul recounted his surprising volte-face and cathartic reconciliation with Naipaul. Despite all their bitterness, Naipaul had softened with illness and old age: "You will laugh, but really it was all jolly—hugs, jokes, long evenings; Vidia mellow as anything and Nadira very friendly. Life is strange, and better with forgiveness." In their photo Naipaul—with puffy face, grey goatee and rather grim expression—is crumpled up in his chair. Paul—wearing an Indian shirt and vest, a tattoo on his hand and wedding ring on his finger—leans toward and towers over his old friend, and attempts a slight smile. After their reunion Paul rarely mentioned him to me again. But he was in fairly close touch, generally with Nadira as go-between. She once said to him, "People are amazed that we're friends now, after your book about Vidia. But I tell them, 'I was the one who caused the rupture of your friendship.'" All is now well between them.

Paul would vaguely comment, "If I am in the Bay Area I look forward to seeing you for longer than two minutes." But he never told me when he planned to read in Berkeley or San Francisco. I was not able to pin him down for drinks or dinner—though he was curious about my house, view and library—or meet him in Honolulu when I traveled to Maui or Kauai. He seemed to have no close friends except Naipaul and Jonathan Raban.

In response to my questions, Paul clarified the portrayal of his *isolado* character in the autobiographical passages in *My Other Life:* "Friends: the narrator does not seem to have any, or any close ones. Am I describing my own situation? Yes, in a way. I was in London in April for a week and did not see a single English person I had known from the past. . . . I hate parties, I tend not to make long-term plans, because (it's true) I don't like to be pinned down." He may have sought freedom and solitude because, as the third of seven children, he grew up in a large, competitive family and found it difficult to secure his own privacy and freedom.

Paul sometimes touched on personal matters. He bought a twelve-acre island with a cottage and deck, near the town of Thomaston and the painter Jamie Wyeth, on the mid-coast of Maine, and retreated there to write in solitude and quiet. As he grew older there were inevitable health problems. In 2005 he seriously injured his spine in a fall, but hoped to make a full recovery. The following year he had difficult eye problems, alluded to in *Blinding Light,* and after several operations ended up with "middling to bad" eyesight. His mentally alert mother died four days before her 104th birthday: "She was not ill, took no medicine, but just wore out, and was found with the day's crossword puzzle on her lap."

Often concerned with domestic matters, Paul remarked, "I am very curious about family reactions in the lives of other writers because my family members usually don't read my books—they seem to make a point of not doing so; but when they do they are deeply critical, particularly when they perceive versions of themselves in my work." I remembered that his brother Eugene was a prominent attorney when he noted in 2006, "I did write a novel last year but could not publish it because my family members would have gotten lawyers. It will be in limbo for a while." He was deeply wounded by a corrosive review in October 1996 by his older novelist brother, undoubtedly jealous of Paul's success: "Should you have the stomach for it, look at the long, angry, tormented review of *My Other Life* by my brother Alexander, yes, my brother, in *Boston Magazine. . . .* It is absolutely the oddest response I have ever received, and it is unprecedented in literary history." Despite the dangerous storm warnings and threat of litigation, Paul pressed on. In 2017, thinking perhaps of Naipaul's *A House for Mr. Biswas,* he described his forthcoming novel *Mother Land:* "It's about a large dysfunctional family not unlike my very own but with some differences. My *David Copperfield.* Twelve years in the making."

In his most revealing and rather guilt-ridden message, he described the breakup of his first marriage, to the BBC radio producer Anne Castle, the mother of his two sons:

Marriage: much too complex to go into in detail, but in general I was an unfaithful husband, but with my unreasonable double-standard I would have objected to my wife behaving that way! My wife and I separated for three months, just to examine our lives. I set sail for the Pacific. I realized I was done with London, done with city life, looking for a new life elsewhere, in a more salubrious climate. My wife and I saw a pair of counselors for some time to explain what we wanted (with referees), divided our earthly goods in half, and off I went into the sunshine.

He moved to Hawaii, where he lives for the wintry part of the year, and married a Hawaiian resident of Chinese descent, but is sometimes absent on his solitary travels.

Whenever I managed to track him down, Paul always greeted me with a warm embrace, and we met briefly before or after his talks. An excellent speaker who liked to perform on book tours, he enlivened his fiction and answered all questions from the audience with full-throated ease. He interrupted his talk to mention my biographies and, when asked if it were better for travel writers to go alone or with a companion, shifted the spotlight to me and said, "Ask Jeffrey." Luckily, I could answer the query by quoting Kipling's "Down to Gehenna, or up to the Throne / He travels the fastest who travels alone." Afterward Paul introduced me to his cousin, married to Harold Smith, a professor of nuclear engineering at Berkeley who'd been deputy secretary of defense in the Clinton administration. We talked for two hours in a lowlife Irish bar just next to the bookstore, and I became a tennis-playing friend of Harold. When I was out of town during one of his readings, my daughter Rachel brought books for him to sign and introduced herself to Paul, who stood up and greeted her as if she were an old friend.

Always generous, Paul signed all his books for me in person or by mail. His most interesting inscriptions were on my copies of his rarest book and first work of nonfiction, *V. S. Naipaul: An Introduction to His Work* (1972). Quoting me, with a proviso, he wrote: "'The first and still the best book on Naipaul'—perhaps," and more self-critically, "This early gushing view of the younger Naipaul by the even younger PT." He quoted me on Samuel Johnson and Ernest Hemingway in *The Tao of Travel* and promised, "I must send you the new paperback with an Afterword quoting you extensively. Your bon mots are not wasted on me, you see."

Since my daughter was in the Foreign Service, Paul gave me the name of a neighbor and potentially useful contact, the former ambassador to Tajikistan. He also introduced me to Loren Rothschild, the Los Angeles collector of Samuel Johnson, Somerset Maugham and Paul himself. Loren gave me generous help and hospitality as I studied his valuable books while researching the lives of the first two authors. Paul got me a commission from *Architectural Digest* to describe Marilyn Monroe's modest house in Los Angeles and I earned $5,000 for writing 500 words in one morning.

Isolated in Hawaii and on his travels, and starved for intellectual stimulation, Paul always responded enthusiastically when I sent him my books and articles. After reading four of my biographies he offered effective and influential blurbs. He wrote that *Samuel Johnson* "is a superb book, not only an intellectual history of one of English literature's greatest and most restless minds, but to me an incomparable portrait of a man who was physically an oddity and a marvel. Dr. Johnson with his tics and his appetites and his lopsided wig is depicted with the full-blooded gusto he deserves." He stated that *George Orwell* "is admirable for its portrayal of Orwell the man and writer—dark, disturbed, obsessing, contrary—a much more helpful and believable portrait than the many that depict him as St. George. This book is both moving and edifying."

Grateful for his help, I tried to reciprocate whenever I could. Like most writers, Paul was both thankful and annoyed with himself and his editors when I pointed out errors in the proofs of *Mr. Bones*. I asked a professor to invite Paul to lecture at the University of Hawaii, but she said that would be quite impossible. He'd defied political correctness by severely criticizing the torpid Hawaiians and the lack of intellectual life on the islands. Paul was often as satiric as Naipaul and equally indifferent to whomever he offended.

Far from good libraries in those pre-Google days, Paul often asked me questions and I always tried to answer them. He wanted to know where to buy for his son an edition in Russian of Varlam Shalamov's *Kolyma Tales*. He asked me to recommend the best biography of T. E. Lawrence; to describe what D. H. Lawrence's family thought about his writings; and to identify the source of Saul Bellow's provocative quote: "Who is the Tolstoy of the Zulus, the Proust of the Papuans?" He believed, "You're the only person I know who can answer this Orwell question. Somewhere he writes of an unemployed man who says with feeling, 'Send us work!' I think it's in an 'As I Please' column."

He also had many queries when researching *The Tao of Travel*. Did I know, he asked, who besides Graham Greene and his cousin Barbara Greene wrote separate accounts of the same trip? He also inquired about "writers who did not travel to the place they wrote about—Bellow in *Henderson*, Kafka in *Amerika*." He asked, "Do you know off-hand how long Hemingway spent in Africa for his *Green Hills of Africa*? I am compiling a list of the length of time travelers spent in a given place. Lawrence wins the prize for shortest, I think: seven days in Sardinia." The next day he added, "Lawrence just lost the 'shortest stay' prize. Kipling gets it for spending 'not more than a few hours in Rangoon' (just in time to visit the pagoda) and then writing poems and travel pieces about it." Now I understood why Kipling got the geography all wrong in his poem "Mandalay."

I thought Paul was underrated as an author, and enjoyed reviewing seven of his books for the *Financial Times, New Statesman* and other journals and newspapers in America and Canada. After his pioneering *The Great Railway Bazaar* (1975) and *The Old Patagonian Express* (1976), which established his reputation, he's published fourteen impressive travel books. He stands, I believe, with Wilfred Thesiger and Norman Lewis as one of the best travel writers of our time.

As a travel writer Paul observes other people and engages with strangers, but keeps a cool distance in his personal life. More interested in people and landscape than in history and art, he combines description and interpretation with social criticism and political commentary. He prefers a rough to a comfortable journey, popular to high culture, colloquial to mandarin style. He is engagingly frank about backward and brutal people, boring voyages and self-created torments, and believes the great traveler must also be a great masochist. Theroux would agree with D. H. Lawrence that "travel seems to me a splendid lesson in disillusion." I once asked if he liked lecturing on a cruise and he said the people were "horrible. No, worse than horrible."

The excellence of his travel books has overshadowed the achievement of his fiction, but he is one of the best novelists now writing about Africa. *The Lower River,* his finest novel since *Saint Jack* and *The Mosquito Coast,* is elegantly written, captures authentic African speech and is filled with vivid details. When a hippo opens its wide jaws, the hero "could see the reddish flesh of the mouth and the blunt pegs of its thick round teeth and the raw mottled skin of its fat body."

I wrote about how Paul's work had been nourished by the exotic locales, outcast characters and moral themes of his master, Joseph Conrad, who'd first brought us together. *The Family Arsenal* (1976) updates the Russian anarchists in *The Secret Agent* and satirizes the morally squalid London underworld of IRA revolutionary bomb throwers, who merge at times with a cross section of corrupt upper-class society. In *The Mosquito Coast* (1981), as in *Victory,* three villains invade a remote jungle outpost, threaten the vulnerable inhabitants and are killed. After a storm, the family floats away on a barge named *Victory.* There's an additional pleasure for readers who can recognize the Conradian echoes and see how Paul translates Conrad's fiction into a contemporary idiom.

The impact of *Lord Jim* on Theroux's best novel, *Saint Jack*

(1973), is even more significant. Like Lord Jim, Saint Jack (the titles are equally paradoxical) is a white man who has lost his social and professional status and lives on the fringe of a lonely, alien world in Singapore. Paul emphasizes the themes of disillusion and decay in his description of the once seedy port city: "There was something final in the decline, an air of ramshackle permanency common in Eastern ports, as if having fallen so far they would fall no further." Jack, who has been charged with possession of drugs during a police raid in the United States, has jumped bail (as Jim jumped ship) and become a sailor in the Indian Ocean. An immoral but fundamentally decent character, Jack seeks moral redemption and sacrifices himself for salvation. For low pay but in return for a work permit that allows him to remain in Singapore, he toils as a water clerk (Jim's job) and, through his contact with European ships, brings trade to the Chinese chandler. Captain Brierly's suicide in *Lord Jim* is reflected at the end of Part I of Paul's novel when William Leigh, the accountant who has come from Hong Kong to examine the company's books, suddenly dies of a heart attack. The apparently ironic title of the novel contrasts the conventional idea of sin to a more idiosyncratic but equally valid morality. The novel reveals goodness beneath evil (Jack's entrepreneurial whorehouses are the equivalent of Jim's adventures in Patusan), describes a religious quest, portrays the salvation of a sinner and—despite his vices—suggests the possibility of achieving grace.

When I dedicated my life of John Huston to him in 2011, Paul hesitantly replied: "Many thanks for your handsome offer. Naturally I'm flattered, but I feel unworthy since all I have ever done is respond to your work, as any delighted reader would do." But he soon clarified his feelings: "I hope you did not interpret my reply as a rebuff. As I said, I was deeply honored by your suggestion but felt unworthy, and this is not false modesty. Maybe you can persuade me that I'm worthy!" He admired the flamboyant and adventurous Huston and remarked when my book appeared:

"I imagine that he lived an ideal life: wine, women, song, and money. . . . In a way we all want to be Huston, his life seems so rich, so complete, so full of satisfactions—though as you indicate he wore himself out with his indulgences. I am so pleased for my name to be on the dedication page."

My work on modern writers often sparked Paul's perceptive novelist's-eye response. He described D. H. Lawrence's essential qualities and how he had absorbed elements of Lawrence's restless wanderings into his own personal and literary life. He noted "the breathless haste of DHL's travels, his monkish non-materialism, his amazing creativity. I am going to read his intro to the Maurice Magnus book. . . . Odd, how one's reading becomes part of one's travel." After reading my biography of Scott Fitzgerald he felt "horror for such a painful life." But he said, "It inspired me to reread *Tender, Tycoon* and some stories. I think the last part of *Tender* is rather a mess, indeed the book has structural problems, but it is full of delights—real writing brilliance. Except for Stahr himself—a magnificent portrait—I don't see anything in *Tycoon*. . . . I am now reading Cowley's edition of his stories. I like 'The Crack-Up' immensely. Altogether, you can see how your book inspired me."

He agreed to read my film scripts of *The Magic Mountain* and Orwell's colonial novel, and usefully replied: "I know *Burmese Days* pretty thoroughly. I think you've done a good job, though the early scenes are overlong—esp. the club. The confrontation in the church between May and Flory would have been better in Burmese—May screaming, I think. . . . I always thought Orwell was describing colonialism as a dead end." But he'd had a lot of trouble when writing his own screenplay for *The Mosquito Coast* (whose title refers to a real place in Honduras), hated film work and no longer had any useful contacts in Hollywood.

In a witty reaction to my essay "Bluebeard Bellow," Paul was "amazed at Bellow's obtuseness in choosing these five women. And why marry them—why not have them as mistresses? To marry a woman to 'get into her pants' as he says is utterly absurd. He's weirdly masochistic and is a victim in all these relationships, yet as you say he found 'material.' God, there are easier ways of finding material than marrying, surely?"

Paul sometimes sent me vivid portraits of writers he had known. He'd spent some uneasy time with Robert Lowell when both ex-patriates were living in England. But Lowell's self-absorption and emotional demands could be frustrating and exhausting. Paul re-called: "In April 1973 we were fishing in Appleby, Westmoreland, and on the Sunday the reviews of my novel *Saint Jack* appeared in about six newspapers—they were at the hotel, I read them over breakfast, all of them praised the book. I was over the moon. Low-ell was at the table. He took no interest at all. 'Pass the marma-lade.'... After another visit Lowell said, self-consciously, 'thanks so much. I have clung to you'—aware of the fact that it was very late and that I had been longing to get away."

Paul did not succumb to the fabled charm and brilliance of Bruce Chatwin. He defined himself in opposition to his rival's in-authentic mode of travel writing and thought real journeys had to be both solitary and difficult. In an acute analysis of Chatwin's character, Paul called him "the deeply flawed and very weird man, whose life was a relentless pose. I found him exhausting and as for his 'physical beauty,' once a person becomes tedious they stop seeming beautiful.... Chatwin in his whole life never traveled alone or at risk, and he made a huge meal of the few little scrapes he had on the road. He was afflicted with Munchausen's Syndrome, among other syndromes.... He couldn't sit still. He was not only a know-all but like a lot of know-alls he was tiresome to be with, always trying to impress. Maybe, au fond, a really unhappy person."

I'd once spent an invigorating day showing Anthony Burgess around Canterbury before he gave the T. S. Eliot lecture at the University of Kent and agreed with Paul's favorable judgment: "Burgess was the most generous and friendly writer I have ever known, and one of the hardest working and cleverest. He could also be wonderfully self-mocking." Paul also shared my enthusiasm for the witty and satiric J. F. Powers, who wrote mostly about disillusioned Catholic priests in the Upper Midwest. He stated: "I adored J. F. Powers and read him v. early in my career—the stories . . . of priests were helpful in ridding me of any religious feeling. . . . Powers was one of the first writers who truly reflected the cultural Catholicism I knew growing up. I read him when I was fairly young (*Prince of Darkness*) because my older brothers were reading him. That story 'The Eye' knocked me off my feet. Where did JF get this southern info?"

In an unusually long message Paul described—in a mixture of hostility and admiration—the English novelist and poet D. J. Enright. He was the head of the English department when Paul taught from 1968 to 1972 at the National University of Singapore. I'd met Enright in Singapore in 1966 after my year of teaching in Japan. He'd sent an assistant to fetch me in a Rolls Royce and force-fed me on hundred-year-old eggs. Paul recalled:

Dennis Enright was extremely puritanical, and my youthful excesses (drugs, women) bothered him. He was a tetchy Mr. Chips and was dismissive of anyone who had a successful book. When my early novel *Girls at Play* was optioned for a movie by the husband and wife team who made *David & Lisa,* Enright became quite miffed. By the way he had read the telegram with the news. I was in Penang, with my wife, living it up. He used to boast about how he'd turned down well-paid jobs in the USA. He had that strange envious ambivalence that many English people have for the US. He was also a fearful gossip. So my three years in Singapore were hard work. When I left, I thought: Fuck academia if it's like this. I wrote *Saint Jack,* which was a modest success, and later a movie, and kept at it. . . . Enright, a heavy smoker, died a painful death. He was a brilliant teacher, gifted in languages, widely read and loyal to his circle of flatterers, of which I was not one.

Always on the move, like a foreign correspondent, Paul would send me surprising bulletins from remote places: "I am picking up your message on a 24-hour train ride from Bombay to Madras"; "I am in Tokyo starved for felicitous prose. I am here for a while and then to Siberia." He asked me for contacts in Alabama when writing *Deep South* (2015), but traveled only in rural areas and didn't get in touch with my friends in Birmingham. He liked my condemnation of Harper Lee's wildly overrated *To Kill a Mockingbird* as "a sentimental, simple-minded rip-off of Faulkner's *Intruder in the Dust,* though no one seems to have noticed or cared," and quoted me in *Deep South.* He contrasted his mode of travel in that book to Naipaul's more superficial approach in *A Turn in the South* (1989):

> I read all the fiction I could find. My book is not about me or my relations with blacks, except when I discuss the word nigger. I stayed away from all cities, keeping to rural areas, went to church services, football games, gun shows and even went camping and paddling down the Buffalo River, talked to KKK types and Civil Rights stalwarts. I loved traveling in the South but it would drive me mad to live there (as I believe you did at one point). At the heart of my book is the question: Why are Americans devoted to uplifting Africa when almost a quarter of the people in the Deep South live in poverty that is worsening?

In November 2011, at a time when I was taking more comfortable voyages, Paul continued his Conradian journeys. He dragged himself to the former Portuguese colony of Angola, which had never recovered from the apocalyptic civil war that lasted from 1975 until 2002. In several characteristic messages he described the depressing events he would soon portray in *Last Train to Zona Verde* (2013):

> I have just arrived back from seven weeks in Africa, much of it spent in the hard-to-enter and even harder-to-leave country of Angola. Just the sort of place John Huston would have chosen to film in—an impossible place. Virtually all the places he used in Africa are inaccessible now. They were pretty inaccessible then. . . .
>
> I was lucky to get a visa to Angola (I had to pull some strings). They hate tourists—and there are none. The country is never written about—they hate journalists. There are no animals in the country. The roads are appalling. The country is fabulously rich on oil, diamonds, gold, but as you might guess none of the money goes to enrich the people, who are extremely poor and mostly living in slums in Luanda. . . . Angola was one of the hardest places I've been—very slow and uncomfortable travel, revolting food, xenophobic govt, but the people are pretty jolly. Maybe I'm too old for this?

At the age of seventy the intrepid Paul was still willing to endure the grim and brutal journey into what Conrad, describing the Congo, had called "one of the dark places of the earth." As a welcome change, he has recently been taking trips to Mexico to improve his Spanish. He now plans an extensive journey in Mexico, with an idea for a book that may rival those by D. H. Lawrence, Aldous Huxley, Evelyn Waugh and Graham Greene.

Our talks about books and ideas, in correspondence and in person, stimulated my mind and enhanced my life. Though Paul remained an elusive loner who preferred to maintain a remote intimacy with me, I valued his acute perceptions and was willing to accept him on his own terms. As Rat says of Badger in *The Wind in the Willows,* "You must not only take him *as* you find him, but *when* you find him."

9

Patrick Leigh Fermor

(1915–2011)

The handsome, charming and dashing Sir Patrick Leigh Fermor belongs with authors as men of action—Melville, Conrad, Hemingway, Malraux and Orwell—who did not go to university and learned their lessons from violent experience. Fermor, whose reputation is based on three impressive achievements in travel, war and literature, has enjoyed after death a well-deserved revival of interest in his life and work. In 1933–34, in his late teens and after expulsion from school, he spent a year walking southeast across Europe, passing through nine countries from Holland to Turkey. In his leisurely 1,700-mile ramble, rough when solitary and poor, hedonistic as guest and lover, he moved effortlessly between peasants and patricians. Though his journey did not equal the agonizing treks of Henry Morton Stanley through Equatorial Africa or of Wilfred Thesiger across the Empty Quarter of Arabia, it was a considerable feat of social and cultural exploration.

Fermor played a significant role in the war in Crete. In May 1941 German paratroopers led by General Karl Student launched the first major airborne assault in history. The Germans controlled the skies and had superior firepower; the Allies were defeated and evacuated to Egypt by the Royal Navy. Evelyn Waugh's novel *Officers and Gentlemen* (1955) portrays a commando raid while the Allied soldiers were bombed by the Germans and retreated to the south coast for escape by sea. Olivia Manning's *Balkan Trilogy* describes the British escape from Athens to Cairo.

In April 1942 Fermor returned to Crete by parachute and set out, with resourcefulness and courage, on his second and most famous Byronic adventure. He spoke modern Greek and joined a handful of British Special Operations commandos sent into the mountains of the Nazi-occupied island to organize the resistance and unleash a guerrilla uprising. His men attacked airfields and blew up a fuel base. He also watched helplessly as the Nazis took revenge by destroying whole villages and massacring thousands of civilians. While on Crete, he fired a rifle he thought was unloaded and killed a Greek comrade, setting off a blood feud that was not settled for many decades.

Fermor's greatest wartime achievement was the daring capture of a German general, Heinrich Kreipe, on April 26, 1944. Dressed in German uniforms, Fermor and his men set up a road-block. As the car slowed down around a sharp curve, the armed soldiers poured out of the darkness and restrained the general, who shouted, swore and punched until he was handcuffed and shoved onto the floor of the back seat. They then smuggled their prisoner through the main town, Heraklion, west along the coast and into the mountains.

The general turned out to be a cultured captive, well versed in the classics, and had many lively talks with Fermor before he was taken to Egypt and then to a POW camp in Calgary, Canada. A moment of true understanding came when Kreipe, gazing at the white hills, quoted Horace's *Odes* 1.9—"*Vides ut alta stet nive candidum Soracte*" (See, the snows of Mount Soracte glare against the sky)—and Fermor quoted the rest of the Latin poem from memory. In April 1972 they appeared congenially together in a Greek television program. When asked if he'd been treated well, the general replied, "*Ritterlich! Wie ein Ritter*" (Chivalrously. Like a medieval knight). Fermor's heroic exploit, still famous all over Greece, boosted morale during the dark days of the German occupation and gave a glimmer of hope for the final victory.

Fermor's bold exploit inspired a novel, *Ill Met by Moonlight* (1950), by his comrade-in-arms Stanley (Billy) Moss and a film of that name with Dirk Bogarde (1957). (The title comes from *A Midsummer Night's Dream*.) Moss—handsome, six years younger than Fermor and a veteran of the North African campaign—was educated at Charterhouse and spoke French and Russian but not Greek or German. He does not provide any historical or military background, bases his memoir on the diary he kept at the time and writes in a plain, often clichéd style. The first rather uneventful half—mostly marching, hiding and planning, with a few close calls—expresses admiration for the Greek partisans and leads up to the daring capture of the much older General Kreipe, who was born in 1895.

Fermor carries "an ivory-handled revolver and a silver dagger" and cuts a dashing figure. They'd hoped to capture General Friedrich Müller, a cruel "tyrant much loathed by the islanders" who was later hanged as a war criminal, but he was unexpectedly replaced by Kreipe. The capture takes place between German headquarters and the general's residence in the Villa Ariadne, built by Sir Arthur Evans during his excavations of the ancient Minoan palace of Knossos. After driving through Heraklion in the Opel, with Fermor wearing the general's hat, they bluff their way through twenty-two German checkpoints—though one map shows only four checkpoints. (The gullible sentries, some suspected of complicity, were arrested and probably shot or sent straight to the Russian front.) The commandos evade all the German patrols searching for Kreipe and, with many difficulties, bring him through the slopes of Mount Ida and down to a British ship on the south coast.

Kreipe—"a thick-set man ... with thin lips, bull neck, blue eyes, and a fixed expression"—had been sent to a comparatively restful post in Crete after two tough years on the Russian front.

Concerned more for his dignity than for his life, he worries about the lost symbols of his rank and valor: his general's hat and his Knight's Cross of the Iron Cross. Though fairly stoical and cooperative, he complains about his minor injuries, poor food and lack of sleep. He and Fermor also exchange Greek verses from Sophocles, but do not establish a comradely connection. Though the commandos leave evidence suggesting only the British, not the Greeks, had captured the general, the Germans razed the nearest village and eventually killed two thousand civilians. The 1957 film of the same title begins with a map of Crete and a voice-over that gives the essential background. The film closely follows the structure of the book: planning, capture and escape. The Greek partisans, who provide local color, are heroic and sacrificial, but noisy rather than secretive. Dirk Bogarde, miscast as a tough fighter, appears as a rather wooden brigand in Cretan costume. This boys' adventure movie is competent, but not terribly tense or exciting. Kreipe speaks English to make their conversation more meaningful, and the film has two clever inventions. A Greek boy, bribed by the general, remains loyal to the British and leads the German soldiers away from the beach where the ship will arrive. And Kreipe slyly leaves behind a trail of his possessions, which are quietly picked up by his captors and returned to him on the ship.

Fermor's short book on the same subject, *Abducting a General* (2014), is blatantly padded. The foreword provides useful historical background. Only half the 189-page book contains the main text. Seventy pages print his hastily written intelligence notes sent by radio from Crete to headquarters in Cairo. The most interesting dispatches describe his accidental but fatal shooting of his close Cretan friend and his part in the executions, without trial, of Cretan traitors. (When I asked Sir Alec Kirkbride, the last surviving officer of T. E. Lawrence's Arabian campaign, if he had really killed a lot of lawless Arabs after the capture of Damascus in 1918, he casually replied, "Oh, not that many.") The last twenty pages provide a detailed guide to the abduction route though the mountains that few visitors to Crete, apart from fanatics, would willingly endure.

Fermor's account had already appeared in his anthology *Words of Mercury* (2003) and been the basis of the two chapters on Crete in Artemis Cooper's biography (2012). Based on memory rather than diaries and written twenty-two years later in 1966, *Abducting a General,* like his earlier travel books, is filled with invented details. He gathered intelligence, carried out sabotage and prepared the Cretans to help the British when they recaptured the island. His major difficulties were faulty radio transmitters, lack of transport, "rain, arrests, hide and seek with the Huns, lack of cash, flights at a moment's notice, false alarms, wicked treks over the mountains, laden like a mule, fright among one's collaborators, treachery, and friends getting shot."

He is excited by the constant danger and, when disguised as a Cretan, by his close proximity to German soldiers. His book is more detailed than Moss' about the history and geography of the island, more stylish and lyrical. As he leaves Crete, "the coast retreated east and west in a score of towering folds and each succeeding cape, in the clarity of this lens-light air, was as precise in detail as the rocks where we lay; they only dimmed as they sank under the surface." He is devoted to his brave, loyal and sacrificial Cretan friends and comrades, whose language he speaks and whom he idealizes: "We could not have lasted a day without the islanders' passionate support: a sentiment which the terrible hardships of the occupation, the execution of the hostages, the razing and massacre of the villages, only strengthened." But he ignores the conflicts between the Greek Communists and the pro-British partisans, which led to a civil war after the liberation of Greece. His hyperbolic and Homeric tributes to the numerous Cretans (often under code names) — "their capacity to cross several mountain ranges at the same lightning speed on an empty stomach after swallowing enough raki and wine to lame other mortals for a week" — are excessive.

The main dangers of the abduction were the possibilities of stopping the wrong car, encountering other German vehicles and provoking savage reprisals. The identification and immediate escape in April 1944 (the exact date is not mentioned in the book) were helped by Kreipe's colored metal pennants on the front fenders of his car. When seized, he lashed out with his fists, was manacled and had his legs tied. The whole episode took only seventy seconds. His badly injured driver, who could not keep up with the escaping partisans, had to be killed.

Since Fermor could also speak German, he writes more fully and positively than Moss about his relations with Kreipe, who bears up stoically under humiliating circumstances. The youngest son in the large family of a Lutheran pastor in Hannover, he was forty-eight years old and unmarried. He had a broad pale face, grey hair and jutting chin. A professional soldier, he'd served in the army since 1914 and had recently won a Knight's Cross on the Russian front. His moods during this ordeal ranged from cheerfulness to depression, and he sometimes slept under a blanket with Fermor and Moss, huddled together against the piercing mountain cold. Fermor writes in comradely fashion, "The General's behaviour was most friendly and helpful throughout and he put up with the hardships of mountain travel and living rough with fortitude. Moss and I had the impression that he had lost his nerve a bit after the first contact with us. He certainly made no attempt to escape." If he had broken his word, he would have been shot by the Cretans. On May 14, 1944, after eighteen anxious days in the mountains, they all boarded the ship to Cairo. Spared the disastrous German defeats in Russia and in Greece, Kreipe remained in British custody until 1947.

The crucial military and moral question, which Moss ignores and Fermor answers with qualified affirmation, is whether the abduction of General Kreipe was worth the brutal German reprisals. In August 1944 the Germans destroyed whole villages and slaughtered masses of men, women and children. The survivors rejoiced, the dead remained silent.

The memoirs by Moss and Fermor are first-person, eyewitness accounts. The popular histories by Wes Davis and Rick Stroud have a wider focus, but they are not nearly as good as Anthony Beevor's authoritative history *Crete: The Battle and the Resistance* (1991). Davis' *The Ariadne Objective: The Underground War to Rescue Crete from the Nazis* (2013) gives a brief and now familiar account of Fermor's early life and activities on the island before his capture of Kreipe. It also describes his life in wartime Cairo, and portrays Moss and three other leading commandos.

Stroud, a professional military historian, had Greek translators and had read the typescript of Fermor's *Abducting a General* and Cooper's biography of Fermor. His account of the war in Crete is livelier and more detailed than Davis' book. *Kidnap in Crete: The True Story of the Abduction of a Nazi General* (2014) starts in 1941 with the British retreat from mainland Greece and describes the German airborne attack on Crete, the British evacuation and the savage German occupation of the island. The plan for Fermor's abduction does not begin until page 100, the description of the capture (with the wrong date) until fifty pages later. Stroud is especially good when analyzing Fermor's fatal shooting of his Cretan friend and describing his hair-raising drive with Kreipe through the German crowds and barriers of Heraklion.

Fermor's third major achievement was the travel books about his youthful European journey that appeared decades later: *A Time of Gifts* (1977), *Between the Woods and the Water* (1986) and the unfinished and posthumously published *The Broken Road* (2013).

A slow, procrastinating writer, blocked for much of his life by the weight of too much material, he resembled Penelope unwinding at night what she had woven by day. His wanderings abroad to write without spiritual yearnings in Benedictine and Trappist monasteries, which he described in *A Time to Keep Silence* (1953), were also an escape from writing.

Fermor often indulges in unseemly displays of erudition. His learned digressions and serpentine style, his mannered mandarin, even baroque prose, which Lawrence Durrell called truffled and dense with plumage, were influenced by the elaborate work of Charles Doughty, T. E. Lawrence and Norman Douglas. This florid style clashes with his descriptions of colorful gypsies and cave-dwelling bandits. Dressed in sheepskin jackets, high boots and billowing breeches, with daggers tucked into their belts and bandoleers charged with cartridges, they are all rioting, feasting and firing their carbines into the air—or, during a vendetta, into their enemies.

I corresponded with Paddy (as everyone called him) while writing my biography of Errol Flynn. He had written the screenplay of one of Flynn's best movies, *The Roots of Heaven* (1958), and been on the scene during the disastrous filming in French Equatorial Africa. He thought Hollywood screenwriting was a lark that enabled him to cavort and drink with colorful characters in an exotic setting. Flynn, Trevor Howard and Paddy were all drinking heavily, and there was some conflict when Paddy fell in love with the French singer Juliette Gréco, the costar and mistress of his boss, the producer Darryl Zanuck. In a vivid letter of May 5, 2000, Paddy described the horrendous conditions—heat, disease, swarming insects and dangerous animals—while making the movie in the tropics. He got on well with the flamboyant Flynn, a kindred spirit, and gave a perceptive account of his character:

Errol seemed distinctly more intelligent than the run of
actors. Full of original tangents, a great narrative gift, and a
great sense of humour. He often referred to his learned father,
a marine biologist at Belfast University. He loved reminiscing,
largely about Hollywood. I asked him what the leading and
most beautiful stars of the day were like. "Well, pretty good,"
he said. "They've all got my scalp, I'm afraid." There were lots
of memories of his early days there, and his adventures. He
was very funny about a yacht he shared with David Niven,
and the girls they would take on trips. "We looked on them to
supply the food. One pretty girl came on board with nothing
but a loaf and a contraceptive device." He took his acting
seriously, and was absolutely adequate in his not very exacting
role. He was on very good terms with all the other actors.
His physical condition wasn't too bad, troubled by hangovers
now and then. Darryl was worried that he might have been
on some drug, though I didn't see the evidence of it.

When I wrote again while working on my life of John Huston,
who directed *The Roots of Heaven,* Paddy vividly recalled the savage Darwinian scene. Bangui, now in the Central African Republic, was the roughest and most primitive place of all: "The forests
near Bangui were inhabited by very intelligent pygmies. We were
'shooting' in the forest when the clouds broke and a large deluge
of rain came down. Our procession of vehicles headed back to the
ultra-modern hotel, like an up-ended mouth-organ on the banks
of the Shari river, which was full of crocodiles. I got there with
Errol and his girl, and we were astonished to find the whole of
the ground floor a foot deep in termites, over which small bright
green frogs from the Shari were leaping about in parabolas, while
Juliette's mongoose ran riot among them, killing and swallowing
as many as he could, two legs sticking out of his mouth. A strange
sight."

I also got in touch when writing my life of Somerset Maugham. Paddy was an Old Boy of Maugham's alma mater, the King's School in Canterbury, and as a student had read *Of Human Bondage*. He was also a close friend of Maugham's admirer and confidante Ann, the wife of Ian Fleming. After the war he'd visited Maugham's luxurious Villa Mauresque on Cap Ferrat. Since Paddy lived in Kardamyli, a remote village in the southern Peloponnese, and my daughter was a Foreign Service officer in Athens, it was a perfect time to see him. In May 2002 we rented a flat for three weeks overlooking the sea and a few kilometers from Paddy's village.

I rang him up from a local shop and he immediately invited me to come round for a talk. Since his house was hidden away and hard to find, he walked up to the main road and hailed me as I approached. Tall and straight, white-haired and suntanned, he was at eighty-seven still a virile and impressive figure. He'd designed his low, rambling, whitewashed and red-tiled home himself, and called it "a loose-limbed monastery and farmhouse with massive walls and cool rooms." It had a shaded patio facing the Mediterranean, a flourishing garden and a huge library filled with books in ancient and modern languages. He'd created the setting he wanted and the life he wished to lead, traveled widely and wrote well, charmed everyone and seemed content.

Paddy wanted to correct Ann Fleming's version of his embarrassing visit to Maugham, which she'd exaggerated—with shattered drinking glasses and blood on the floor—to amuse Evelyn Waugh. Maugham had asked Ann to bring Paddy with her for dinner, and then (always generous to good-looking young authors) had invited him to stay on as his guest and write at the villa. Unnerved by Maugham's severe expression and icy manner, Paddy drank far too much. Falling victim to the perverse tendency to talk about the very thing he was strictly forbidden to mention— Maugham's debilitating speech defect—Paddy quoted the absurd belief that everyone in the College of Heralds had a stammer. That was bad enough. But noting that the day was the Feast of the Assumption, he mentioned Correggio's painting of that subject in the Louvre and repeated a stammering friend's bon mot: "*That* is a m-most un-un-w-warrantable as-assumption."

Deeply offended, Maugham became even icier. Rising from the table and taking his leave, he rescinded his invitation by saying: "G-G-Good-bye. Y-Y-You will have left b-b-before I am up in the m-m-morning." The wretched Paddy, who did not intend to wound his host, contrived to make matters even worse. Instead of waiting for the valet to pack his bag, he hastily threw his things together and caught a precious monogrammed sheet trimmed with Belgian lace in the zipper of his suitcase. He rushed down the stairs with the rest of the sheet trailing behind, frantically tore part of it off and escaped from the villa with shreds of fabric hanging out of his bag.

After our talk, Paddy signed some travel books I'd brought along. Specially buying another one in the village shop, he inscribed his book *Mani: Travels in the Southern Peloponnese* (1958), surrounding his words with a cloud and a sketch of birds flying around the title page. When he mentioned bees and my daughter used the unusual word for "buzz"—*zouzounizo*—which he hadn't heard for years, he praised her fluency in Greek. After drinks in his house Paddy invited all of us to dinner at a simple restaurant, set on a promontory overlooking the glistening sea, which he'd bought for Lela, his former and now ancient cook. I noticed that the cook's son Giorgos—who greeted us warmly in excellent English and recommended the best dishes—was tall, blond, blue-eyed and very un-Greek looking.

Paddy, who didn't see well at night, asked me to drive him home in his battered old Peugeot, which had stiff gears, negligible brakes and holes in the rusted metal of the floor. As we went down a steep hill toward the sea, which had no barrier, I suddenly realized that the brakes didn't work and had to swerve violently to avoid submersion. Paddy, who'd had many close calls, was jovial and unconcerned about the dangerous episode. As we descended the dirt road to his remote house, I was astonished to find myself in a traffic jam. I couldn't enter the driveway, which was blocked by his maid's car. My daughter's car, following close behind, prevented me from backing up. And an impatient young Greek, trying to drive past us to dally with his girlfriend on the secluded beach, blew his horn at us and was cursed by us in several languages. My instinctive feeling that Giorgos was Paddy's son was confirmed when my daughter returned to Athens and impressed her Greek friends by mentioning that she'd dined with a national hero.

Paddy was the Byron of our time. Both men had an idealized vision of Greece, were scholars and men of action, could endure harsh conditions, fought for Greek freedom, were recklessly courageous, liked to dress up and displayed a panache that impressed their Greek comrades. Paddy also reminded me of a Bedouin chief's tribute to another famous warrior, T. E. Lawrence: "Tell them in England what I say. Of manhood, the man, in freedom free; a mind with no equal; I can see no flaw in him."

PART II

10

Anthony Blunt

(1907–1983)

In his major works of art history the enigmatic and elusive Anthony Blunt created a covert intellectual autobiography. His books on Nicolas Poussin, Francesco Borromini, William Blake and Pablo Picasso—the first three originally conceived as lectures, where his arguments seemed more persuasive than in print—reveal the connection between his high-minded scholarship and his subversive espionage. They show what George Steiner called "the coexistence within a single sensibility of utmost truth and falsehood." Blunt led separate and contradictory lives as a then illegal homosexual and distinguished public figure, Communist and courtier, journalist and scholar, soldier and (beginning in 1934) Russian spy. One friend called him "the most compartmentalized man I ever met." Though he was never able to resolve his personal conflicts, he lived vicariously by writing about kindred spirits in art.

A reviewer of his *Art and Architecture in France* (1953), noting Blunt's close identification with his subjects, observed that "there was a kind of personal and emotional revelation in Blunt's writing that manifested itself in his choice of artists and the intense personal engagement he seemed to have with them." Focusing on French, Italian, English and Spanish artists from the seventeenth to the twentieth century and trying to connect Poussin and Picasso, Blunt repeatedly exposed the opposition between the antithetical sides of his personality: stoical-hedonistic, harmonious-chaotic, withdrawn-committed, moderate-excessive, rational-passionate, serene-anguished, austere-sensuous, reticent-exuberant, tranquil-tumultuous.

Blunt established his formidable reputation by challenging traditional interpretations and by reviving the declining reputations of artists who were not generally admired at the time he wrote. John Ruskin, the greatest Victorian authority on art, had condemned Poussin (1594–1665)—who focused on biblical, mythological, classical and literary subjects—as an unemotional, chilly and forbidding artist. In *Modern Painters* he declared that Poussin's "want of sensibility permits him to paint frightful subjects, without feeling of any true horror: his pictures of the Plague, the death of Polydectes [a mythological Greek ruler] &c., are thus ghastly in incident, sometimes disgusting, but never impressive." Though Blunt ignored Ruskin's harsh judgment, he quoted negative critics who called Poussin "a dry, pedantic artist ... [who] relied too much on ancient art and [whose] figures looked like statues and not like human beings."

Yet, like a gallant knight rescuing a maiden in distress, Blunt personally identified with his subject and exclaimed that "Poussin has always remained my first love." Announcing his own intellectual standards of perfection, he stated that Poussin has now "come into his own. His classical ideals of reason, harmony, balance, economy, moderation, clarity and concentration have been once more seen as the source of one kind of great art." Unlike Ruskin, Blunt admired Poussin's ability to involve himself in frightful activity without feeling true horror, and Blunt imitated such dissociation in his own life. Running counter to prevailing opinion, he confidently declared, sometimes with more enthusiasm than discrimination, "I believe Poussin to be one of the supreme masters of formal design and, when he wishes, as exquisite a colorist as one could imagine."

Influenced by the art-historical methods of the German-Jewish exiles—Walter Friedlaender, Rudolf Wittkower and Johannes Wilde—who in the 1930s had come to the Courtauld Institute where Blunt was a prominent lecturer, all his books emphasized the dominant ideas that had influenced the artists' work: "In order to appreciate [Poussin] as an artist it is essential to understand the intellectual climate in which he worked and the ideas—religious, philosophical or aesthetic—in which he believed and which affected his method of work as well as his paintings." Poussin's emphasis on clarity, logic and order were similar to the philosophical method and ideas of his close French contemporary René Descartes (1596–1650), whom Blunt only briefly mentions.

Blunt devoted a whole chapter to Poussin's Stoicism—his rationality, scepticism, repression of emotion and self-abnegation—which he himself admired, tried to emulate and desperately needed to sustain him after he was publicly exposed as a spy in 1979. Like Blunt, who had tried to escape from his treacherous past, Poussin told a friend, "My nature compels me to seek and love things which are well ordered, fleeing confusion, which is as contrary and inimical to me as is day to the deepest night." When Poussin failed as a court painter (as Blunt finally failed as a spy) Blunt praised him for preferring "to live apart from the world of public affairs" and in his last years to "become even more completely detached from the world." Blunt's disappointing description of Poussin's penetrating self-portrait (1650) missed a promising opportunity to analyze his complex character: "It is not a lovable face, and that hardness which appears in Poussin's thought is to be seen in the frowning wrinkles of the brow. The mouth is set, and the eyes stare piercingly and almost threateningly at the spectator."

When describing Poussin's qualities as a painter Blunt conceded his weaknesses, but gave these traits a positive interpretation. He stated that Poussin's compositions are simple and static, and have "no surprises, but lead the spectator . . . by a series of visible—one could almost say predictable — steps to a conclusion which seems inevitable from the beginning." Ignoring Poussin's *froideur*, detachment and lack of human drama, Blunt claimed that "he works out carefully planned, motionless compositions made up of rocklike figures who gaze into infinity, unaware of what is going on around them. His paintings . . . embody an absolute refusal to make any concession to the senses."

Blunt wrote that *The Massacre of the Innocents* (late 1620s) — which he would later compare to Picasso's *Guernica*— "shows the whole tragedy [in Matthew 2:16] concentrated in a single group of mother, child and soldier, an almost *Racinien* concentration." But Walter Friedlaender, to whom Blunt paid tribute in his preface as the great pioneer "who laid the foundation of Poussin studies," echoed Ruskin by stating that in this lifeless painting "the cruelty and terror are static. . . . The face of the desperate mother is frozen in terror, like a theatrical mask." In an unconvincing attempt to achieve a synthesis, Blunt endowed Poussin with diametrically opposed qualities, and claimed that he was both impersonal and emotional, rational and mystical. Another forced use of the qualifier "almost" (as in my three previous quotations) undermines the weak argument: Poussin "created paintings which, though impersonal, are also deeply emotional and, though rational in their principles, are almost mystical in the impression that they convey." Despite Blunt's crude distortions and special pleading, his views have prevailed in the modern era. As his former pupil Christopher Wright notes, "So much of the writing on Poussin consists of undeviating admiration."

Blunt identified with the Italian architect Francesco Borromini (1599–1667) as he had with Poussin, who was five years older. Just as Poussin was his "first love," so he confessed (in a canine metaphor) that "once Borromini has bitten you he never lets go." Just as the French painter had been criticized for excessive reliance on ancient art, so "Borromini was vilified as the great anarchist of architecture, the man who overthrew all the laws of the Ancients and replaced them with disorder, and who corrupted the taste of many architects." Blunt used similar methods to rescue both Poussin and Borromini. After discussing Borromini's sources and theories, he gave "a clear account of the artist's career, a convincing analysis of his style and an estimate of his achievement." Blunt based his account of the architect's style on the influence of the ancients, Michelangelo and (rather vaguely) nature. He argued that the architect struggled "between imaginative energy and intellectual control," and that his bizarre inventions—curvilinear, ornamental and fantastic—"were in fact variations based on an almost [his favorite adverb] ruthlessly logical method."

Borromini was a hands-on stonemason and draftsman as well as an architect. A contemporary praised his diligence, expertise and mental power: "He guided the builder's shovel, the plasterer's darby [leveler], the carpenter's saw, the stonemason's chisel, the brick-layer's trowel and the ironworker's file, with the result that the quality of his work is high but not the cost, as his detractors claim, and all this springs from his intelligence and his industry." But he had a bitter, jealous rivalry with the more charming and successful Gian Lorenzo Bernini, who won all the best commissions. Unable to finish many of his ambitious projects and give complete expression to his ideas, suffering from hypochondria and morbid introspection, Borromini finally became misanthropic, manic and frenzied.

Blunt (with yet another "almost") observed that Borromini alienated his patrons. "Though physically of a fine presence, he lacked all the social graces. He was melancholy, nervous and uncompromising, and these qualities soon turned to a neurotic fear of all human contacts and a suspicion of people, which almost reached the stage of persecution mania." Yet Borromini had two things in common with Blunt: his "devotion to art and unhappiness in his life." When describing Borromini's character and career

Blunt seemed to be writing about himself. Like Blunt—who desperately tried to cover his tracks and avoid his inexorable fate, and was finally repudiated by former companions who did not want to be tarred by his treachery—Borromini "was a neurotic and unhappy man, constantly dogged by disaster, often largely of his own creating, quarreling even with his best patrons and closest friends."

Borromini was the first major artist to kill himself. After his botched suicide attempt, and with amazing objectivity, he managed to dictate a morbid account of his experience before dying a few hours later. He seized a convenient weapon and followed the Roman tradition—described in Plutarch's *Life of Brutus*—of falling on his sword: "In despair I took the sword and pulling it out of the scabbard leant the hilt on the bed and put the point to my side and then fell on it with such force that it ran into my body, from one side to the other, and in falling on the sword I fell on to the floor with the sword run through my body and because of my wound I began to scream. . . . [Friends] pulled the sword out of my side and put me on my bed; and this is how I came to be wounded."

Blunt, who himself had contemplated suicide after his humiliation and disgrace, was deeply impressed by Borromini's morbid memoir and (rather illogically) connected the architect's internal conflict to his artistic power: "To have been under a strain so violent that it drove him to this act of violence—if not of madness—and yet immediately afterwards to be able to dictate such a lucid account of the event, reveals a combination of intense emotional power and rational detachment which are among the qualities which go to make him such a great architect."

Always consistent in his approach, Blunt used the same methods in his book on Blake as he had on Poussin and Borromini. He examined "the sources of his style, his relation to his contemporaries' painting, his development as an artist." In a rather strained effort, Blunt began and then immediately abandoned a false comparison of two wildly different painters: "One artist might at first sight seem to provide an analogy with Poussin . . . William Blake. With him it is certainly true that his philosophical and religious beliefs formed the starting point of his creation, but the analogy would not be fair."

Blunt saw Blake, paradoxically, as both a traditionalist and a revolutionary: "He used the works of his contemporaries as freely as he did those of the dead—and in the same way, because what he took from them he made wholly his own. . . . When he borrows a pose from some other artist, he so completely transforms the figure that it seems to be wholly Blakean." Like all artists, Blake was certainly influenced by other painters. But since he re-created their work in his own extremely personal style, he did not follow tradition but broke it.

Blunt shared one significant characteristic with his subject. The ideas of the French Revolution had a similar impact on Blake as those of the Russian Revolution later had on Blunt, and both revolutions provoked their liberation from the old order. Blunt's biographer Miranda Carter notes that he "made Blake's tangle with revolutionary politics, and his subsequent retreat from them, the central drama of the poet's life. What he most directly responded to in Blake was the natural opposition to authority." Blunt also supported and then retreated from the Revolution. He first subverted the authority of the British government, then tried to break away from his Russian authority and was finally broken by British authority.

In his 1943 article "Blake's Pictorial Imagination," Blunt wrote that the ideas of the French Revolution "seemed intensely real and vitally important, and Blake expressed them in a series of revolutionary works, in the political as well as in the literary sense." In a self-reflective passage, he concluded that Blake's "interest in politics had always been more emotional than practical, and after the [reign of terror] of 1794 he withdrew entirely into the field of the intellect." But there was also one important difference between author and subject. Blake was, according to his painter-friend Samuel Palmer, "one of the few to be met with in our passage through life who are not, in some way or other, 'double minded' and inconsistent with themselves." By contrast, these contradictory qualities ruled Blunt's double life.

Just as Poussin was Blunt's favorite painter, so Picasso was his favorite living painter. Just as Blunt had called Blake both a traditionalist and a revolutionary, so he also said that Picasso, a very different kind of artist, "in addition to being a great revolutionary, is also a great traditionalist." Yet Blunt contradicted himself by stating that Picasso attempted "to create a new reality through the destruction of traditional forms." Blunt also tried to complete the circle and connect his favorite subjects. Focusing on Picasso's brief classical period in the early 1920s, Blunt made a daring leap from the seventeenth to the twentieth centuries by claiming that Picasso was "essentially a calm, detached, intellectual artist, belonging to the tradition of Poussin, Ingres and Cézanne." It is significant that Blunt did not mention Poussin's most important follower, Jacques Louis David. After trying to link Poussin and Picasso, Blunt called *Guernica* (1937)—whose central figures are a sacrificial horse and brutal bull—a modern *Massacre of the Innocents:* "Closer to Picasso in feeling, owing to its economy and concentration, is Poussin's *Massacre* at Chantilly, a painting which Picasso must certainly have known when he planned *Guernica*." In denying the evidence of the eye and arguing for the similarity of two disparate pictures, Blunt substituted bold assertion ("must certainly have known") for solid fact.

Blunt was on even shakier ground when trying to connect Picasso's Cubism of about 1910 to Poussin. In his book on Poussin, and again without citing evidence, Blunt claimed that Poussin (as if he were a late Turner) was a proto-abstract painter: "The early Cubists saw in him the near-abstract qualities which they themselves sought.... The doctrines of the Cubists ... are close to Poussin's ideas on art, and some of them claim descent from him through Cézanne." But John Richardson, the contemporary authority on Picasso, contradicts Blunt by stating, "Picasso has surprisingly little time for Cézanne's theorizing [and said] 'I'm in complete disagreement with his idea about making over Poussin in accordance with nature.' ... He would not have wanted to lay himself open to a charge of Poussinism."

Picasso forced Blunt to confront the crisis of contemporary politics. Like André Malraux's *Man's Hope* (1937), Georges Bernanos' *A Diary of My Times* (1938) and George Orwell's *Homage to Catalonia* (1938), *Guernica* was created during the Spanish Civil War. After the Nazis bombed the sacred Basque capital, a ghastly event that unleashed destructive power against helpless humanity, Picasso painted his political protest in a week of white-hot fury.

Writing in the *Spectator* of August 6, 1937, Blunt completely missed the artistic and political point: "The painting is disillusioning. Fundamentally it is the same as Picasso's bull-fight scenes. It is not an act of public mourning, but the expression of a private brain-storm which gives no evidence that Picasso has realized the political significance of Guernica." Blunt published short books on Picasso's sources in 1962 and on *Guernica* in 1969. In the second work, he was more interested in the origins and well-documented genesis of the painting than in the political meaning, and repeated his claim that "it would not be an exaggeration to describe *Guernica* as a *Massacre of the Innocents*." But Picasso's depiction of cruelty and horror was very similar to the engravings of Francisco Goya and of Poussin's contemporary Jacques Callot (1592–1635), neither mentioned by Blunt, and quite different from the work of Poussin.

To fortify himself and heal the fissure in his own subversive character, Blunt—deceptive in life and art—distorted the facts and denied the evidence. He identified with his various alter egos, and exalted the qualities he sometimes lacked and most admired: Poussin's idealistic Stoicism and resignation in the face of adversity, Borromini's ruthless logic and intellectual control, Blake's defiance of authority and support of the Revolution, Picasso's imaginative transformations and political commitment.

11

Basil Blackwood

(1909–1945)

Basil Blackwood, the clever and charming 4th Marquess of Dufferin and Ava, died in Burma at the age of thirty-five in the last months of World War II. Neither family nor friends ever knew how he had died. My discovery of eighty pages of unpublished documents in the National Archives at Kew reveal for the first time his military mission, and the exact place and precise circumstances of his death. These papers provide a brief history of his short life. They include his photograph and describe his religion, education, knowledge of French and official travels in foreign countries. They list his interests, the books he read during military service, his personal possessions and instructions about returning them to his family in Northern Ireland. They contain a sorrowful account of the failure to recover his body and his presumed burial in an unknown place by the Japanese.

Basil Blackwood's grandfather, a descendant of the eighteenth-century playwright Richard Brinsley Sheridan, was the cultured and worldly 1st Marquess of Dufferin and Ava (1826–1902). Dufferin is in County Down in Northern Ireland; Ava, near Mandalay, was the ancient capital of the Burmese kings. One of the most prominent diplomats of his time, Dufferin was governor-general of Canada, ambassador to Russia and the Ottoman empire, when he helped settle the future of Egypt, and author of the successful travel book about Iceland *Letters from High Latitudes* (1857). He became viceroy of India and in 1886, after a brief military campaign, annexed Upper Burma to the British Empire. He was painted by the Symbolist artist George Frederick Watts, and was a friend of Kipling, who praised him in the pedantic dramatic monologue "One Viceroy Resigns," in which the poet assumes the viceroy's voice and advises his successor. After India, Dufferin continued his diplomatic career as ambassador to Italy and France. In 1900 he was innocently involved in a financial scandal with the notorious swindler and suicide Whitaker Wright.

The viceroy's four sons fought in Britain's early modern wars and had a tragic history. His oldest son, Archibald, born in 1863, was killed in 1900 in the Siege of Ladysmith in the Second Boer War. Terence, his second son (1866–1918), was a British diplomat who became the 2nd Marquess and died of pneumonia at the end of World War I. His third son, Basil, was born in 1870 and killed in action in July 1917. Frederick (1875–1930), the fourth son, a soldier and politician, became the 3rd Marquess. The father of Basil Blackwood, he was wounded in the Boer War and wounded twice in World War I, and was killed in a plane crash in 1930.

Tennyson celebrated Helen's Tower on Dufferin's 3,000-acre estate, Clandeboye, built in 1800 and twelve miles from Belfast in County Down: "Helen's Tower, here I stand / Dominant over sea and land / Son's love built me and I hold / mother's love in lettered gold." But according to Dufferin's great-granddaughter Caroline Blackwood, who portrayed Clandeboye as Dunmartin Hall in her autobiographical novel *Great Granny Webster* (1977), it was chilly, damp, smelly and filthy, with no hot bath water and stone-cold food. Basil's mother, Brenda, was considered half-crazy. She called herself Queen of the Fairies and thought her offspring were demonic changelings, left by evil sprites as substitutes for her real children.

Basil Blackwood, the 4th Marquess, was educated at Lockers

Park, a "prison-like" prep school in Hertfordshire, won the prestigious Rosebery History Prize at Eton and was a Brackenbury Scholar at Balliol College. A friend described his "beautiful brown eyes, very very alive and deep and large," and said he was quiet and reserved, with fine manners. The biographer Elizabeth Longford called Basil "brilliantly clever . . . very well grown, extremely handsome, very athletic." Lord Birkenhead, another contemporary, recalled "his incessant chucklings at his own sallies, his dark and striking face thrown forward in fierce argument." Evelyn Waugh admired Basil. John Betjeman fell in love with him, and gave him the affectionate schoolboy nicknames of "Little Bloody" and the ironic "Mindless." He noted his lively conversation and described his appearance and character: "Lord Ava had enormous eyes / And head of a colossal size / He rarely laughed and only spoke / To utter some stupendous joke." Betjeman later wrote an elegy that described him as "Humorous, reckless, loyal / My kind, heavy-lidded companion."

Basil's intellect matched his beauty and character. The Oxford economist Roy Harrod praised him as "the most brilliant pupil I ever had." Randolph Churchill, agreeing with Betjeman and Harrod, lauded Basil as "the most lovable man I met at Oxford. His liquid spaniel eyes and his beautiful, charming manner commanded affection. He was the most brilliant of all my contemporaries at Oxford." But Churchill, himself a heavy drinker, added that "an undue addiction to drink blighted what might have been a fine political career." Basil was also addicted to gambling and heavily mortgaged his vast estate to pay his gaming debts. He solved his financial problems in July 1930 by marrying his cousin, Maureen Guinness, heiress to the inexhaustible brewery fortune. Basil succeeded to his title that month, and spent his honeymoon traveling in Burma and shooting big game with the Maharajah of Mysore in India.

Basil's three young children had only the vaguest memories of their busy and often absent father. His son, Sheridan, observing him in the bath when he was on leave from India, was startled to find him covered with mosquito bites. Caroline's most vivid memory was accompanying her father on a massacre of pheasants and being sent out like a retriever to fetch the dead birds. Her younger sister, Perdita, presented with rare wartime chocolates by an American soldier, looked forward to eating them. But when she left them in the library, her father succumbed to temptation and devoured the entire box.

Basil had a dazzling political career and held a series of important government posts in the 1930s. He was private secretary to Lord Lothian, the under-secretary of state for India, in 1932; to Lord Irwin, president of the Board of Education, 1932–35; to Lord Halifax, secretary of state for war, 1935, and Lord Privy Seal, 1935–36. Basil himself became under-secretary of state for the colonies from 1937 to 1940. An effective public speaker, deftly mixing argument and wit, he made his maiden speech in Parliament at the age of twenty-two. The historian William Maguire, who did not think Basil's drinking was an impediment, described him as "a gifted young man of extraordinary charm; like his grandfather [the viceroy] he combined intellectual, literary and artistic gifts with ambitions in public life, and as Under Secretary of State while still in his twenties, he was talked of in some circles as a future Conservative prime minister."

In 1940, as the Japanese troops steadily advanced in Burma, Basil refused a position in Winston Churchill's coalition government and became a captain in the Royal Horseguards. He returned to civilian life as director of the Empire Division of the Ministry of Information from 1941 to 1943, but rejoined the army in May 1944 when his experience in the ministry led to propaganda work in Burma. (Two other dashing soldiers, Orde Wingate and Peter Fleming, were also fighting in Burma.) Basil was posted to Force

136, the Special Operations Executive in Southeast Asia. It specialized in strategic deception and fought against the Japanese and against the Burmese and Indian nationalists who joined the Japanese in the vain hope of achieving independence after they won the war.

SOE's mobile broadcasting stations, operating only thirty yards from the front lines, tried to break Japanese morale. They distributed pamphlets and used loudspeakers to make demoralizing speeches and to play sentimental music that made the soldiers long for home. One message, purportedly from the emperor, used Japanese prisoners to persuade the troops to leave Burma and return to protect their families at home. Though the enemy had been taught that death was preferable to dishonorable surrender, British propaganda urged them to stop fighting the lost war and assured them that they would be treated well as prisoners. Though their perilous task was almost impossible, the propaganda sometimes worked and in the spring of 1944 Force 136 convinced four different Japanese units to surrender.

Basil's jaunty and optimistic letters home during the last week of his life (which reached Northern Ireland after his death) revealed his adventurous spirit and eagerness to confront danger. Writing to his wife on March 17, 1945, he assumed a historical as well as a personal interest in the Burmese campaign by announcing that Ava had been retaken and that the Allies had nearly won the war in Burma:

> I am now in the last camp of one of my journeys across Burma of which I have now made several. I certainly have seen more of the various fronts in the time I have been here than most people have. I have not enjoyed myself so much since the war began.
>
> Fort Dufferin is still but tonight Ava is said to have been

recaptured. So after three years Sheridan's earldom is once again in the family. Please congratulate the little fellow on the successful recovery of his property from the invaders.

I am now halfway between two battles and there is a hell of a glare in the far distance, but whether it is Mandalay or Meiktila I am not sure. The only fly in the ointment is that the road I am taking tomorrow was cut yesterday and I shall have to go in a convoy which means very slow travelling and for a nervous old politician some anxious moments on some of the narrower portions. . . .

It really looks as though the Jap has just about had it in Burma, though how long it will take and how much he will be able to salvage from the wreck is another matter.

In his last letter, written to his children on March 24, Basil expressed excitement about the tough fighting and very real danger. Though surrounded and attacked by the enemy, he was still confident of victory:

At the moment I am in a camp in a plain which has got the Japs all round it, so we have got to get all our food and ammunition and all things dropped to us from aeroplanes every day. But we get plenty so we are all right. I was just about the last car to get through on the road before these Japs closed it, so I was in luck.

So now we are like a besieged city in olden days (like Troy). I am writing this in a slit trench as it is six o'clock and the sun is going down so the Japs are shelling us and I'm afraid they are going to attack us again tonight. They attacked us the night before last and got into the middle of our position but we drove them out and counted 300 dead bodies the next morning which was jolly good, though they killed a few of ours which was very sad.

Printed sources, including the official British history of the Burma campaign, *The War against Japan* (HMSO, 1965), romantically but mistakenly state that Basil died in Ava or even in Fort Dufferin in Mandalay. But on March 25, 1945, on a covert mission with the Indian Field Broadcasting Unit (IFBU), more than one hundred miles southwest of Mandalay, Basil was killed in a Japanese ambush. In *Telegram from Guernica,* a biography of the war correspondent George Steer, who was also killed in Burma, Nicholas Rankin wrote that Basil was filmed just before his death: "Stanley Charles was a combat cameraman with the South-East Asian Command Film Unit, who were roving film reporters. In Burma in March 1945, Charles met a 'very pleasant' captain who invited him to film the IFBU at work. Charles filmed them putting up their apparatus, which included a loudspeaker on a tripod, then broadcasting surrender terms in Japanese to an enemy unit in a tunnel on a hill, with the captain lying prone. He was still filming from about seventy-five yards away when a Japanese mortar fired on the Indian Field Broadcasting Unit and killed the captain." Basil's family was notified of his death through diplomatic channels by the Crown Princess of Sweden. His body was never recovered.

The recently discovered military documents include full-face and profile photographs of Basil in captain's uniform, which show his dark hair and skin and his handsome, aristocratic features. In his SOE Personnel History Sheet he wrote that his religion was Church of Ireland, his profession politics. His education included Lockers Park (c. 1915–21), Eton (1921–27) and Balliol (1927–30). His addresses were Clandeboye, Northern Ireland, and the Mayfair Hotel, London W1; his solicitors were J. D. Langton & Passmore, 8 Bolton Street, Piccadilly. He had "considerable knowledge" of India and Burma in 1930; experience in the Indian Franchise Commission (on voting rights) in 1932; and extensive travel through "all colonial possessions," including Mauritius, Zanzibar, Tanganyika, Aden and Hadramaut on the Arabian Peninsula, as well as Madagascar and Albania, when he was secretary for the colonies in the years before the war. He had a speaking, reading and writing knowledge of French, and noted his other interests as shooting, golf, literature and, more troublesome, racing.

The thirty books in Basil's possession included thrillers by Agatha Christie and adventure novels by C. S. Forester as well as more serious works: Edward Gibbon's *The Decline and Fall of the Roman Empire,* Robert Browning's poems, Sir James George Frazer's *The Golden Bough: A Study in Magic and Religion* and W. P. Ker's *English Literature: Medieval.* Basil's personal effects included a wooden box with letters, personal papers and photos of his wife and three children, all of sentimental value, English and Egyptian money, leather case with sporting guns, leather valise on wheels, tin trunk, kit bag and camp bed. He also had some useful smaller items: passport photos, cigarette case, pocket lighter, miniature compass, traveling clock, fountain pen, book of stamps, sealing wax and clothing coupons. An official asked that Basil's possessions be sent back to Britain either by air or by "safe hand with one of our own officers," and urged that "special care be taken to prevent any loss or damage as the result of extra handling and repacking." But owing to wartime restrictions, the commanding officer "regretted that special permission cannot be given to forward to Lady Dufferin the items listed in the above mentioned letter."

Basil was actually killed in the tiny village of Letse, across the Irrawaddy River and only five miles from what is now a major tourist site: the sprawling ancient city of 2,200 temples in Pagan. On March 27, 1945, Major D. H. Preston interviewed eyewitness survivors of the Japanese attack and gave a dramatic account of how the enemy, whose presence was unsuspected, opened fire at almost point-blank range as Basil was leading his men:

I have now seen SONG [a Japanese-speaking Korean officer]
and the official position seems to be that DUFFERIN must be
regarded as "missing" at the moment.

SONG is not too clear or explicit about the whole business
but briefly the situation appears to be as follows:

On the 25th of March at about 1500 hours the section,
escorted by a platoon of a British Regiment, went out on the
flank of the box with a view to broadcasting in an area where
a previous patrol had reported only dead bodies. The actual
target seems to have been about 400–500 yards ahead of this
position. DUFFERIN and the Jemedar [Indian officer] and the
platoon were ahead of the section about 200 yards, presum-
ably doing a recce. One hundred and fifty yards short of the
dead bodies' position Japs in some strength opened fire. The
platoon and DUFFERIN were more or less in open country and
DUFFERIN was hit in the chest. SONG says he saw him clutch
his chest and stagger about with the platoon as it withdrew.
He himself made several attempts to get up to DUFFERIN but
could not do so owing to enemy fire. Ultimately the rest of the
section had to withdraw with the British troops and although
fresh troops made three more attempts to bring in DUFFERIN
they failed to do so. . . . I think SONG has behaved and is behaving very well indeed.

Two months later on May 23, the regimental chaplain Reverend
A. J. L. Heaver, who'd actually examined Basil's dead body under
fire, vividly wrote of his wounds, the state of his corpse and their
inability to get him out of the battlefield:

I can indeed confirm that Lord DUFFERIN's body *must* have
been buried by the Japs near point 534 [on the 1″ map of
Burma], for our patrols were sent over the same spot repeat-

edly and there was no trace of either his body or that of the private soldier killed near him.

His death must have been instantaneous as we got out to him only a little time after he was reported hit and from my examination I could see that he must have been hit through the heart and lungs for the nature and extent of the bleeding proved it. Also, his body was rigid. I don't think more than an hour and a half at most can have passed before we got to him.

It will always be a sorrow to me that we couldn't bring his body in but though I dragged it for some yards, I had to give it up as the man next to me was hit and we all had our work cut out to bring him in under covering fire.

Two years after Basil's death, Evelyn Waugh gave Nancy Mitford an amusing account of an incident that occurred when both Basil's widow and Randolph Churchill were probably drunk at a London ball: "Maureen gave Randolph a terrific box on the ear. Instead of striking back like a man he tried to pacify her. They stood in the centre of the ballroom sweating & arguing for three minutes and then—another more terrific box. I said to her: 'I am all for Randolph being struck but why particularly do you strike him now?' She: 'He never wrote a letter of condolence when Ava was killed.'"

Betjeman chose the glorious but not entirely accurate words for Basil's memorial at Clandeboye:

A MAN OF BRILLIANCE
AND OF MANY FRIENDS
HE WAS KILLED IN ACTION AT LETZE ON MARCH
25TH 1945 AT THE AGE OF THIRTY-FIVE,
RECAPTURING BURMA THE COUNTRY WHICH
HIS GRANDFATHER ANNEXED TO THE BRITISH
CROWN.

Poets from Tennyson and Kipling to Betjeman and Robert Lowell have celebrated the Blackwood family. In "Runaway," addressed to Blackwood's daughter Caroline, who was his third wife, Lowell followed the memorial inscription and wrote about "your father's betrayal of you, / rushing to his military death in Burma, / annexed for England / by his father's father, the Viceroy." Betjeman exaggerated Basil's heroic exploits; Lowell saw them as a personal "betrayal" of his abandoned children.

Basil Blackwood had an illustrious literary tradition and diplomatic heritage, impressive title and good looks, great wealth and formidable intelligence. As W. B. Yeats wrote of Major Robert Gregory, another gallant Irishman, "Soldier, scholar, horseman, he, / And all he did done perfectly." The detailed documents in the military archives solve the mystery of Basil's death, which occurred nearly seventy-five years ago. His personal charm, difficult to capture and define, impressed everyone who knew him. A brilliant scholar, with a gift for friendship, he was destined for high office but had his career cut off in his mid-thirties. He held an important position in the British government, but showed personal courage by volunteering for dangerous duty. It's sadly ironic that he was killed on a comparatively unimportant and inglorious mission. In Burma, Basil was destined to follow the tradition of his gifted but tragically doomed family.

12

Derek Jackson

(1906–1982)

Derek Jackson, a virtually unknown genius, had a unique combination of talents and achievements. He was a renowned physicist and professor at Oxford, a war hero who shot down five German planes and invented a device that ruined their radar, a jockey who rode his own horses in four Grand National steeplechases and a bisexual who married six times. His arrogant and provocative character inspired the straitlaced and decorous *Dictionary of National Biography,* not given to emotional outbursts, to call Jackson "fearless, wild tempered and wickedly amusing," capable of "devastating repartee and outrageous fantasy." An independent thinker and researcher, he created his own morality and trusted his own judgments. In his arrogant manner and reckless wit he seems to have stepped out of an Evelyn Waugh novel.

His Welsh father, Sir Charles Jackson, was a barrister and politician, art collector and authority on English silver, and owner of the *News of the World,* the most scandalous and successful paper in Britain. Derek and his identical twin brother, Vivian, were born in Hampstead in June 1906, and grew up in a wealthy and cultured family. Their father died when the twins were fourteen, their mother when they were eighteen; and their sister, Daphne, who was ten years older, died during World War I. Derek later complained that their guardian, Lord Riddell, who succeeded their father as chairman of the newspaper, "did the dirty on us." With his power of attorney, he sold a huge block of the young twins' shares in the *News of the World* at a low price, bought them himself and made a handsome profit. Derek, however, remained extremely wealthy and privileged, and used money to satisfy his every desire.

From 1920 to 1924 Jackson was one of six hundred boys at Rugby School in Warwickshire. Thomas Arnold, father of the poet Matthew and headmaster of Rugby from 1828 to 1841, had established the model of the English public school, portrayed in Thomas Hughes' *Tom Brown's Schooldays* (1857). The South African novelist William Plomer, three years older than Jackson, wrote a dispiriting account of the school in the postwar era, and Jackson's experiences were very similar to his. Many of the recent masters and Old Boys had been killed in the war and the remaining teachers were either dotards or weaklings. Plomer hated the compulsory games and military drills and managed to avoid most of them. The water in the swimming bath, the color of strong tea, was filled with tadpoles and slime. There was still a shortage of food and the exiguous portions of sugar, bread and meat had to last all week. In these harsh conditions physical punishment was frequent. Plomer remembered that one of the servants, attempting to comfort the frightened boys before a whipping, insisted, "'Tain't the hagony, it's the disgrace."

Jackson hated the harsh regimen and prevailing cruelty. He was taught by the Reverend Geoffrey Woolley, a major and chaplain who had won the Victoria Cross as a young lieutenant in the Battle of Ypres in 1915 and was the father of Jackson's future wife Janetta. In the school workshop Jackson built his first spectroscope, an optical device for measuring the waves of light or radiation, and was regarded by boys and masters with amused amazement. Later on, when asked what it was like to engage in nighttime aerial combat, he replied, "It wasn't as bad as being at Rugby."

In the summer of 1924, between school and university, Jackson learned German at Heidelberg. He loved the German language and culture, especially the writing of Goethe and music of Wagner, and gave his beloved dachshunds Germanic names. In World War II he even shocked his English aircrew by shouting orders to his pilot in German—*Links! Rechts! Gerade aus!*—while fighting enemy planes.

After visiting Germany Jackson went up to Trinity College, Cambridge, which had an impressive Great Court and a magnificent library designed by Christopher Wren. The college of Isaac Newton specialized in science and math. The Master was J. J. ("Atom") Thomson, who had discovered the electron and won the Nobel Prize in Physics in 1906. Vladimir Nabokov had entered Trinity in 1919, five years before Jackson. Like Nabokov, Jackson avoided all team sports, and dined in Hall under the portrait of his future marital model, King Henry VIII.

Jackson earned a First in physics at the age of twenty and was expected to continue his work at the Cavendish Laboratory under Lord Rutherford, who had won the Nobel Prize in 1908. But he was lured away by Frederick Lindemann, who offered him his own research facilities at the Clarendon Laboratory at Oxford. Born in Germany, Lindemann (later Lord Cherwell) was a model for Jackson of the worldly scientist. He was a wealthy man, an accomplished pianist and a tennis champion who had competed at Wimbledon. He came to England in 1914, qualified as a pilot in the war, and was the first to demonstrate how to get a plane out of a spiral spin. "Oxford *bought* me," Jackson said, using his favorite equine metaphor, "just as you might buy a promising yearling." Despite his academic brilliance in these years, he left almost no trail in the records of his school and college.

Working in Professor Lindemann's lab in the 1920s and 1930s, Jackson investigated the properties of the atomic nucleus. When he was twenty-eight he published his first paper, in the *Proceedings of the Royal Society of London,* which earned him a place in the history of atomic physics. Simon Courtauld explained (sort of) that "the splitting due to the electron magnetic moment is known as 'fine structure' and the very much smaller splitting due to the nuclear magnetic moment is known as 'hyperfine structure.'. . . . Using [the element] caesium as his starting point, Derek's aim was to deduce from the measured hyperfine splitting a value for the nuclear magnetic moment."

Physically unimpressive, Jackson was short, with a small head, regular features, brittle dark hair, grey-green eyes, thin lips, and tiny hands and feet. A friend recalled that his voice had a "gravelly, strained quality as if each word had to be squeezed past recalcitrant vocal chords." He spoke rapidly, with long dramatic pauses, and had trouble pronouncing the letter "R." When excited, as he often was, he would run his hand through his hair, chew his tongue and begin to shout. His third wife, Barbara Skelton, satirically added that his strutting walk "reminded me of a yapping Welsh terrier." He and his brother, strikingly similar in looks and temperament, were both physicists. In the Oxford laboratory Derek's collaborator Heinrich Kuhn, a German-Jewish refugee from Nazi Germany, "was faced with the extraordinary sight of Derek Jackson talking excitedly to what appeared to be his mirror image, in gestures, voice and all"—his twin brother Vivian.

The war hero and travel writer Patrick Leigh Fermor, living in Greece, told Jackson's sister-in law Nancy Mitford, "Derek Jackson has just left, after four days here: all alone, which was nice; and you were talked of with great fondness. . . . He was very bland and easy; but, my word, he's very far from usual." It's not clear if Fermor referred to Jackson's brilliance, eccentricity or homosexuality, and many other friends have tried to describe and decipher his enigmatic character. In January 1931, when Jackson was married to "Poppet" John and moved in Bohemian circles, the Bloomsbury diarist Frances Partridge called him "a lively, spontaneous young man of quick speech and winning ways, whose slanting eyes (half-closed when he smiled) gave him a fawnlike [faunlike?] appearance."

Jackson adopted camp speech along with a superior manner, and his favorite startling word was "pretty." In the war, when his commanding officer asked him to report on a new plane he'd just inspected, Jackson replied, "It was so pretty, I wanted to stroke it." At a foxhunt he challenged the master of hounds by stating, "I'm Derek Jackson, you know *me!*" "No, I don't. Why should I?" "Because I am so pretty." Referring to Barbara Skelton's physically repulsive royal lover and previous husbands, he insisted that after King Farouk, Cyril Connolly and George Weidenfeld, "I was the pretty one."

In a letter to the *Times* just after Jackson's death, Air Vice Marshal E. D. Crew, noting his haughty and prickly character, wrote that he was "intensely intolerant of the second-rate—and sometimes simply amusingly and outrageously intolerant." In a review of Simon Courtauld's biography, Selina Hastings portrayed Jackson as "rich and rebellious, arrogant, provocative, wildly funny, often offensive." He drove cars dangerously fast, took risks on the road and liked to shake his fist menacingly as he passed the more cautious foreign drivers. Barbara Skelton attributed his frequent rages and yelling at waiters to high blood pressure, and described a characteristically violent scene in their married life. She and a friend, she wrote, "were rudely chattering across Derek who lost his temper, grabbed our two heads and cracked them together, like a pair of walnuts. Whereupon I took Derek's hand and bit into his thumb."

Jackson often indulged in deliberately provocative statements, not only to enliven a dull conversation, but also to show off and draw attention to himself. In 1942, for example, before the major Allied victories at Alamein and Stalingrad, he told the diarist James Lees-Milne "that we can't win the war, that he loathes the British lower classes who have forced us into this unnecessary war and that the Germans know the best way of treating them, which is to crush them under heel. We argued, I think he cannot be absolutely in earnest." This sort of outrageous declaration was completely contradicted by Jackson's valiant war service. He knew quite well that the lower classes did not force Britain into the war and that many lower-class Germans supported Hitler. But his willingness to express these reckless ideas allowed his enemies to attribute even more absurd statements to him. Though the British Fascist Oswald Mosley was his brother-in-law, Jackson did not agree with his political ranting and never said "that all Jews in England should be killed and that the war should be stopped 'before we lose any more money.'" Between 1935 and 1939 he published eleven scientific papers with his Jewish colleague Heinrich Kuhn.

Jackson inherited millions from his father and freely spent his great wealth on foxhunting and racehorses, scientific equipment and laboratories. He commissioned portraits of himself by Henry Lamb in 1934, William Rothenstein in 1941 and Oskar Kokoschka in 1960, and purchased valuable paintings by Corot, Pissarro, Sisley, Renoir, Matisse, Augustus John and the German Expressionists. He bought grand houses and stayed in luxurious hotels: Claridge's in London and the Hôtel Normandy in Deauville for the summer racing season. He loved good food and fine wines, and entertained lavishly. Frances Partridge observed, "He was much more generous with his own money than any other rich man I have known, both by coming to the rescue of friends in trouble and by giving presents of crates of superb claret."

Horses and science were the two polestars of Jackson's life, and he named two of his horses—Neon and Xenon—after noble gases. He once half-seriously remarked that his winning horses had supported his scientific work. He met his first two wives at foxhunts, and raising and riding horses were a vital bond between them. He rode the Grand Nationals at Aintree racecourse in Liverpool, as well as many other races as late as 1965 when he was nearly sixty. Mary Lovell noted that Jackson, short and compactly built, "could hunt thoroughbreds when most men needed a heavyweight hunter—thus he had an incomparable advantage when following hounds across fast country."

A professional jockey, underestimating Jackson's ability, called him "a very amateur rider. He was kind to horses, but he couldn't catch hold of them or pick them up. And he didn't really know how to use a whip." His horses fell in the steeplechase in 1935 and 1957 and refused a fence in 1948, but he was expert at falling without getting hurt. Depreciating his considerable skill, he recalled that when boldly jumping over stone-edged banks, "I took to them without any problem at all; never had a fall, relying on the sound principle of leaving it to the horse, and when in doubt shut my eyes."

Jackson behaved as provocatively, even insultingly, at the track as he did on social occasions. When fined by racing stewards for breaking the rules, he would fling a £100 note at them and ask for change. Charged with riding improperly, he gave an Evelyn Waugh-like response: "How dare you accuse me when you allow the jockeys' lavatories to be in such an improper state—quite disgusting, in fact." Using an equine metaphor when friends mentioned a new girl, he would ask, "Have you mounted her?" Like Gulliver infatuated by the Houyhnhnms, he thought men existed to look after horses. His highest praise was "as perfect as someone on *two* legs can be."

In December 1936 Jackson and Pamela Mitford traveled to Vienna on their honeymoon. At the Sacher Hotel the manager informed them that Vivian (as reckless as Derek) had been killed in a freak accident in St. Moritz, Switzerland. Pamela's sister Diana Mosley wrote that "Vivian drove the [horse-drawn] sleigh at full speed on the frozen snow, and at a bend it touched a telegraph pole and overturned. All were violently thrown out. Vivian broke his neck and was killed instantly." Derek felt he had lost a vital part of himself, the person he loved more than anyone else. He was deeply moved by and often recited Goethe's popular poem "Der Erlkönig." It portrays a child, unprotected by his father while riding on horseback, who is attacked and killed by a supernatural being. The poem must have reminded Derek, in a spooky way, of the horse-sleigh accident of the dead Vivian.

None of his wives had the faintest understanding of his highly specialized scientific work and animals formed a crucial bond between them. Though severe with people, Jackson was sentimental about dogs. He was obsessed with long-haired dachshunds, and his letters to his second wife, Pamela Mitford, were filled with trivial gossip and soppy endearments about their dogs. When he woke in the morning he'd sing, to the tune of "Happy Birthday," "Good morning dear Wüda, good morning to you; and dear little Hamelin and big Weser too." He claimed that Wüda was much better than a hot-water bottle because she didn't get cold in the morning, and was delighted whenever his "badger hounds" chased and caught a rabbit.

He maintained, when he flew home from America in a great rush in August 1939, "It's because of our little dog. It's her birthday tomorrow so we must get home." In fact, the military authorities were afraid he might drown if he went by ship. As Lovell explained, he had "been allocated seats because he was carrying top-secret papers. The embassy had asked him to give [the papers to them] for transmission in the diplomatic bag. Derek refused. He said later, 'If I'd accepted, the Russians would have had them next day.'" His caution was prescient. In the 1940s the spies Kim Philby and Donald Maclean infiltrated the British Embassy in Washington.

Partly because of his passionate attachment to Germany, Jackson at first opposed Britain's declaration of war when the Nazis invaded Poland in September 1939. He completely misjudged the dangerous intent of Hitler's demand for *Lebensraum* and maintained that "war with Germany was quite unnecessary since Hitler's territorial ambitions were directed only at eastern Europe, and that [Britain] could never defeat Germany unless America came in on our side." But he changed his mind about the war after Hitler's conquest of Europe and the British retreat from Dunkirk. In July 1940 he enlisted in the Royal Air Force as a lowly aircraftman and rose through the ranks to become a wing commander (the equivalent of a lieutenant colonel). Professor Lindemann did not want to release Jackson from his important scientific work. But Pamela's friend Group Captain William Elliot, assistant secretary to the war cabinet, personally intervened with Prime Minister Winston Churchill, who liberated Jackson from the lab.

Jackson's distinguished wartime service had three phases: specialized training, aerial combat and military research. While training as an air gunner and air wireless operator, Jackson told Pamela that he found the Blenheim bomber "distinctly draughty— I would have been glad of a balaclava," a woolen helmet. Posted to a night fighter squadron, he sometimes piloted his planes, and enjoyed the same sensation of speed and danger in both racing and flying. As a navigator, he located German planes armed with lethal weapons by radar and guided his pilot to within visual range of the targets. He also applied his skills to more personal matters. When his suitcase, with his favorite red silk dressing gown, fell through a loose hatch and out of the plane, he tracked it by radar and told the Wiltshire police exactly where to retrieve it.

During his night operations Jackson patrolled the south coast of England, searching for enemy planes that had crossed the Channel from France or were returning from bombing raids on industrial towns in the Midlands. In the autumn of 1941 he described a dramatic encounter with boyish excitement: "Last night we had a terrific chase ending in a combat; there was a great flash as the cannon hit the Hun; but as it fell into a cloud and we could not see it hit the ground (France!) we could only claim a probable." In December 1942, while testing his new radar, he experienced a serious setback and near-fatal attack. As he wrote to Lindemann, his British planes, mistaken for Germans, were attacked by their own fighters: "The Mark IX seems to be the answer. Unfortunately it has now been lost: I was doing a final test just before Christmas, and the two aircraft we were using were both attacked by a Spitfire. He shot down the Mark IX and damaged, but did not shoot down, the Beaufighter I was in."

Jackson flew sixty operational sorties and engaged in eleven combats. He destroyed five enemy planes, probably brought down two more and damaged two others. By the end of the war he had courageously risked his life by flying 1,100 hours with two hundred different pilots. When a senior officer asked how to improve British planes, Jackson cheekily said it would help to get some superior Messerschmitts. His extraordinary skill with instruments and observations made him chief airborne radar officer in Fighter Command.

Jackson had the unique ability to combine military research with operational experience, and played a major role in winning the scientific war in the air. In 1942 he began work on the top-secret "Window" project, in which strips of metal foil were dropped by British bombers to confuse the German radar system. Alfred Price explained, "Jackson had developed a 'Window' bundle with sufficient tinfoil to produce a 'heavy bomber' echo, while weighing less than two pounds. This meant that the bombers could now use the strips all along their route instead of just at the target, and the result would be far greater protection from the defences." He then devised a completely new type of "Window." "Jackson evolved a system of folding the strips concertina-fashion into manageable lengths; after they had been released from the aircraft the weighted end ensured that the zig-zag unfolded properly." Winston Churchill described the effect of Jackson's invention: "If a cloud of these were dropped by our aircraft the enemy fighters would not be able to tell which were our bombers and which were our tinfoil strips. . . . The device was so simple and so effective that the enemy might copy it and use it against us." But after the first raid on Hamburg in July 1943, Churchill reported, "For some months our bomber losses dropped to nearly half."

In 1940 Oswald Mosley, Jackson's actively pro-Nazi brother-in-law, was interned in Holloway prison by the British authorities, but was released in November 1943 when his health deteriorated. In a characteristic provocation, Jackson immediately invited Mosley and his wife, Diana Mitford, to live in his house, Rignell, in Banbury near Oxford. The invitation inspired sensational front-page news stories throughout the country. The cabinet minister Herbert Morrison, fearful that Mosley might steal war secrets, was furious and ordered Mosley to move out. Jackson replied that no one could tell him which guests he could or could not invite to his own home and claimed—on shaky grounds—that the traitorous Mosley would never steal secret information. Still in uniform and on active service, he defied authority by refusing to take orders from a civilian. "Well, Mr. Home Secretary," he declared, "when you have won the DFC [Distinguished Flying Cross], AFC [Air Force Cross] and the OBE [Order of the British Empire] for valour, you can speak to me again." But Jackson was forbidden to enter his own house when the Mosleys lived there and they eventually had to find more suitable accommodations.

Like Henry VIII and Norman Mailer, Jackson had six wives. Though he divorced five of them, Barbara Skelton strained credulity by claiming, "I have never known a more loyal man." Divorce, unusual in Jackson's generation, was mainly confined to movie stars and playboys. But his wives, who lived in squares and loved in triangles, were—like Jackson himself—uncommonly promiscuous. They married as many as four times and took casual lovers in between. He liked the thrills of courtship and seduction more than the constraints of marriage, raided the fashionable jewelry stores and did everything he could to satisfy the whims of his current woman. Once a week in Paris, Skelton reported, "he came into my room and placed a wad of francs on the dressing table."

Marriages for Jackson, who was both outrageous and conventional, were short-lived experiments rather than permanent commitments. Like runners in a relay race, his wives faithfully passed on the torch to their successors. He married Elizabeth "Poppet" John in 1931, Pamela Mitford in 1936, Janetta Woolley Kee in 1951, Consuelo Eyre, Princess Ratibor, in 1957, Barbara Skelton in 1966 and Marie-Christine Reille in 1968. His first, third, fourth and fifth marriages lasted less than two years. His marriage to Pamela continued for fifteen years, but he was away at war for much of that time. He remained in his final marriage, begun in his quiescent sixties, until the end of his life.

The lively, amusing and flirtatious Poppet John, a peripheral member of the bohemian Bloomsbury circle, had no conventional education and married the twenty-five-year-old Jackson when she was only nineteen. Her father, the distinguished painter Augustus John, was jealous of his daughter's love for Jackson and boldly defended his turf. Michael Holroyd wrote: "After Poppet's wedding to Derek Jackson, [Augustus] hopped into the car at Fordingbridge beside his daughter and . . . was driven off with her while Jackson sat disconsolately next to the chauffeur. . . . With his herd of women and children round him, interlopers were beaten off."

During Jackson's courtship of Pamela (born 1907), one of the six attractive and politically notorious Mitford sisters, he gave her bountiful diamonds from Cartier's and convinced her to move into his house near Oxford. Her youngest sister, Deborah, while still a schoolgirl, "fell madly in love" with Jackson and when he became engaged to Pamela "fainted dead away." In a love letter to Pamela he poured out his emotions in hyperbolic but effective flattery: "Darling, you are so wonderful and beautiful and I adore you and always [sic] will; all the time I am not with you is only time wasted, it is time spent in misery." She had several miscarriages both before and after the war. Selina Hastings noted that Pamela, "calm and childlike, with a gift for cooking and domesticity, provided a comfortable haven for her highly-strung husband, a respite from the stress of his wartime occupations."

Jackson met Janetta Woolley (born 1922) when she was still in her twenties, but had already been married to the South African writer Humphrey Slater and to the British historian Robert Kee and had a child by a third man. She was introduced to Jackson in a London theater and he made immediate passes. During her horrid marriage to Kee, she thought Jackson was funny, complimentary and delightful, and didn't take him seriously. But she was desperate to leave her marriage and when he said, "Come to Paris to me," she suddenly and impulsively decided to join him.

Patrick Leigh Fermor, a connoisseur of women, described her as "a marvellous fine-boned beauty. . . . There is something magical and quiet about her." During Jackson's courtship of Janetta, whose liberal politics were diametrically opposed to his own, he promised to turn the *News of the World* into a left-wing paper if she agreed to marry him. In 1953, just after Janetta gave birth to their daughter, Rose, Jackson—who didn't want children—suddenly announced that he was leaving her. He then ran off with her even more glamorous half sister, Angela Culme-Seymour.

Jackson's lovers, during and between marriages, included the eighteen-year-old daughter of a Canadian lumber tycoon, Anne Dunn, who'd painted his portrait but refused to marry him, and the much-married Mary Campbell, former wife of the same tycoon, Philip Dunn. But his liaison with the alluring Angela was more serious. Lees-Milne ecstatically wrote that "she had camellia-like skin of the softness of satin, large glowing dark eyes of a dreamy quality, which smiled even when her lips were solemn." She lived with Jackson for three years while he was still legally married to Janetta. Frances Partridge enigmatically wrote that he asked Janetta "not to divorce him, saying that he would only make a fool of himself" in court—after his cruel behavior and third marital failure. He confessed that "he was good for nothing but work and that was nine-tenths of his life." Then, quite unexpectedly, "at some mention of their life together he burst into tears."

Jackson abandoned Rose, didn't see her until she was three years old and took very little interest in her life. They argued violently about politics when she was a Communist sympathizer and she disappointed him by studying philosophy, a "pointless subject," at London University. She then worked for the BBC. Lucian Freud had an affair with Janetta, and in 1979 he also slept with Rose. She became his muse and model and posed naked when she was pregnant. He stopped seeing Rose after she had the child, and Jackson gave Anne Dunn, pregnant with another child by Freud, £100 to pay for an abortion. The teenaged Dunn also got drunk in an Irish railroad station and was raped by a porter.

Consuelo Regina Maria Eyre, born in 1909, was the daughter of a South American mother and Irish-American father, and widow of the German Prince Ratibor. Though she had a strong character and was intelligent and cultured, Jackson tired of her after only fourteen months and ungallantly maintained, "Ratibor was inclined to be ratty, and was frequently a bore."

Barbara Skelton, born in 1916, was a model for Pamela Fitton in Anthony Powell's *A Dance to the Music of Time*. Jackson's most colorful and scandalous wife liked to entrap her lovers before humiliating and torturing them. The biographer of her first husband, the impecunious writer Cyril Connolly, described her as "the daughter of an unsuccessful soldier and a former Gaiety Girl. She had worked as a model for Schiaparelli before the war; affectionate, waspish and disconcertingly detached, she had lived, sometimes simultaneously, with a series of adoring admirers, flitting unconcernedly from one to another, raising blood pressures in the process, and leaving behind her a trail of devastation." Her second husband, the wealthy and still infatuated publisher George

Weidenfeld, longingly recalled that she "liked intellectuals. She was strikingly good-looking, with a honey-coloured complexion, reddish-blonde hair and slightly slit eyes. She had a slim figure and wore clothes with unstudied elegance. Her voice was unforgettably distinctive—there was melody in her speech, and a faintly accusatory and doubting tone in her questions. She had a gift for narrative and could be extremely funny."

Barbara confessed that she married Jackson for money and security rather than for love, and he shrewdly tried to shield himself from her rapacity. Before their marriage, she recalled, "I was taken to see his lawyer in Switzerland and asked to sign a document whereby I relinquished all claim on my future husband's millions." She added that when their Paris apartment was finally renovated and ready for occupancy, they agreed to a friendly separation and eventually a divorce.

Jackson finally found stability, in another unhappy marriage, when he lived in Paris, Lausanne and Gstaad, Switzerland, with Marie-Christine Reille. A handsome French widow of a baron, she was in her thirties (when Jackson was in his sixties) and had two daughters. She shared his keen interest in horse racing, seemed fond of him and looked after him until his death. Like Consuelo, Marie-Christine tried in vain to convert Jackson to Catholicism. But he'd condemned the work of Bach as "church music," called God "that grey-bearded monster," and prompted Pamela to confess, when he took Catholic instruction, "I feel so sorry for the priest." Firmly rooted in the empirical proofs of physics, Jackson could not swallow the myths and fantasies of religion. Each of his wives had a distinctive background. Poppet's father was an eminent artist, Pamela's father was Baron Redesdale, Janetta's father had won the Victoria Cross, Consuelo's late husband was a prince, Barbara had been the mistress of a king and Marie-Christine (who still lives in Gstaad) was the widow of a French baron.

At a time when homosexuality was illegal in Britain, Jackson's adventures had to be furtive and fleeting. But his behavior with men was as provocative as his speech at dinner parties. He said that he'd married Poppet "only because he was in love with her brother." He danced with transvestites in Paris nightclubs. While taking a shower in the jockeys' weighing room he showed off his painted toenails. After racing victories he hugged and kissed the astonished riders. When embracing the stiff and reserved Mosley, he pinched his bottom and kissed him on the mouth.

Though Jackson had no long-term male lovers, he found all his acquaintances fair game. He did not pursue and pick up working-class men, but confined his activities to his own social circle. He had encounters with Consuelo's cousin and with Anne Dunn's nephew, who turned up in bed wearing her distinctive pajamas. To prove his love for Pamela's nephew, the handsome Eton schoolboy Desmond Guinness, Jackson chewed and swallowed his photograph. The endlessly cruising painter Francis Bacon, well satisfied with their connection, exclaimed, "Don't you think Derek is the most marvellous person you know?" Jackson also boasted about his bisexuality and his wives were well aware of it. He once declared, "I don't see why my wife should be surprised. I slept with the butler on our wedding night."

After the war Jackson continued his valuable research and extensive travels. He joined the British Liberation Army in Holland and Belgium and inspected captured German radar equipment. In the spring of 1945 he made an eleven-week tour of America and was awarded the U.S. Legion of Merit. He was a visiting professor in the physics department at Ohio State University in Columbus in 1949–50 and again in 1960. He witnessed a clear solar eclipse in Khartoum in 1952 and a cloudy one, two years later, in Bornholm, Denmark. He liked to claim that the East German astronomers, fearing dire consequences if they returned empty-handed, had committed suicide.

In 1947 Jackson was elected a Fellow of the Royal Society and appointed professor of spectroscopy at Oxford. That year, however, after his distinguished war service, he was outraged when the Labour government planned to take 95 percent of his £20,000 annual income. To avoid this prohibitive tax, he and Pamela moved to Tullamaine Castle in County Tipperary, Ireland. Despite many horse events and occasional visits to the Dunsink Observatory outside Dublin, he soon got bored with the lack of stimulation and remoteness from scientific centers. He moved again and spent the last thirty years of his life, with his last four wives, in France and Switzerland, often working at the Bellevue spectroscopy laboratory in Paris. But he remained an Englishman abroad, and after three decades he still spoke French with a strong English accent.

In the fall of 1981 Jackson developed arterial sclerosis, which interfered with the circulation in his leg. After an unsuccessful bypass operation and ten days of excruciating pain, he agreed to have his leg amputated. Unable to adjust to his new prosthesis, he bitterly said that he was hobbling toward the grave. Though he seemed to recover from the operation, his condition deteriorated and he died in Lausanne in February 1982.

Jackson's pioneering research continues to influence contemporary science. During World War II he'd talked about traveling in space and how he might send a rocket to the moon. Courtauld wrote that Jackson's early work on spectroscopic measurement led indirectly to the development of modern Magnetic Resonance Imaging (MRI), "which uses the magnetism of atomic nuclei to gain an extraordinarily detailed view inside the human body."

Brilliant and courageous, angry and arrogant, Jackson was gifted with intelligence, imagination and insight, and was capable of sustained scientific work for five decades. Yet he was also a man of mysterious contradictions. His great wealth allowed him to defy social conventions and behave with astonishing egoism. He led a life of compulsive philandering in a series of unstable marriages, but women found him irresistible, partly because of his ambiguous sexuality. The loss of his twin brother affected him deeply, and his homosexuality may have been a kind of displaced incest, a narcissistic attempt to recover a lost part of himself and to reunite in the flesh with his dead brother. He valued courtship more than marriage, companionship more than wedded sex. He was not monogamous and could not remain faithful to one woman or to one man. But he still craved, as domestic diversions from intense work, the formal security—or deceptive mask—of marriage. Jackson had the amazing ability to unite the disparate aspects of his life: science and war, racing and flying, affairs with men and unions with women.

13

Nicola Chiaromonte

(1905–1972)

You pronounce a name, but it is not known to anyone.
Either because that man has died, or because
He was famous on the banks of another river.
Chiaromonte.
— Czeslaw Milosz, "Whence the Sun Rises to
  Where it Sets"

In 1985 the critic and biographer Joseph Frank declared that Nicola
Chiaromonte "was a remarkable personality, who left an indelible impression on all those who knew him, and whose work . . . is
more and more coming to be acknowledged as a precious part of
the Italian cultural patrimony." Frank emphasized Chiaromonte's
Italian rather than American influence, and did not explain why
he had such a profound effect on the New York intellectuals, who
absorbed him into their group and enhanced his reputation.

Chiaromonte arrived in New York in 1941 unknown, out of
nowhere and with an imperfect knowledge of English, yet came
to dominate some of the leading cultural figures in America. He
exerted his powerful personal and intellectual impact through
his knowledge and idealism, his tragic exile and narrow escapes
from death. A left-wing anti-Communist, like George Orwell and

Albert Camus, he was praised for his honesty and integrity, and like them was regarded as a secular saint. A refugee from Mussolini's Italy, Chiaromonte had risked his life by fighting against the Fascists in Spain and as an exile in Nazi-occupied France. To the New York intellectuals on the Left he became a moral and political touchstone—he was the man, he'd suffered, he was there—who frequently appeared in the lives and was praised in the works of Dwight Macdonald, Mary McCarthy and their circle. Chiaromonte seems obscure, yet his character and experience, his warmth and friendships, were highly influential during and after World War II. He deserves—to use his own favorite theatrical metaphor—to be brought out of the shadows and into the spotlight.

In the early 1940s Chiaromonte's adventurous background provided a striking contrast to the New York writers who were cut off from Europe by the war and searching for a hero. His moral convictions and critical intellect made a tremendous impression on those sharp-tongued infighters. The philosophy professor William Barrett stated that "Chiaromonte had lived through, or actually fought in, all the major conflicts of the time about which most of the intellectuals of New York had only argued." Macdonald took him up, published him in his journal *Politics* and sent his work to the editors of the leading highbrow magazines: *Partisan Review, New Republic, Nation, Commonweal, Dissent, Atlantic Monthly* and *Encounter.* (Many readers may have thought "Nicola" was a woman.) He "enfolded me," Macdonald wrote, "in his affection and intelligence . . . like a father to a son." He also taught Macdonald the principles of the leading Italian anarchists. As William Phillips, coeditor of the *Partisan Review,* wittily remarked, Dwight found "a disciple who will tell him what to think."

The New York intellectuals' personal admiration of Chiaromonte inspired intense friendships and generous assistance. Macdonald sat at his feet and arranged for the sale of his papers to Yale.

McCarthy persuaded her publisher, Harcourt Brace Jovanovich, to bring out *The Worm of Consciousness*. Joseph Frank invited him to give the prestigious Christian Gauss lectures at Princeton in 1966. Both McCarthy and Frank wrote enthusiastic essays about him that were later reprinted as introductions to his books.

Chiaromonte was born into a middle-class family in Rapolla (Potenza), in the "primordial, stagnant and ossified" province of Basilicata in south central Italy, about fifty miles east of Salerno and the Mediterranean coast. His sister was a social worker; one of his brothers was a Jesuit, the other a doctor. Rigorously educated at the Jesuit Collegio Massimo in Rome (though he did not remain a Catholic), he earned a law degree at the University of Rome, and joined the libertarian socialist group Giustizia e Libertà. He was active in the anti-Fascist underground and in 1934, as Mussolini's rule became increasingly oppressive, went into exile in France.

Despite his pacifism, Chiaromonte went to Spain when the Civil War broke out in 1936 and served as a bombardier, with André Malraux as machine gunner, in the ancient airborne coffins of the Escadrille España. In *Man's Hope* (1937) Malraux portrayed him as Scali, an art historian whose "face had the somewhat mulatto cast characteristic of the peoples of the western Mediterranean." Malraux's novel gives Scali military experience that Chiaromonte, who was suddenly thrust into battle, did not actually have: "Scali, the bomber on the second International machine, had been watching the bombs falling nearer and nearer the road. He had a thorough training in the Italian Army behind him, and, till he left his country, had put in a yearly reserves course. Three raids on the Sierra had restored his skill." Effectively echoing Malraux's terse style, Chiaromonte portrayed his own experience in one of his best essays, "Spain: The War." He begins in a cramped plane over Medellín in western Spain, then, expanding to a view from the sky, describes the effect of bombs and the destruction of an acrobatic German aircraft: "I am sitting in a sort of funnel-shaped space, my

knees doubled against my chest; I peer through the small opening from which the machine gun protrudes. . . . On the ground . . .
yellowish flames shoot up from the buildings, a locomotive is torn
open, a long red roof disappears. . . . Far away against the sky a
plane is slowly turning over, so slowly that one would think it was
executing a maneuver. It was a Heinkel, and our gunner at the rear
turret got it."

Chiaromonte and Malraux were good friends, saw each other
in the officers' mess and discussed the Italian's favorite author,
Plato. In Malraux's novel, "a little copy of Plato, in Greek, [was]
filched that morning from Scali (who had raised hell about it)."
In his posthumously published essays *The Worm of Consciousness*
(1976), Chiaromonte explained what Plato meant to him: "The
Platonic form of reasoning inevitably appears as the only point
from which we can again glimpse, if not the truth, at least the light
of truth. . . . *The Republic* is simply a *model* whose natural purpose
is to inspire thoughts, not direct actions." Malraux wrote that
Scali—a conscientious thinker who did not belong in the arena of
ruthless action—was "a good intellectual [who] not only wanted
to explain, but to convince. And as for physical violence," the paradoxical warrior "had an aversion to it amounting to disgust." Chiaromonte's active involvement in history and bitter disillusionment
after the military defeat in Spain gave him a fundamental distrust
of the political effectiveness of governments, armies and action,
which was confirmed by the brutal German occupation of France.

Joseph Frank observed that Scali represents "the ethical dilemma of [*Man's Hope*]—the problem of whether it is possible to
safeguard the moral values of revolutionary action in the midst of
an armed struggle against the Fascist threat. What distinguishes
Scali is the absolute refusal, even while risking his life for a cause,
to surrender his critical capacity and his moral sense." In May 1937,
when the Communists in Barcelona were killing the POUM anarchists, who were also fighting the Fascists, Chiaromonte con-

demned "the absurdity and the inconsistency of all political action in the present situation. The inanity of every dogmatic standpoint must finally be recognized." After Malraux defended the Communists, Chiaromonte (like Camus) found him all too submissive to political expediency. Escaping to France, he found refuge in Paris, where he sought out like-minded intellectuals.

Eileen Simpson (ex-wife of the poet John Berryman) recalled that in Paris Chiaromonte "met and married [Annie Pohl] an Austrian artist who had come to live there with her parents. His wife's father had been the editor of an important newspaper in Vienna and was said to be a Communist. When the Germans marched into Paris, Chiaromonte's father-in-law killed himself." In June 1940 most of the Italians living in France headed for Toulouse in the unoccupied southwest. "One step ahead of the Nazis," Simpson adds, "Chiaromonte had escaped with his wife to Toulouse, where, stranded and waiting for exit papers, she died of tuberculosis." He had to dig his wife's grave. He was eventually able to secure transparently forged papers and, when stopped by a Vichy policeman, dared to ask, "Do you want the false ones or the real ones?"

In a series of narrow escapes, Chiaromonte made his way from Toulouse to Marseilles and across the sea to a temporary refuge in Algiers. Since that city was controlled by the pro-Nazi Vichy government, he pressed on to Oran where, in troubled times, he met the young Camus. The two Mediterranean men swam in the sunlit sea and formed a close friendship. (In return, he would guide Camus around New York in 1946.) Finally, like the desperate refugees in the film *Casablanca,* after so much deep pain and many narrow escapes, he traveled to Morocco and sailed to safety in America.

Eileen Simpson wrote that the newly arrived refugee seemed ill equipped for the intensely competitive literary scene in New York: "In 1941, when Chiaromonte had turned up at the door of a New York City high school teacher with an introduction from George

Santayana [who lived in Rome], he had presented a far from prepossessing figure. The suit he was wearing did not fit him properly. He could read English and understand it perfectly, but did not speak it very well. That first evening he had seemed uncomfortable and embarrassed and sad. With some misgivings, [she] agreed to help him with his English." The following year Chiaromonte married the teacher, Miriam Rosenthal (1912–2008), who taught English at Washington Irving High School near Union Square, and they lived in an apartment at 23 West 8th Street in Greenwich Village. Miriam, who must have helped him when he wrote in English, later edited *The Worm of Consciousness.* He described her as "an affectionate and intelligent girl."

William Phillips portrayed her as "reserved, but always ready to put herself out for friends. Though she was clearly very devoted to Nicola, in an almost Italian pre-feminist way, there was no sacrifice of personal dignity." Perhaps in recognition of Miriam's devotion and Chiaromonte's status, there's no mention in all the writing about him of his serious love affair in the promiscuous and adulterous milieu of the early 1950s in New York. Macdonald's biographer, Michael Wreszin, refers to Chiaromonte's unusually revealing confession about his marital woes in an "open and personal letter" to Macdonald on February 2, 1953. Wreszin rather vaguely notes that his "disciplined sense of morality dictated the way he dealt with the disruption in his marriage," but he does not quote this letter.

Chiaromonte's lover, in fact, was Patricia Blake (1925–2010), whom he'd met through Camus in New York in April 1946 when she was twenty-one years old. Blake had studied history at Smith College, worked for *Vogue* magazine and wrote articles for the *New York Times Book Review.* Stunningly beautiful, with blue eyes and brown hair (her photo appears in Olivier Todd's life of Camus), she had an excellent command of French. Camus thought she represented an ideal type of American girl and found her "astonishing." In 1948 she became the third wife of the Russian composer Nicolas Nabokov, an official in the CIA's Congress for Cultural Freedom, and they lived in Paris. Nabokov called her "a thorough-bred intellectual, brilliantly intelligent and good-looking." Blake later learned Russian and became an expert on Soviet literature. Chiaromonte's affair with Blake ignited in 1952 after the end of her marriage to Nabokov. He was madly in love with her and she wanted to marry him. Miriam knew about the affair and suffered, but their marriage survived this crisis.

On February 3, 1953, Chiaromonte sent Macdonald a self-tormenting letter, which was written in a contorted style and did not mention Blake. He confessed the truth about his affair and his agonizing decision to remain married to Miriam:

> My troubles (plainly, the fact that I was in love with a woman, and torn between her and Miriam) were still unsolved. I finally decided in favor of Miriam. But it has been a horrible torture both for me and Miriam, whom I finally told every-thing. Knowing Miriam you know how difficult for me it would have been to act differently. Still, I would not maintain it was the right thing. Except that I found it impossible to go beyond telling M. the truth and finally letting her decide, that is, insisting that I would not repudiate her if she did not feel that our life together had become impossible. This is what I did, and I would not maintain that there was reason or morality involved in my decision. Simply an impossibility on my part.

Carol Gelderman, McCarthy's first biographer, described the short Chiaromonte as a "dark and handsome man who looked like a monk. . . . His manner was shy and modest, slow and grave." Bowden Broadwater, who married McCarthy in 1946, resented her infatuation with the charismatic man and referred to him ironically as "the Master." Broadwater noted his mouthful of Italian gold teeth and dandyish costume, "a spot of off-red in the cravat, a dark coat buttoned high, and corduroy pants of a soft, delicate green." In a 1966 photo that suggests the congenial social atmosphere, he appears—with dark hair, high forehead and unshaven face—sitting on a couch, smiling gently and chatting intimately with McCarthy. Robert Lowell, seated on her left, ignores them and with clasped hands stares straight ahead and holds forth to no one in particular. Macdonald, Hannah Arendt and their spouses stand benevolently behind them.

A Polish friend of McCarthy, favorably comparing Chiaromonte to her other European mentor, said that he "shared Arendt's high intellectual and ethical standards, but was more modest and possessed of some humor." McCarthy praised Chiaromonte as "a dense writer, a compact writer, [whose] insights, *aperçus,* brief analyses, pungent observations are packed together in a continuous flow."

Lionel Abel, critic and translator of Jean-Paul Sartre, could "honestly say I've never known anyone I've liked better or respected more." Niccolò Tucci, another Italian exile-writer, noted Chiaromonte's tonsured head and praised his spiritual quality and elegant style: "He was like a Benedictine monk. Very much so. One of the very few Italians who use language politely and precisely. He was a great man. He was both brilliant and truly good." Phillips noted how his tragic gloom and laconic withdrawal amid the loquacious belligerents of New York gave him a holy aura: "Chiaromonte had great charm and made his presence felt; he was generous and friendly, though usually in a manner that created a feeling of distance, and he was moody, often morose, and given to periods of silence, especially with talkative people—a trait that reinforced the role of saint assigned to him by many of his friends." In a self-reflective passage about his contemporary Alberto Moravia, Chiaromonte defined his own strengths. He wrote that Moravia had "the self-assurance of a man who has plumbed the depths of his own experience, who, when he speaks, arrives immediately at the heart of the matter."

McCarthy, with characteristic wit, told Arendt that "some demon seizes Chiaromonte when he's in the company of women he considers brainy. Which must mean he looks on *me* fondly as rather dumb." He didn't like McCarthy when they first met, but she eventually conquered him. So, as he gratefully acknowledged, she also had a beneficial influence on him: "You won me over, Mary, yours was that magic touch that broke my sullenness and my shyness." She provided what Kafka called the ax that "breaks the frozen sea within us."

Though the sexually liberated McCarthy did not have a love affair with Chiaromonte, she freely admitted that her friendship with him was the crucial conversion experience in her life. In an unusually tender letter of March 1968, she wrote, "Nicola, I've long wanted to tell you . . . that seeing you on the Cape in the summer of '45 was a crossroads in my life. In fact, *the* crossroads. I became a different person." He agreed, telling Macdonald, "My best summer vacations were the ones I spent in Truro in your company and Mary's. How far away those days now seem. We must thank the gods that our friendship has withstood the test of time."

Chiaromonte had a pensive seriousness and capacity for friendship that transcended the caustic feuds of the New York literati. "The *change*," McCarthy later wrote, "from someone like Edmund [Wilson] and his world and most of the *Partisan Review* boys was absolutely stunning. . . . [They] had no moral core. It never occurred to them that there should be a connection between what they read and wrote and their own lives, how they were living and what they believed in." But she wrote this retaliatory and inaccurate condemnation after ending her unhappy affair with Philip Rahv (coeditor of the *Partisan Review*) and her bitter marriage to Edmund Wilson. In fact, Wilson had served in World War I, traveled through the impoverished regions of the United States and wrote about them in *The American Jitters: A Year of the Slump* (1932), and had described his disillusioned journey to Russia in *Travels in Two Democracies* (1936). Unlike most of his left-wing colleagues in the 1930s, he was an independent thinker who opposed the Communists and never swallowed the party line. In his review of Wilson's *Europe without Baedeker* in the *Partisan Review* of February 1948, Chiaromonte himself wrote that Wilson had humanely considered the effects of World War II in Europe and that Wilson's themes (like his own) ranged "from the beastliness of modern man to the future of western civilization." Nevertheless, McCarthy glorified Chiaromonte in opposition to the other men in her political and literary circle.

Though McCarthy conceded that Chiaromonte, brooding over his tragic past, had a "saturnine cast" and "rasp of sarcasm," she frequently extolled his noble idealism: "As a man he is wholly lovable. And his mind is full of justice.... Anyone who knew and loved Chiaromonte will recognize that an intransigent and fearless honesty was a basic trait of his character." Though he was very fond of McCarthy, and may even have been in love with her, he sometimes cast a cold eye on her insincere character and theatrical behavior. During her engagement to her fourth husband, the diplomat James West, he wrote, "Mary acted all through the period ... as if this was her first love, and was going to be her first marriage—sweet, but slightly false, nevertheless more than false, unreal and unconvincing, like some of the psychological cracks in her novels." Using the same word that McCarthy applied to him, he concluded, "Anyway, she is a lovable woman and a wonderful friend." After hearing reports of her immaculately planned and luxurious wedding reception in Paris, which his heart attack prevented him from attending, he justified her grandeur and told Macdonald: "That's her style—a fairy-tale style, I should say—occasions are to Mary challenges to the imagination, which is one of her most charming traits, probably the most charming, since her wonderful generosity is part of it."

The Chiaromontes and the Wests spent several postwar summers together at the fashionable, arty fishing village of Bocca di Magra on the Ligurian coast near La Spezia. Given his instinctive austerity, he naturally disapproved of McCarthy's glamorous but rather misguided expatriate life in France and thought she would be happier residing in Rome. "All considered, I don't think living in Paris is very good for her," he told Macdonald in March 1965. "French literary people have snubbed her and she has gone the wrong way about making inroads in their milieu. Too much show of money, parties, dresses, dinners, cocktails etc. Moreover, she has no real sensitivity for things French, except cooking and fashions. She would be much better off in Italy." Though he told her that Romans never invite guests to their homes and almost never use their parlors, except for funerals, he was a delightful host when she visited Rome: "We, and the Roman literary circles as well, managed to have her entertained and feted all the time. She loves that, as you know, and her pleasure is communicative."

Though McCarthy, influenced by her admiration for Chiaromonte, tended to overvalue his work, he could be severe about her contentious books, urged her to strive for a higher standard and was benevolently critical of her flawed personality. In a letter of April 1949 on *The Oasis*—her satire on the conflicts of Macdonald, Rahv and the *Partisan* crowd who try to live their ideas in a Utopian community in a remote region of New England—he criticized her inability to imaginatively transform reality: "I should have liked to be enthusiastic about the story, but alas I am unable to do so. Mary is certainly a brilliant girl, but why she should be so hopelessly literal, I can't understand." He must have recognized a revealing passage in the novella where McCarthy (echoing Broadwater's "the Master") refers to him as "Monteverdi, the Founder" of the idealistic group, who had an American wife and was now absent and presumed dead. She also adopts Phillips' idea of Chiaromonte as a secular saint and Tucci's comparison to a "monk": "The only saint with whom the colonists were personally acquainted . . . was an Italian anarchist in possession of his first [immigration] papers, a veteran of the Spanish war and of Vichy's prisons, a lover of Plato and Tolstoy, a short pink-and-black man with a monk's tonsure of baldness and a monk's barrel chest." He had taught them "certain notions of justice, freedom and sociability." In April 1949 Macdonald wrote Chiaromonte, "You, of course, are the Holy Ghost, hovering over the scene but exempt, by virtue of your sacred character from either criticism or (alas) specific description."

Chiaromonte's 1952 letter on *The Groves of Academe,* McCarthy's witty satire of the corrosive feuds at Bard and Sarah Lawrence colleges, disapproved of her lack of clear structure, penchant for clever remarks and frivolous tone: "I found it very clever and confused. If Mary only learnt to stick to some line of consistent development, instead of showing off in all directions. She has a genuine talent for satire, and she is really intelligent. But she should make up her mind about some conclusion—nihilistic satire, or just play. But not both at the same time. . . . However, I like Mary's mind very much. There is something really generous and passionate about it, for all her smartness." He wrote a favorable, compendium-of-quotations review of *The Stones of Florence* in the summer 1960 *Partisan Review,* but told Macdonald that since McCarthy was not entirely serious, she could not be taken seriously. He admired her research and readability, but saw "many questionable ideas or cracks, as usual. But that is Mary, an overly intelligent woman, with a streak of foolishness."

The Group, McCarthy's novel about the sexual lives of a cadre of Vassar graduates, was her first popular and financial success. In 1963 Chiaromonte repeated to Macdonald the kind of paternal and moral guidance he often gave to her. He exaggerated its pornographic element and deplored her lack of modesty, but conceded that the novel was better than her earlier works: "I hear Mary's book will be the most obscene ever published. Apparently, obscenity pays a lot, too. Mary says she has become rich just on the [$100,000] sale of the book for the paperback edition. Rich, and, I am afraid, also very full of her own importance as a writer. Let's hope not too much. . . . Mary's sarcastic attitude to her characters, which made her previous novels (with the exception of *The Company She Keeps*) quite unbearable to me, has mellowed, and become real novelistic interest."

In 1967 he discouraged McCarthy—who was opposed to the war in Vietnam and all too sympathetic to the Communists—from going to that dangerous country as a foreign correspondent. He warned her that "she risked her 'position' as a writer as well as her personal safety." But when he read her *Vietnam* that year he was tremendously impressed and graciously admitted his mistake: "May I say that it is simply masterful? Nothing (by a long shot) so devastatingly simple and direct has been written about Vietnam. And I do not know of anything at all that can be compared to your piece of *writing* in contemporary journalism. It was done through simplicity and *true* concern. . . . I won't forget to eat some humble pie for having doubted your ability to come out of this victoriously."

Saul Bellow later respectfully dissented to all the praise lavished on Chiaromonte. Aided by hindsight, he perceptively analyzed the reasons for the Italian's powerful influence and justified his own scepticism:

> I knew Nicola Chiaromonte well, liked him, occasionally agreed with him, considered him to be one of the better European intellectuals of the Fifties and Sixties. But Nick was, in many ways, a standard product, often deficient in taste, snobbish. . . .
> I had a more reserved view of Chiaromonte than the rest

of them did—partially because he held such sway over the New York intellectuals. I thought there must be something wrong somewhere. Of course he was everything they admired. He had been in Spain with Malraux. He had had a tragic first marriage. He was a very romantic character. He talked classics and especially Plato to them. And they behaved as if they'd never heard of Plato. Anyhow, they sat at his feet, listening to him. I was never a great one for sitting at anyone's feet.

Bellow ignored the fact that he himself had sat at the feet of Allan Bloom and had been subservient to his domineering wives.

Chiaromonte, after living in New York for seven years, returned to Europe in 1947, but maintained his influence on American friends through his extensive correspondence and their visits to the Continent. He worked under Julian Huxley for UNESCO in Paris, the United Nations organization designed to promote peace through education and culture, which seemed to be a congenial place for a man with his philosophical and literary gifts. But he soon found he was ill suited to bureaucratic machinations. He felt "demoralized by the empty and absurd routines of life in a large organization," and complained, "Here I am doing extremely little, but bound ... to office hours, the language of idiots and stuffed shirts, feeling that every day I lose more hold on my own life and brains." He then went back to Rome, where he remained for the rest of his life, and surprised his friends by becoming a theater critic for *Il Mondo*.

His writing from this point on reveals that Chiaromonte was primarily a moralist who'd been reluctantly forced to plunge into the maelstrom of politics and war. Like his beloved Plato, he wanted to inspire thought, not action. In a characteristic passage of *La Situazione Drammatica* (1960), he emphasized morality, truth and commitment: "In a deep sense good drama and good farce are always moral ordeals, and [there must be] simply a certain willingness on the part of the audience to undergo a test of how much truth it can stand." McCarthy's essay "Nicola Chiaromonte and the Theatre" in the *New York Review of Books* (February 20, 1975) was intended to introduce his uncollected theater criticism, edited by Miriam. McCarthy helped secure a grant from the Agnelli (Fiat) Foundation, but this book—perhaps because of Miriam's poor health—never appeared.

Chiaromonte made many of his political pronouncements in theatrical terms, and portrayed significant political players as if they were actors on the stage. He wrote that Malraux, de Gaulle's head of cultural affairs from 1958 to 1969, "was a minister much in the same way as he was an aviator in Spain; he simply stuck to the role he had chosen, impersonating in dead earnest the character he wanted to play on the world stage." Chiaromonte discussed Robert Oppenheimer in a similar fashion. The brilliant nuclear physicist, head of the Los Alamos project that developed the atomic bomb in World War II, was suspected of Communist sympathies and had his security clearance revoked in 1954. McCarthy reported that Chiaromonte "doubts that Oppenheimer is mad and sees him, rather, as a man playing a role of which he's uncertain—an actor not quite sure of his part."

Chiaromonte was used to being a commanding and authoritative presence to whom others deferred. But he could not play that role in his meeting in 1966 with Arthur Schlesinger, a professor of history at Harvard who'd been special assistant to President Kennedy from 1961 to 1963 and was deeply engaged with and expert in American politics. He found Schlesinger haughty, "insupportably stuffy and pretentious and equivocal as well," and declared that the smug and self-important Schlesinger had actually put him down by insisting, "'I, who am an historian' (while you are not) or 'I, who was in government.' Now that's intolerable." Chiaromonte was vexed when Schlesinger pulled rank and rejected his outsider's view of the political situation.

From 1956 to 1968 Chiaromonte and Ignazio Silone edited the highly regarded *Tempo Presente,* which echoed the title of Sartre's journal *Temps Modernes.* In 1967 Chiaromonte discovered that his journal was secretly subsidized by the CIA's Congress for Cultural Freedom, an organization set up to counter Soviet propaganda through literary and political writing in the West. He did not voice the automatic outrage others felt, but justified the covert funding precisely because it allowed him to maintain editorial independence. Macdonald's biographer wrote that "when Chiaromonte saw Dwight's name on the *Partisan Review* statement denouncing secret funding and expressing a lack of confidence in magazines that had received it, he dashed off an angry letter asking Dwight whether he meant that he didn't trust the *Tempo Presente* editors."

Though warm and loyal, Chiaromonte refused to follow friends whose views he could no longer support. Andrea Caffi (1887–1955) was his closest friend and political-anarchist mentor, "the best, as well as the wisest and most just man I have known." Born in Russia of Italian parents, Caffi took part in the 1905 Revolution, was a student in Berlin, a member of the Parisian avant-garde in the early twentieth century and a radical exile between the wars. In his "Letter to Andrea Caffi" (1970), Chiaromonte distanced himself from his old teacher and explained why he rejected his views on revolution and the duty of the good citizen. He disapproved equally of Malraux's turn to the right and of Caffi's belief in violent nihilism.

Bellow vividly described the self-absorbed Caffi as "tall but frail, with an immense head of hair, and a small nervous laugh, but he was a serious man. . . . Caffi had formal manners, loved conversation (with men, he disliked women), and passed most of the day in bed drinking coffee and writing learned notes to himself." When

Miriam was about to leave for America to take care of her sick mother, the Chiaromontes joined Caffi and Lionel Abel for a farewell luncheon in Paris. Abel reported that Caffi, noticing a gold medallion that Miriam was wearing, asked her, "'Is that a medal from the Daughters of the American Revolution?' Miriam kept her poise, made some amiable reply, and soon after that excused herself." Caffi's ambiguous but insulting remark meant either that Miriam was ostentatiously wearing valuable jewelry or snobbishly pretending, as a Jew, to belong to the DAR—though her medallion had absolutely no connection with it. Abel concluded that the misogynistic remark, which Chiaromonte also ignored, was provoked by envy. Caffi, who received money from Chiaromonte, "was jealous of Nicola for having a wife, and having the means to pay for her trip to America."

Chiaromonte rejected not only the dogmas of Marx and Freud, but all doctrines. McCarthy affirmed that "all abstractions but two—justice and freedom—were anathema to him." He perceived, before the Nazis took power in 1933, the "morphological affinity" in the regimes of Mussolini, Stalin and Hitler. Chiaromonte had met Camus in 1941 after Hitler had conquered most of Europe. Germany had just invaded Greece and the swastika waved over the Acropolis. In his obituary essay on Camus, Chiaromonte declared, "We had arrived at humanity's zero hour, and history was senseless; the only thing that made sense was that part of man which remained outside of history, alien and impervious to the whirlwind of events." He condemned the glib slogans and violent rhetoric of the nihilistic student rebellions of 1968, and their mindless worship of tyrants like Mao, Ho and Fidel. But he did not explain how man could remain impervious to the whirlwind of history and, if he did, what he could possibly achieve from outside those senseless events. As McCarthy had suggested in *The Oasis,* the establishment of small anarchist-pacifist communities, inspired by Chiaromonte, were impractical and could not effect significant political change. His belief was actually a contradiction, since anarchists were violent and pacifists—except for Gandhi—almost never achieved their political goals. "Independence involves isolation," Chiaromonte acknowledged in *The Worm of Consciousness,* "isolation means to be outside history . . . and consequently to be, by definition, in the wrong."

Perhaps because of his determination to stay "outside history," some of Chiaromonte's political views seem surprisingly reactionary. In 1948 the art critic Clement Greenberg opposed awarding the Bollingen poetry prize to the *Pisan Cantos* of Ezra Pound, who had broadcast virulent anti-Semitic propaganda on the Fascist radio in Italy and been accused of treason in America. Yet Chiaromonte, who had had two Jewish wives, dismissed Greenberg's opposition as "Jewish chauvinism." He was also furious with Greenberg for his cowardly physical attack on the much smaller Lionel Abel during their heated dispute about the merits of Sartre. Defending his anarchist hero Pierre-Joseph Proudhon, who frequently made the anti-Semitic connection between Jews and international finance, Chiaromonte argued that this connection "was not, after all, altogether arbitrary and without foundation."

Writing in Macdonald's *Politics* in May 1947, Chiaromonte refused to exonerate individual Germans from collective guilt: "The notion that Germans are people like any other people is not rejected, but simply does not work. Through the Germans, Europe committed suicide. But still the Germans did it. The guilt might be general. But still the Germans actually did it." Disagreeing with the Communist Sartre, who remained a supporter of the Soviet Union despite Stalin's savage rule, Chiaromonte insisted that it was *not* "treasonable to desert the Soviet bureaucracy and criticize the Soviet state." But in 1948 Chiaromonte—who'd condemned Stalin's slaughter of the POUM anarchists in Barcelona—changed his mind and excused the evils of Stalinism. He maintained that it was dangerous to talk about those evils "without trying to show to what extent Stalin's foreign policy is, if not justified, at least made intelligible by the conduct of his adversaries." But Stalin had actually helped his Nazi adversaries by wiping out almost all his senior military officers shortly before the start of World War II.

Chiaromonte's best book, *The Paradox of History* (1970), was influenced by Simone Weil's essay "The Iliad, or the Poem of Force," translated by Mary McCarthy in 1939. He approached the relations between history and the individual through works of fiction rather than more conventionally through philosophers and historians. He analyzed the interplay of history and morality in the battles of Waterloo in Stendhal, Borodino in Tolstoy, World War I in Roger Martin du Gard, the Chinese revolution in Malraux and the Russian Revolution in Pasternak. In contrast to the Victorian optimism expressed in W. E. Henley's "Invictus"—"I am the master of my fate, / I am the captain of my soul"—he believed, "the faith in History, which was shattered by an historical event—the impact of the First World War—cannot in good faith be restored, since the confidence in Progress underpinning it, tacitly or explicitly, is no longer there." Following Tolstoy, he thought that "historical events escape the control of human reason and will." The belief that history can be made to serve ethical ideals is paradoxical, he argues, because the attempt to convert these ideals into reality inevitably fails. Unlike most people, who believe their actions can improve society, Chiaromonte came to a negative conclusion: though totalitarianism is unacceptable, political action is futile. In his life he retreated from politics into criticism, yet continued to bestride the paradox of history, maintaining his intellectual ideals while accepting the realities of politics.

In March 1961 McCarthy wrote Arendt about the beneficial psychological results and harmful intellectual effects following Chiaromonte's recent heart attack: "In Rome, I've been seeing the Chiaromontes every day and sometimes twice a day, taking walks and talking. Nicola has achieved serenity, like a smiling sage and commentator, but unfortunately this is the result of a disability. He has been having some heart trouble (angina or a coronary condition) and his brother, who is a doctor, has put him on a diet ... and allows him to smoke only three or four cigarettes a day. The effect of this natural regime has been to make him very peaceful and indeed simple and natural but it has deprived him (he says) of any inclination to intellectual work." Chiaromonte managed to survive for another decade, and then died suddenly. McCarthy told Arendt, "It happened in an elevator in the Italian Radio building; he had just given a broadcast on the [Jean-François] Revel book [*Without Marx or Jesus*] and was dead in a minute.... That morning he'd been well and in bright spirits."

A brave and revered idealist—intense, serious, passionate— Chiaromonte had many close encounters with death and exerted a powerful moral influence on the New York intellectuals. The political chapters of *The Worm of Consciousness* perceptively identified the corrupt thoughts and feelings that allowed totalitarianism to flourish in our time. Chiaromonte's colleague and admirer Joseph Frank summed up his impressive achievement: "[He had] the moral passion that one feels in every line; the unwillingness to lose sight of, or betray, the simple, humble, pathetic bedrock realities of human experience; the refusal to surrender the substance of the socialist dream to the play of vast historical forces or the compulsive grip of ironclad ideologies."

14

Xan Fielding

(1918–1991)

Lord Byron's need to escape boredom and quest for adventure; his realization of egoistic fantasies, flamboyant costume and theatrical behavior; his union of thought and action, art and politics; his idealism and fight for liberty; his desire to free Greece by his own courageous effort and achieve military glory by fulfilling the destiny of a nation—all these qualities inspired the romantic adventurer Xan Fielding.

The frontispiece of Xan's book *The Stronghold* (1953) imitates the famous portrait *Byron in Albanian Dress.* Xan assumes a swaggering pose in profile and wears a Cretan costume: a fringed headcloth, white buttoned shirt, embroidered black vest, baggy Turkish trousers, wide cloak and cummerbund with curved dagger. Patrick Leigh Fermor, Xan's comrade-in-arms during the guerrilla war in Crete and lifelong friend, was also fond of operatic costume. A historian wrote that "his clothes included a bolero, a maroon cummerbund which held to his waist an ivory-handled pistol and dagger. His corduroy breeches were tucked into long black riding boots." Paddy told another warrior, "Xan and I like the locals to think of us as sort of dukes." Both handsome, charismatic and popular men achieved the rank of major and were awarded the Distinguished Service Order military medal.

Xan and Paddy shared more than a love of colorful dress. Xan was born in India, the son of an officer in the Indian Army whom he never knew until adult life. Paddy's father, who directed the Geological Survey in India, only returned to England every three years and Paddy scarcely knew him. Yet these fatherless sons became great masculine heroes. Both were public-school boys, but did not have university degrees. Both traveled extensively in their teens. But in *Hide and Seek,* his memoir of the war in Crete, Xan recalled their differences: "Like Paddy, I had tramped across Europe to reach Greece; like him, I had been almost penniless during that long arduous holiday—but there the similarity between our travels ended, for whereas I was often forced to sleep out of doors, in ditches, haystacks or on public benches, Paddy's charm and resourcefulness had made him a welcome guest wherever he went."

After the war Xan and Paddy lived on the Continent with older, wealthy, previously married wives, but did not have children of their own. In *The Stronghold* Xan admitted, "I never feel really at home in a nursery; its gurgling inmates fill me with embarrassment; I can only pretend to admire them." The two friends and their wives traveled together in Spain, France, Germany and Greece, in Morocco, Syria and Yemen, and frequently visited each other. When the sixty-nine-year-old Paddy swam the Hellespont in Turkey, Xan and his wife watched his Byronic achievement with binoculars from a hotel balcony, waiting for the hero with a chilled bottle of champagne.

Xan and Paddy sometimes appeared in each other's works. Paddy wrote a nostalgic "Introductory Letter to Xan" in his travel books *A Time of Gifts* (1977) and *Between the Woods and the Water* (1986), and Xan annotated Paddy's translation of George Psychoundakis' *The Cretan Runner [Messenger]: His Story of the German Occupation* (1955). Xan used an epigraph from Paddy in *The Stronghold;* and in *The Money Spinner,* his book on Monte

Carlo (1977), he acknowledged his special debt to Paddy, who raked the typescript "with the eye of a friendly hawk" and whose criticism and advice greatly improved the final version.

There were also significant differences. Paddy was three years older, but lived twenty years longer and wrote Xan's obituary. Xan was short, dark, thin and fine-boned; Paddy was tall, fair, solid and strong. Following Xan's bold idea in a well-publicized exploit, Paddy captured the German general Heinrich Kreipe on Crete, hid him in the mountains, sent him by ship to Cairo—and on to a POW camp in Canada. But Xan, who didn't look like a German, despite his stolen uniform, couldn't take part in that daring mission. Paddy became a national hero and lived in Greece after the war; Xan lived in four other Mediterranean countries. Paddy, a better writer than Xan, earned more recognition during his lifetime and after his death. Paddy was knighted in 2004 and all his books have remained in print; two of Xan's books were reprinted in 2013.

For the first time, we can now release Xan from Paddy's overwhelming shadow, place him center stage, tell his equally impressive story and reveal his intriguing background. Xan's father, Major Alexander James Lumsden Wallace, was born on August 8, 1889, in Kirkcaldy, Scotland, north of Edinburgh, the son of a solicitor. His family had a long tradition of military service in India. He studied Greek, French, logic, mathematics and (during his last three years) military subjects at the University of St. Andrews, and graduated with an M.A. in January 1912. He entered the 52nd Sikhs Frontier Force, an Indian infantry regiment in the British Army, in February 1912 and was promoted to captain in September 1915. In 1917–19 the Frontier Force fought in Mesopotamia, Kurdistan and Iraq.

His son, AleXANder Percival Wallace, was born on November 26, 1918 (two weeks after the end of World War I), in Ootacamund (now Ooty) in the Nilgiri Hills, a temperate resort in south central India. Xan was brought up in a château in Nice by his maternal grandparents, who owned valuable property there. In his introduction to *Hide and Seek,* Robert Messenger wrote that "in the late 1960s, Fielding learned that his 'mother' was actually his grandmother. His real mother had died [two weeks after] childbirth. The newborn was adopted into the older generation, and his father, Major Alexander Wallace of the 52nd Sikhs Frontier Force, was simply never mentioned again. His brothers and sisters turned out to be aunts and uncles. According to Fermor, he related this tale with 'considerable humour and bewilderment.'"

The unusual maiden name of Xan's grandmother, Mary Fielding, was Yackjee. The mother of the English actress Vivien Leigh was also called Yackjee—a Bengali name, like Bannerjee and Chatterjee. So Xan's grandmother and mother were probably all or part Indian. It was common during the Raj for Englishmen to take native mistresses, and the newly arrived memsahibs despised and hated the half-caste Eurasian offspring.

Xan's Indian blood would help explain why his grandmother in Nice cut him off from his family in India, why his father was never mentioned, why the family changed Xan's surname from Wallace to Fielding and why the dark-complexioned Xan—who looked like a Greek—could not pass for a Nordic German. It might also explain why he was secretive about his early life, why he disliked institutions such as public schools, military regiments and universities that might discover his background and why he had no children. In his Oxford University application in the fall of 1947, Xan described his father as Percival Wallace Fielding, a businessman whose address was the Travellers Club in Pall Mall. According to the *Dictionary of National Biography* Xan had been adopted by Fielding, who may have been his uncle, and given his surname. He died before 1963. At the same time the records at the University of St. Andrews describe Xan's real father, Alexander James Lumsden Wallace, as a barrister. He lived in North London until 1968.

After prep school at Orley Farm in Harrow, Xan won a classical scholarship to the elite Charterhouse School, which was founded on the site of an old Carthusian monastery in London in 1611. He entered the modern Charterhouse in Surrey in the fall of 1932, when he was almost fourteen, and departed in the spring of 1936. The dark horse left no outstanding record in the archives and no hint of his future achievements as a military leader. He lived in Bodeites House, where he played fives and football, and was also a prefect, studied Greek and published two competent drawings in the school magazine, *The Greyfriar,* in March 1933. He did well academically and was rapidly promoted to the highest form. Instead of going on to university like most of his classmates, the teenager traveled roughly and on foot to achieve what Paddy called, in his "Letter to Xan," "A new life! Freedom! Something to write about!"

In 1936–37 Xan studied briefly at the universities of Bonn and Munich. During these years the Nazis intensified their persecution of Jews and reoccupied the Rhineland, supported the Fascists by bombing Guernica in the Spanish Civil War and prepared to invade Eastern Europe. According to the *DNB,* Xan moved from Bonn to Munich, "became involved in anti-Nazi student agitation, and was arrested and run out of Germany by the Gestapo. An attempt to join the International Brigades in Spain also foundered in arrest." Back in London in 1938, he lived at 74 South Audley Street, off Grosvenor Square. In 1939 he turned up in Cyprus, where he was fired as subeditor for the *Cyprus Times* in Larnaca, a port city on the south coast of the island. He then unsuccessfully ran a bar, and added modern Greek to his French and German.

Though well aware of the Nazi menace, Xan did not enlist when the war broke out in September 1939. Instead, he strangely retreated to a tiny Greek island, St. Nicholas, in the narrow bay of Khalkis between Euboea and the mainland. The island was rented for £3 a year by the archaeologist Francis Turville-Petre (1901–41), who was dying of syphilis. He belonged to an aristocratic Catholic family, and became famous in 1926 when he discovered a fragment of a Neanderthal cranium in a cave near the Sea of Galilee. A homosexual friend of W. H. Auden and Christopher Isherwood in Germany, Turville had drifted away from archaeology, worked for the sexologist Magnus Hirschfeld in Berlin and then retreated to his island hermitage, where he survived on bread and brandy, enhanced by a weekly shot of beef tea.

Isherwood, who'd visited St. Nicholas in May 1933, found it hot and windy, primitive and extremely uncomfortable. He hated the horrid food, and disliked the overbearing Turville and his servile entourage. But he admired the scenery and wrote that the island "was beautifully situated . . . so that one looked across the blue water to mountains on every side, rearing up out of olive groves and standing out against a vast sweep of sky. The island itself was about a kilometer long, much of it densely wooded, and with a small hill at one end." Xan enjoyed the hardships and remained on the island for a year.

Xan returned to Cyprus in August 1940 and joined the newly formed Cyprus Regiment, whose lack of a regimental customs appealed to his rebellious character. But the army offered him order, discipline and duty. Like the officer in Pierre Boulle's *The Bridge over the River Kwai* (which Xan translated in 1954), "he had always dreamed of tackling a really big job without being badgered every other minute by administrative departments or maddened by interfering officials." When he heard that the British military attaché in Athens was recruiting officers who knew Greek, he applied for a lieutenant's commission and was asked, "Have you any personal objection to committing murder?"

His answer deemed satisfactory, he was transferred to the Special Operations Executive (SOE), which fought behind enemy lines, and was sent to Cairo for a commando course in explosives and sabotage. In 1920 Ralph Partridge wrote to his friend Gerald Brenan (in a volume of letters that Xan edited in 1986) about

World War I, in which they had both served as officers. He expressed the idea, which Xan shared, about the difficulty of sustaining a sense of adventure in an increasingly drab and uniform world: "What an exciting life that was; there was always something terrific impending even at the dullest times. . . . The element of risk is perhaps the greatest pleasure of all"—and Xan would soon experience this risky pleasure.

In May 1941, after a high-casualty but spectacular parachute attack, the Germans seized Crete and drove off the Allied troops. In January 1942 Xan landed by submarine on the island, which had become the main staging ground that supplied Erwin Rommel's army in North Africa. Xan's meager equipment included only a flashlight, pistol, useless map and thick wad of Greek drachmas worth only £16. Many young Cretan men had fled to the remote mountains to organize guerrilla resistance against the brutal German occupation. As Paddy wrote of the warriors in his introduction to *The Cretan Runner,* "Crete is famous, throughout Greece, for the revolutionary past [against the Turks], for its feuds and its lawlessness, and for the violence and the impetuosity of the islanders." Xan and Paddy celebrated this primitive but colorful way of life in their books.

Xan was disguised as a Greek and had a good knowledge of the language, but he could not attack the Germans, who would retaliate for casualties by massacring entire villages. If the men fled, they would murder the women and children. Instead, Xan sent valuable information about troop movements, shipping routes and plane flights by radio transmitter to Middle East headquarters in Cairo. The British were then able to sink and shoot down many enemy ships and planes. Xan also helped to evacuate thousands of stranded Allied troops by ship to Egypt, and prepared the Greek guerrillas to support the future Allied invasion. But the Allies invaded Sicily from North Africa, not Crete, and German troops held the island until the end of the war.

Paddy described their difficult and dangerous work in Crete: "My six months seem to have been one long string of battery troubles with the wireless sets for sending messages back to Cairo, transport difficulties, rain, arrests, hide and seek with the Huns, lack of cash, flights at a moment's notice, false alarms, wicked treks over the mountains, laden like a mule, fright among one's collaborators, treachery and friends getting shot." Promoted to major at the age of twenty-five, Xan became responsible for the western part of the island, Paddy for the eastern.

In his best book, *Hide and Seek: The Story of a Wartime Agent* (1954), Xan refers to his stinging messages on the incompetence of headquarters in Cairo and provides an admiring portrait of Paddy's impressive character: "His frivolity was a salutary contrast . . . to my own temper, which had lately grown progressively shorter. It was also a deceptive quality, for although it enhanced his patent imaginative powers, it concealed a mind as conscientious and thorough as it was fanciful. His pre-war experience of Greece combined with an instinctive philhellenism gave him an immediate grasp of local problems." Xan also reveals how they assumed Byronic roles as secret agent and heroic warrior, with Paddy becoming the natural leader: "[Each of us] saw himself playing a role created only by his own imagination. I, for example, affected to regard myself as the Master Spy, the sinister figure behind the scenes controlling a vast network of minor agents who did all the dirty work. Paddy, obviously, scorned such an unobtrusive and unattractive part. He was the Man of Action, the gallant swashbuckler and giant-slayer, a figure who would be immortalized in innumerable marble busts and photogravure plates."

Apart from the struggle to survive on meager rations and hide in freezing caves, Xan experienced the constant danger of capture by German patrols and execution by firing squad. His memoir describes his attack of influenza, his head grazed by a bullet, his boat crashing on the rocks during his second landing on Crete, the capture of his Greek comrade and bitter quarrel with the self-styled but inept Greek leader. He saw the killing of a Greek traitor and dealt with many captured enemy troops after the Italian surrender. He botched the execution of a German deserter and saw the remains of his head splattered on the rocks. His account of these hardships is relieved by humor when Xan has difficulty passing as a deaf-mute imbecile and when pigs gobble up one of his precious diaries—the source of his future war book.

His happiest nights on Crete are his rare, life-enhancing reunions with Paddy and other English comrades, a welcome relief from the tedious exchanges with uneducated Greeks. It was delightful to be "able to talk to people whose conversation was not limited to discussing the merits of one make of pistol compared to another or the advantages of rubber boot-soles over soles made of leather and other similar concerns that seemed to be uppermost in the average peasant mind." In a sly comparison with Paddy, Xan proudly noted that when studying the German list of most wanted men, "the entry under my local pseudonym [Aleko], which outlined in detail my physical characteristics, aliases and activities for a period of eighteen months, took no less than three-quarters of an octavo page in closely set small-point type." His main political achievement was arranging a pact between the two most powerful armed and hostile groups, which prevented a postwar civil war in Crete.

After two dangerous years (with a two-month break) on Crete, Xan returned to Cairo in February 1944, had six weeks leave in Syria and took a parachute course in Haifa. He was then sent to a ciphering course in a military camp outside Algiers. Eager to escape to his next perilous assignment behind enemy lines in France, he vented his anger in a letter to Paddy: "I now realise what they mean by 'the horrors of war.' Since I arrived here four days ago I've been living in a physical and mental squalor which has no parallel in Egypt. Picture me stationed miles away from anywhere, in a camp similar but infinitely inferior to Middle East 102. The food is bad, the accommodation is vile and the company beyond description. There is no transport to get me out of here into town and no 'beau part du monde' in town, even if one could get there."

In August 1944, two months after the D-day landings in Normandy and six years after his last stay in western Europe, Xan was dropped into the Vercors region of southeast France. He'd survived many narrow escapes in Crete. But two days after his arrival his car was stopped in Digne, in the mountains about fifty miles from the French Riviera, and he and a Resistance colleague were arrested (Xan for the second time) by the Gestapo. The Nazis discovered that their papers were forged and that they were carrying a huge number of banknotes with consecutive serial numbers. There was no possibility of escape and they felt certain they'd be shot. Instead, the Polish-born Resistance leader Christine Granville risked her life and rescued them with threats of retaliation from the Allies, who were about to land on the south coast of France, and with a bribe of two million francs, dropped by the SOE. Led out of their cell and expecting death, they were hurried into a waiting car and driven away to safety. Xan's friend Lawrence Durrell greatly improved the story by telling Henry Miller that the R.A.F. "BOMBED THE FRONT DOOR OF THE PRISON FROM LOW LEVEL AND KNOCKED THE WHOLE PLACE DOWN ABOUT HIS EARS, and he escaped."

While visiting Durrell in Rhodes in 1946, Xan confirmed his daring reputation by leaping a couple of yards from a high wall to a twelve-foot Ionic column that rocked frighteningly before he regained his balance. Durrell's brother Gerald called Xan "a really fabulous creature," and Xan's execution of the German prisoner of war on Crete inspired an episode in Lawrence Durrell's novel *The Dark Labyrinth* (1947).

In the spring of 1945, before atomic bombs forced the Japanese surrender on August 15, SOE sent Xan to India and planned to drop him in Tokyo. Xan documented his restless movements in Asia until April 1946 in five free-verse poems, privately printed by Durrell on the army press in Rhodes, by listing the places and dates of composition at the end of each work. The poems reveal his personal feelings about exotic travel, steamy sex, colonial women and postwar uncertainties. After arriving in Calcutta in July, he traveled to Kalimpong in the Himalayas and crossed a mountain pass connecting Sikkim to Yadong, a frontier market town in Tibet. In "Crossing the Natu-La," reminiscent of Walt Whitman's semimystical self-portrayal, he expressed his response to the high mountains: "By this magnificence myself / am magnified. / I command the contours. / I preside / over this vast conspiracy of mountain."

In the fall of 1945 Xan returned to India and journeyed through Ceylon to Saigon in Vichy-controlled French Indochina. In his biography of Billy McLean he noted that despite the French-Vietminh war, "Saigon was pleasant, easy and safe. The hotels were full, the restaurants thronged. There was no shortage of food—fresh meat and vegetables often arrived by air from France." "An Awakening," echoing Matthew 6:10, describes a Graham Greeneish sexual encounter with opium and a Vietnamese lover: "Our will was done on the floor in an inner room of the stilted house, / on the rush matting with a lamp between us, a pipe and a few little pots, / with the silk loose on our loins like a second skin and sensitive / feeling more for the floor than the smoothness of our flesh."

Xan proudly recalled that in November 1945, "I arrived sedately at the fabulous court of Cambodia." After fighting the Nazis in Europe, he spent several months that winter fighting the Communists in Asia and, with a Japanese driver, secretly operated against the Vietminh. In "On the Mekong" River, a poem written in Stung Treng on the Laotian border of northeast Cambodia, he remembered his lovers and longed to see them again: "will you be with me later, / later beside me yawning at the dawn, / stretching darker limbs or displaying / yet another head of golden hair?"

In February 1946, at an army base in Meerut, India, forty miles northeast of Delhi, he satirized the colonial Englishwomen, constricted in mind as in clothing, in "Memsahibs: A Five O'Clock Impression": "Prim and trim as a tonga-pony / her tortured curls are planted like a lawn / and fenced across her forehead with a ribbon. / A scaffolding of corsetry conceals / her body's architecture."

Back in Cairo in April 1946, Xan was depressed by his uncertain prospects after six years in the army. Echoing John Keats' "Now more than ever seems it rich to die" in "Ode to a Nightingale," he imagines in "Demob," after escaping death in war, a worse fate when condemned to an anonymous existence: "Now more than ever . . . / we drift into specific death, / into the tomb of congregations, / crowds and the beetle brotherhood, / unrecognized."

In 1946, after meeting Durrell in Rhodes and printing these poems, Xan spent six months with the Secret Intelligence Service, operating against Soviet agents in postwar Germany. He may also have rooted out former Nazis and recruited the most useful ones as British spies. Then, just after Tito's partisans, with the help of the Red Army, had defeated the pro-Nazi Croatian Ustashe in November 1945 and established a Communist state, he became a United Nations peacekeeping observer in the Balkans.

As Xan suggested in "Demob," he didn't know what to do with himself after all the tremendous excitement and life-and-death responsibility in the war. In D. H. Lawrence's *Lady Chatterley's Lover* (1928), the professional soldier Tommy Dukes expresses Xan's dilemma when he says, "The army leaves no time to think, and saves me from having to face the battle of life." In *My Own River Kwai,* translated by Xan in 1957, Pierre Boulle described the difficult transition from war to peace: "What happens after the tumultuous elation of the turmoil depends on the intensity of the emotions experienced, on the degree to which the mind has been affected and on the particular manner in which each individual reacts to the return to normality, his ears still buzzing at night with persistent memories."

In the fall of 1947 Xan, almost twenty-nine years old, entered New College, Oxford, to read philosophy, modern Greek and French. His tutor, the professor of Byzantine and modern Greek, reported that the always independent Xan "had made a good start, was an extremely good linguist, but in his essays tended to overlook facts in favor of impressions." But he rarely saw his tutor, left after the first term and lost all contact with his college. He then shared a flat with Paddy and his future wife, Joan, above the Heywood Hill bookshop on Curzon Street in Mayfair, and worked unhappily and briefly for the Beaverbrook press.

On July 31, 1950, Xan placed an advertisement in the *Times* that didn't mention his rank and medals and described his character as, "Tough but sensitive ex-classical scholar, ex-secret agent, ex-guerrilla leader, 31, recently reduced to penury through incompatibility with the miserable austerity of post-war Britain: Mediterranean lover, gambler, and general dabbler: fluent French and Greek speaker, some German, inevitable Italian: would do anything unreasonable and unexpected if sufficiently rewarding and legitimate." But he had no private income, was a dilettante and linguist with no university degree, and a self-declared misfit who could not adjust to contemporary reality. There were no takers for this daring adventurer and soldier of fortune who was ex-everything and currently nothing.

Xan's future wife Daphne (whose name was Greek) described her first journey with him in her memoir *Mercury Presides* (1955):

My first professional commission was to illustrate a travel book by Xan Fielding, whom I had met in 1948 at a hilarious luncheon party in London. Two years later he asked me to

join him in Crete to take photographs of the White Mountain district where he was then collecting his material.

I flew out to Athens, where he met me, and a few days
later we sailed for Crete, travelling the cheapest way: as deck
passengers. It was September and we had hoped to be able
to sleep on deck, but a storm broke and we were forced to go
below to quarters that looked like the hold of a convict ship.

In the sweltering heat bodies were wedged tightly together
on a double-tiered wooden platform. We squeezed our way in
between some happy soldiers returning home on leave.

Daphne could surely have afforded a first-class ticket. By insisting
on deck class, Xan attempted to wean her from her luxurious life in
a stately home, to toughen her up, test her resolution and prepare
her for rough travel. Undaunted, she passed the test and gamely
put up with continual discomfort for months on end. During the
course of the journey they found more comfortable accommodations and became lovers.

Daphne Bath (1904–97), fourteen years older than Xan, was
the daughter of the 4th Lord Vivian, who was educated at Eton
and served with distinction in the Boer War and World War I.
Daphne was one of the Bright Young Things of the 1920s, portrayed in the early novels of Evelyn Waugh. In 1927 she married
Henry Thynne, later 6th Marquess of Bath and master of Long-
leat House in Wiltshire, and had four children (one a suicide)
with him. Henry, educated at Harrow and Oxford, spent most of
the war as a POW. Their marriage ended in 1953 when she abandoned her children and ran off with Xan. Though she came from
a wealthy family and divorced a wealthy husband, she didn't seem
to have much money of her own.

Daphne was a tall, attractive, libidinous author of popular
books on London high society. Her close friend Deborah, Duchess

of Devonshire (one of the famous Mitford sisters), said, "She went in for almost childish excesses of all kinds which, with her beauty, courage and imagination, made her an irresistible companion." Waugh's biographer satirically wrote that he quickly became infatuated with the married Daphne. "But it was much the same story as it had been with Diana Guinness. Waugh's puckish gallantry secured him a permanent place in their affections. He was their loyal squire, their eunuch, their pet, paramour and licensed fool. It was flirting without tears, for he was no sexual threat."

Both Deborah and Waugh were in love with the charismatic Xan, who could say of Daphne, as Othello said of Desdemona: "She loved me for the dangers I had passed, / And I loved her that she did pity them." In 1959 Deborah gushed to Paddy that "Xan becomes nobler, smarter, more beautiful & less confident as the years go by & I WORSHIP HIS BODY, but what's the good, one never gets past idiotic chat & one has the strong feeling that he is hating it all." Waugh, who had gone through a homosexual phase at Oxford, added, "I can't blame Debo for falling in love with Mr. Xan. I am a little in love with him myself. But it will make her very unpopular if she robs Daphne." Though Deborah didn't rob her, another woman would.

Xan's first book was *The Stronghold: An Account of the Four Seasons in the White Mountains of Crete.* A mixture of travel and history, the book was dedicated to his many Cretan friends who were killed during the four-year German occupation of the island. He returned to Crete in peacetime in 1951, ten years after he first saw it and only two years after the Greek civil war had ended in 1949, when there were no foreign tourists. Xan has difficulty sustaining the reader's interest in the numerous, indistinguishable Greek characters he meets.

Xan portrays the attractions of village life which draw the émigrés back to their homeland, such as the congenial square and coffee shop, proximity to the vineyards and olive groves, talking, drinking and cardplaying in the comforting sun. In *Hide and Seek* he had glorified the tough mountain men, with their cult of virility, mania for weapons and primitive way of life. But in *The Stronghold* he feels overwhelmed by the aggressive hospitality and tedious vows of eternal friendship, by the compulsory feasting on poor food and rough wine and by the frantic dancing during the endless cycle of baptisms, weddings, holidays and funerals, which sometimes continue for as long as twelve hours and last all through the night. The book ends with a feeling of extreme disillusionment: "The idea of Crete had haunted me ever since my departure after the war; I had pictured it as an unattainable never-never land. That conception had been modified during the last year, during which the idea had given place to reality; the ghost had been laid in the daylight of tangible fact."

In 1954, a year after his marriage and the publication of *The Stronghold,* Xan translated *The Bridge over the River Kwai,* the first of twelve works from the French of his close contemporary Pierre Boulle (1912–94). Like most translators, Xan earned a straight fee and did not share the stupendous royalties when *Kwai* and *Planet of the Apes* became popular movies and sold millions of copies throughout the world. Like Xan, Boulle had worked as a secret agent in Indochina; was captured, faced execution and escaped from prison; and was awarded well-deserved medals after victory in war.

Xan and Daphne first lived in Looe, a fishing village on the southeast coast of Cornwall. Not interested in food except for his own homemade curries, and writing in a monkish cell with no distracting view, he led a rather austere life. Their fortunes changed when Daphne suddenly discovered that their marriage was bigamous. Since both sets of aristocratic parents had strongly disapproved, Daphne had had a secret first marriage to Henry Thynne in 1926 and an officially sanctioned wedding in 1927. When she divorced him in 1953, she declared only the date of the second wedding. But the first one was deemed valid and she appeared to be married to both Henry and Xan. Her legal appeal was eventually granted, but the case provoked a lot of bad publicity and the litigation was very expensive. In 1956 she and Xan moved to Tangier in Morocco to avoid taxes and live more cheaply, and began their twenty-year wandering through Mediterranean countries.

The initial attractions, Daphne wrote in her second memoir, *The Nearest Way Home* (1970), were "a free port, no customs, no taxes, no government even, just an international administration, the nearest approach to freedom you can get in the modern world." She added that on their first visit to the town, "we were enchanted by the house, as compact as its inhabitants, tiny in fact, but with an air of spaciousness due to open archways instead of doors leading from one room to the next." Built into the ancient battlements of the Arab town, it had a fine view of the modern city and the sand-fringed bay beyond. Deborah Devonshire, used to grandeur, gave Paddy a more realistic account of their cramped and horrid tenement in the Arab quarter: "Their little, damp and badly lit house was squashed in a busy street so narrow that the continuous noise never got out, roamed by packs of dishevelled children with runny noses, and no European nearby."

Though Xan and Daphne lasted for three years, they never crashed the barrier of Moorish exclusion and came to hate the squalid and suffocating atmosphere. They suffered from an army of bugs and slithering snakes, the intolerable racket of roosters crowing throughout the night and the muezzin calling the faithful to prayer at dawn, the clattering garbage collectors and herds of goats driven through the narrow alleys. Xan, knocked unconscious by carbon monoxide leaking from a water heater in the bathroom, was rescued from asphyxiation by Daphne. Their soft-top car was vandalized and chained luggage stolen on their first night in the Kasbah. They could not leave their house without being mobbed by hostile beggars and sometimes fell prey to pickpockets. It was a far cry from the glamorization of the North African Arab town in Jean Gabin's film *Pépé le Moko* (1937) and in the works of the presiding literary deity, Paul Bowles. In April 1959 Xan told Durrell that Tangier had been "a bad mistake; for I now have a completely uncritical hatred of the Moors, Islam, and all things Arab."

This hatred was reinforced in his third autobiographical book, the Byronically titled *Corsair Country: The Diary of a Journey along the Barbary Coast* (1958). Daphne, who again took the pedestrian photos, wrote that they were well supplied for another arduous expedition: "Our Land Rover was piled high with tents and camping equipment, jerrycans for water and extra petrol, medicine chests and tin trunks, suit-cases and map-cases, cameras and binoculars, picnic baskets and thermos flasks, tropical kit and emergency rations"—everything that Xan had lacked during the war in Crete.

They drove east from Tangier to Tripoli, hugging the coast for 1,100 miles through Morocco, Algeria, Tunisia and Libya, on the "long strip of Mediterranean Europe soldered on to the sands of the Sahara." Though Xan had lived for years on intimate terms with Greek peasants, he now adopts the satiric tone of the travel writer Peter Fleming and assumes an English pukka sahib superiority, mocks the American tourists and despises the Arabs. He's irritated by the importunate beggars, merchants and guides, and condemns the Arabs' subconscious craving to destroy all Western machines: "Trust the native mind to function with unswerving stupidity." Opposing the prevailing Anglo-Saxon admiration of the Arabs, he praises the French and Italian colonists for bringing European civilization to backward North Africa.

The dominant theme of this travel book is disillusionment. Tetuan is beastly. Oran (the setting of Camus' *The Plague*) is hideously ugly. The worst place in Algeria has no redeeming feature to justify his visit. Djijelli in that country shatters another romantic illusion. The best times occur when they escape from the Arab towns to little French hotels on empty beaches and do nothing but eat, swim and sleep. His conclusion, chauvinistic but honest, resonates today: "After these months spent in the shadow of Islam I've never before been so conscious and proud of my European and Christian background."

It was infinitely more pleasant in the summer of 1956 to serve with Paddy as technical adviser to the movie *Ill Met by Moonlight* (1957). Shot in the Maritime Alps above Menton and with Dirk Bogarde playing Paddy, the film focuses on the daring capture of General Kreipe and ignores Xan's role in the war. When Bogarde was reluctant to meet Paddy, Xan reassured him with a self-reflective description of his friend: "Don't worry, Paddy's not a typical army officer or guerrilla leader. He's not a typical anything, he's himself, a romantic figure, in the Byron tradition. Very erudite, a sort of Gypsy Scholar, with an inexhaustible fund of incidental knowledge."

Embarrassed by the greatly exaggerated heroics in the movie, Paddy told Deborah that he was "having a terrific tussle getting them to change these bits in the film, not because I really mind, but because anyone who also knows anything about the operation knows that it's all rot." When the movie was completed, Bogarde and his advisers stopped on the way to Paris in a luxurious hotel in Digne. It was right next door to the house in which Xan had been imprisoned and sentenced to death, and could be seen from his bedroom window. Bogarde apologized for the contretemps, but Xan didn't mind and was pleased to return after twelve years in infinitely more pleasant circumstances.

In 1959, after moving from Tangier to Portugal, Xan told Durrell about his new country house: "We've just bought this little quinta, which you can reach from Lisbon in half an hour though when you get here you're miles away from it all—no proper road, no electricity, a hamlet of washerwomen as nearest neighbours, and country like the rather more pastoral lowlands of Crete. . . . Scenically the background's stupendous, but neutral socially—which happens to suit me after three years in Tangier." Their guests included Evelyn Waugh, Henry Miller (met through Durrell), Daphne's friend Diana Cooper (Viscountess Norwich) and the bohemian English poet and actress Iris Tree, the subject of Daphne's biography in 1974. But after five years the incorrigibly damp house, the universally dull people—"inertia unrelieved by the slightest trace of high spirits"—the dislike of Antonio Salazar's oppressive dictatorship and, as the final blow, the erection of a huge, hideous pylon on their land forced the gypsies to take to the road once again.

Their next stop, in 1964, was Uzès in France, an attractive market town in Languedoc, north of Nîmes and about forty miles from the Mediterranean coast, where they visited Durrell. They bought a house called the Galerie des Pâtres (shepherds) and lasted for nine years. But they were plagued by scorpions (much worse than bugs), and by the fierce mistral that blew down the Rhone Valley and made the unheated house horribly cold. When they ran out of money, the wealthy Diana Cooper came to the rescue and bought half the house from them.

Their Byronic wanderings in Cornwall, Morocco, Portugal and France formed a discernible pattern. Always restless, they liked moving around, buying old houses and fixing them up, but they were careless and impulsive, made poor choices and bought cheap places that didn't suit their needs. They had frequent difficulties with workmen and spent too much on renovations. For decades they counted on a prospective fortune that never appeared and sometimes ran out of money. They sought out remote places, didn't socialize with local residents and then complained of their isolation. They failed to see the obvious problems with the Arab quarter in Tangier, the dampness in Portugal and the mistral in Uzès.

In an important letter to Durrell of April 1959, Xan wrote that he'd done a radio version of his friend's travel book *Bitter Lemons*

(1957), which was never produced because of the current rebellion against British rule in Cyprus, and praised the *Alexandria Quartet* as "the best thing to have come out of this century." He also admired Paddy's *Mani* (1958), a travel book about the Greek Peloponnese, but rightly thought the rather precious and mannered style was ill suited to the primitive setting and subject: "Have you read Paddy's *Mani*? He's really done it this time, though the puritan in me would have liked to see less of that nasty Sitwellian brocade showing through the sackcloth." When the sequel to *Mani*, *Roumeli: Travels in Northern Greece,* came out in 1966, Xan wrote Paddy the kind of enthusiastic letter a writer always hopes to get from a friend: "Your *Roumeli* reached me this morning. I have devoured it almost without drawing breath. In this case *l'appétit vient en lisant* [increased while reading] and I mean [to have] a second, more leisurely, less orgiastic reading. Meanwhile I want to tell you at once how delighted, chastened, awed, beguiled, spellbound I am by this initial gobble."

Then, in a rare confessional and self-lacerating passage, Xan compared himself unfavorably to Paddy and Durrell, undermined his claim to happiness and admitted that he'd become, despite his lofty ambitions, a domesticated second-rate writer:

> I envy you both, not only your success, but because you're both producing something worth while—which is more than I'll ever do, I now know. Translations, reviews for the T.L.S., long turgid articles for *History Today,* and once every five years a less-than-mediocre travel book—that's about my level, I'm afraid. . . .
>
> That's how I feel these days—utterly fed up with myself, though perfectly happy. And I don't think the reason is just bad work, it's being the sort of person I never meant or wanted to be. Fuck it all, I think I've actually become HOUSE-TRAINED!

Xan was also frustrated by financial and legal problems, which repeated his bigamy litigation. Since 1933, when he was fifteen, a French lawsuit of Byzantine complexity and tremendous strain had been slithering through the courts. The editor of Waugh's correspondence with Diana Cooper explained the background in 1965: "Xan Fielding's grandmother, Mary Fielding (née Yackjée), owned a large villa and some land in Nice. She let a strip of her land to the municipal authorities, for the purpose of building a boulevard; but the road was never built, and the land should have reverted to her heirs. The heirs (including Xan) took it to court, and won after years of litigation; but the case had been so badly handled by Xan's brother-in-law that almost all the millions were eaten up in legal fees."

During the financial difficulties in his marriage to Daphne, Xan had waited for the great fortune which, despite many definite assurances of immediate settlement, never materialized. In September 1965 Waugh told Diana Cooper that "Xan's inheritance has risen to one million [pounds]. 11 million was the sum of which 2/3rds have gone in bribery and 100,000 on costs over 32 years— now if de Gaulle dies or the government changes the bribes will have to be repeated to the new gang." Three years later, with legal fees continuing to exhaust the last remnant of the potential fortune, Paddy told his wife that Xan had spent a huge amount of money in the lawsuit: "this delay and worry over the case has driven Xan nearly mad; terrifically nervy and frowning and anxious. . . . Daphne, in spite of her several drawbacks and a dash of arrested development, is very good and calming and kind." The legal documents in the protracted case may have led Xan, in the late 1960s, to the disturbing discovery that his putative mother was actually his grandmother and his supposed father was not his real father.

Xan seemed to have spent most of his time in Uzès on French translations. From 1960 to 1975 he also worked on an unfinished book, "Imperial Vendetta: The History of the Fight of Two Corsicans," Bonaparte and his political rival Carlo Andrea, Count Pozzo di Borgo (1764–1842). In 1977, nineteen years after *Corsair Country*, he published an apparently commissioned potboiler, *The Money Spinner: Monte Carlo and Its Fabled Casino*. Xan had grown up in Nice, a few miles from Monte Carlo, and was fond of gambling. He and Daphne were given a free room at the Hermitage Hotel in the town while he did research on the history of the casino. The luxurious gambling den was developed in the nineteenth century by French millionaires who lured the aristocratic and fashionable world to the tables, and was later controlled by the German arms dealer Basil Zaharoff and by Aristotle Onassis. At the height of the season in the early 1900s, twenty-three gaming tables were manned by five hundred employees.

The opening sentence of the book—"On 1 March 1815, towards eleven o'clock at night, a berlin travelling eastwards along the coast road of the South of France was stopped by a troop of armed soldiers"—clearly echoes the first sentence of Stendhal's *The Charterhouse of Parma* (1839). Xan discusses Dostoyevsky's disastrous gambling at Wiesbaden, which the Russian novelist described in *The Gambler*. He also provides a number of intriguing facts: to prevent swindles croupiers wore suits without pockets, one famous gambler always carried a million francs in cash, no one ever broke the bank and there were many suicides after gamblers had lost everything. In the best part of the book he explains how roulette, trente-et-quarante and baccarat actually work, and how the casino maintains absolute control of the astronomical profits.

Daphne's lively and readable novel *The Adonis Garden* (1961) was published when she and Xan were living in Portugal, and many events in the book are close to their actual experience. Rose Penhaze (based on Daphne) is a peer's daughter with some money of her own. She has enjoyed a luxurious former marriage, loves horses and has two daughters, but cannot conceive a child with her second husband. She refers to the Greek myth of Daphne and fondly mentions Dirk Bogarde several times. While married, she travels cheaply with a lover who's photographing an article on the slave trade in North Africa. She portrays their tiny flat in Tangier, where her purse is snatched and their equipment stolen. Another character is almost asphyxiated by gas leaking from a water heater.

Giles Penhaze (based on Xan) is very attractive and vulnerable to predatory women. Daphne lovingly describes "the dark wing of hair falling over his forehead; the pale skin, lightly freckled, stretched tightly over high cheek bones, eyes the colour of a goat's, gold-flecked; the curling half-smiling mouth in contrast to the brow which was at times clouded with despair." Later on, he's burned dark by the sun. Giles' parents were killed in a flying accident when he was in school. He grew up in a château in the South of France, famous for its lavish parties that squandered his inheritance, which he partly recovers in a protracted lawsuit. He went to Winchester, and a friend opened a bar in prewar Cyprus. Parachuted behind enemy lines, he organized the Resistance and won a DSO. He found it very difficult to adjust to civilian life, but writes a promising novel.

Daphne's novel reflects Xan's restless mood and her anxiety, and a major theme is her fear of losing him to another woman. The character of Baby—a rich, sexy American with two young children who poses nude while Giles sculpts her—foreshadows Magouche Phillips, who later broke up their marriage. But in the novel, dedicated to Xan, the husband and wife, after brief love affairs, are happily reunited.

But the real Xan was weary of his uncomfortable house, domesticated existence, money problems, agonizing lawsuit and frustrations as a writer as well as the increasingly obvious difference in age between himself and Daphne. In 1973 he seized the last opportunity to rejuvenate himself with a rich, glamorous and sexy new woman who was seventeen years younger than his wife.

The sixty-nine-year-old Daphne, who'd left her wealthy husband and small children for Xan, must have been devastated when her marriage failed and she was abandoned after twenty-two years with him. In a letter of January 1975 to Paddy, Ian Fleming's wife Ann said, "Daphne is being very brave and good about Xan and Magouche." In 1997, the last year of Daphne's long life, Deborah asked what she did in the evenings and she replied, "Reading and R-r-remembering rogering!" Deborah thought Daphne was still "rather fast."

Agnes (Magouche) Magruder (1921–2013) was born into an old and distinguished family in Boston. The daughter of a U.S. Navy admiral, she was educated in Washington, The Hague and at Brilliantmont, a finishing school in Lausanne. When her father was stationed in Shanghai in 1939, she rebelled against her parents, rashly supported the Communists in the Chinese civil war and was sent back to America with a modest allowance. She was married to the volatile painter Arshile Gorky—who gave her the name of Magouche, an Armenian endearment—from 1941 until his suicide in 1948. In a photo of Xan disguised as a Greek peasant—with thick back hair, week-old beard and heavy mustache—he looks remarkably like the swarthy Gorky. Magouche was married to the Boston painter John Phillips from 1949 to 1959, and had two daughters with each of her husbands.

Gorky's biographer described Magouche as "five foot seven, slim, and graceful, with full, sensuous lips, a firm jawline, and slightly bulging hazel eyes that often twinkled with a kind of impudent amusement." The Bloomsbury diarist Frances Partridge praised "her thick dark hair, low rich voice, warm smile and large eyes. In fact, she's very attractive indeed." Between her divorce from Phillips and marriage to Xan, Magouche took the much older writer David Garnett as one of her many lovers.

Xan was divorced in 1978 and married Magouche on March 8, 1979. Both his wives were previously married and had four children. But Magouche, the heir to Gorky's valuable estate, had much more money than Daphne. The couple bought a house in southern Spain, in the Sierras between Gibraltar and Málaga, and in 1980 Paddy told Deborah that "their abode above Ronda has become delightful, with thick walls, blazing fires, mountains all around, twenty minutes' walk to the amazing town, where a wonder-bridge spans a deep chasm full of swallows." Paddy found it a fine place to work and in his "Letter to Xan" in *Between the Woods and the Water* thanked him "for diligent spells of cloistered seclusion."

Writing from Ronda in 1978, Paddy mentioned Xan's *Aeolus Displayed* (1991), a slim, fifty-one-page book privately printed by Typographeum Press in New Hampshire, about winds in myth and literature from Homer to Joyce. He was most enthusiastic and reported that "Xan's Wind-Book is absolutely tip-top. He's totally *emballé* [absorbed] by it, charts are everywhere, and excitement reigns, which I beg him to let infectiously rip. I bet it'll be a great success." In a letter to me the publisher Terry Risk wrote that he'd contacted Xan on June 19, 1991, when the author was living at 194 rue de Rivoli in Paris: "I explained my interest, and my limitations as a private press printer. He replied on July 2nd formally offering me the project, *Aeolus Observed*. We corresponded about it until August 16th, then I learned of his death. He never saw the book. Magouche wrote however to say: 'The book you are working on was a great happiness to him. He had loved writing it & [despite the German translation in 1988] it was so disappointing not to find a publisher in English. But your beautiful printing & your enthusiasm coming so unexpectedly & at such a remarkable time seemed, was, a miracle.'"

In 1978 Xan told Paddy,

I have at last finished the mystery of 'the four winds of the sky'. . . . I want to get a real move-on with the book this summer, but at the same time we both long for Greece. Do you realise it's three years since we've been there? Much will depend too on how the new book progresses, on how much more time and money it will take to finish it. Then we shall have to see about selling the house; otherwise we'll be in Queer Street. Meanwhile there are two gardens and two olive groves to attend to. Why on earth does one saddle oneself with so much? I sometimes think how nice it would be to have no more than a couple of rooms in which to keep one's books and things, or a small pension in which to work, and the rest of one's time and money free for seeing friends and traveling.

Paddy also noted that Magouche "has a heart of gold and is awfully good with Xan's once-in-a-blue-moon snickety-snaque [nasty] utterances."

In 1978 the narcissistic travel writer and novelist Bruce Chatwin, who was living nearby, also praised Magouche: "Usually I go for a swim at the pool of a friend called Magouche. She is an old friend, magnificent, stylish, the daughter of a U.S. Admiral: her name was once Agnes Magruder, that is, until she worked for Edgar Snow's 'Support Mao' campaign in New York in the '40s, met the painter Arshile Gorky and married him. She still lives off the contents of the studio, is haunted by Gorky's suicide and quarrels frantically with all but one of her four daughters."

But Chatwin also egoistically emphasized the negative aspects of Xan's character: "The bore is Xan: apparently when I came up with some more 'Wind' information, he took offence and thought I was trying to patronise him. Also resents my friendship with Magouche. I've tried my best to like him, gave Maro [Magouche's daughter] endless lectures about how stupid she was being [about Xan] but I've come to the conclusion she was right. He's a silly, jealous A1 shit. He picks rows with Magouche the whole time and reduces her to a bag of nerves. She's deeply in love with him." Xan and Magouche had both liked the bisexual Chatwin and admired his film-star good looks. But when he turned up uninvited for lunch every day, tediously boastful and interfering with Xan's work, they had to find a way to get rid of him.

While living in Ronda, Xan wrote an excellent introduction, with clear and concise annotations, to *Best of Friends: The Brenan-Partridge Letters* (1986). He also brought out *Images of Spain* (1991), a book of spectacular photos with a brief, illuminating text, divided into four geographical regions of the country and its islands, which shows his deep understanding and appreciation of the Spanish landscape and culture. At one point he compares Ronda to his birthplace, the Indian hill station of Ootacamund. In this book Xan celebrates the traditional Spanish way of life that is slowly being eroded by mass tourism.

Xan's last book was a biography of a soldier with whom he had a great deal in common: *One Man in His Time: The Life of Lieutenant-Colonel N. L. D. ("Billy") McLean, DSO* (1990). Xan and Billy (1918–86) were born the same year, knew each other in wartime Cairo and—like Paddy and Pierre Boulle—led similarly adventurous lives. Both men had Scottish fathers who were professional soldiers; both belonged to SOE and had fought in guerrilla warfare behind enemy lines. Xan self-reflectively wrote that Billy had "no wish for regimental soldiering and looked forward to whatever unorthodox assignment Middle East headquarters had to offer." Like Xan and "many people who are capable of extreme physical exertion when it is absolutely necessary, Billy did not believe in exercise for its own sake. He had never enjoyed games or athletics." Both men were born leaders, the human epitome of dash and swagger, and in both a "charming and lackadaisical façade concealed a toughness of steel, great powers of physical endurance and a needle-sharp intelligence." Both men were awarded the Distinguished Service Order. Billy's wife, like Daphne, was an aristocratic divorcée with four children who'd remained in the custody of their father.

After a brief discussion of Billy's background—Eton, Sandhurst and the Scots Greys—Xan's brisk, exciting narrative (like *Hide and Seek*) goes straight to his war experience. Fighting alongside Orde Wingate and Wilfred Thesiger, Billy helped defeat the Italians in Ethiopia and again in the Albanian campaign. He even traveled as far as Kashgar, in the western Chinese province of Sinkiang, to battle the Communists. In 1954 Billy was elected Conservative M.P. for Inverness, supported the ill-fated British invasion of Suez and became influential in Middle East politics. Xan concludes, as if writing about himself, "Many will remember him as the last of the paladins, and an inspiration to *beaux sabreurs* [bold adventurers] of the future."

On October 23, 1990, the year the life of McLean appeared, Paddy suddenly informed Deborah that Xan was stricken by rapidly spreading cancer: "The bad news, of course, is about Xan, the dread disease running riot everywhere, when thought to be only what's called a spot." Two months later he quoted a mutual friend in Spain and reported, "The Xan news isn't cheering. They both sound very chipper on the telephone, but that's as expected. Janetta [Parladé] says Xan is a bit better, as they've knocked off the wretched chemical treatment." Anticipating his obituary of Xan, Paddy added, "He's very difficult to pin down, a strange and rare specimen." In May 1991, after moving to Paris for medical attention and still seriously ill, Xan managed to attend the ceremonies in Greece to commemorate the fiftieth anniversary of the Battle of Crete. Three months later, on August 19, Xan died in Paris, and Paddy and Magouche buried his ashes in the mountains of Crete.

Paddy's obituary in the *Daily Telegraph* of August 20 defined Xan's extraordinary character and memorialized one of the great literary friendships of the twentieth century: "He was a gifted, many-sided, courageous and romantic figure, deeply committed to his friends, civilised and bohemian at the same time, with a thoughtful style leavened by spontaneous gaiety and a dash of recklessness. He was altogether outstanding." A month later, both delighted and (for once) envious of all the attention Xan had posthumously received, Paddy said their traditional roles were reversed and he was now portrayed as the servant who hands the shotguns to the master shooting the birds: "It was marvellous the spread newspapers gave to poor old Xan, tho' some of them made it look as though he'd won the war single-handed, with me as his loader. But I *was* pleased, for his sake and all his pals, not to vanish unsung." Three years later in his foreword to Xan's *A Hideous Disguise*—a Typographeum reprint of the last chapters of *Hide and Seek* about his capture and escape from the Gestapo—Paddy praised his old comrade as a "gifted, many-sided, courageous and romantic figure." He continued to admire Xan in his letters to Deborah (2008) and *Abducting a General* (2014).

Despite his personal disappointment and inability to produce a masterpiece, Xan underrated his own achievement. He had a heroic war record and an accomplished career as a writer. He wrote a fine war memoir, two travel books, a history of gambling and a biography of a soldier, as well as poems, two pamphlets, a book of Spanish photos, an edition of the Brenan-Partridge letters and thirty-one French translations. Best of all, he led a free life, resided in beautiful places and remained a romantic adventurer. Like the hero of Byron's "The Corsair" (1814), he "Still sways their souls with that commanding art / That dazzles, leads, yet chills the vulgar heart."

BIBLIOGRAPHY

The bibliography provides references for Part II of this book, based on research. Part I is based on personal experience.

Anthony Blunt

Blunt, Anthony. *The Art of William Blake.* New York: Columbia UP, 1959.

———. "Blake's Pictorial Imagination." *Journal of the Warburg and Courtauld Institutes* 6 (1943): 190–213.

———. *Borromini.* Cambridge, Mass.: Harvard UP, 1979.

———. *Nicolas Poussin.* New York: Bollingen Foundation, 1967.

———. *Picasso's "Guernica."* New York: Oxford UP, 1969.

Blunt, Anthony, and Phoebe Pool. *Picasso: The Formative Years. A Study of His Sources.* Greenwich, Conn.: New York Graphic Society, 1962.

Carter, Miranda. *Anthony Blunt: His Lives.* New York: Farrar, Straus and Giroux, 2001.

Friedlaender, Walter. *Poussin.* New York: Abrams, 1964.

Richardson, John. *A Life of Picasso. Volume II, 1907–1917.* New York: Random House, 1996.

———. *A Life of Picasso. Volume III, 1917–1932.* New York: Random House, 2007.

Ruskin, John. *Modern Painters.* 5 volumes. 1843–60. London: Routledge, n.d.

Steiner, George. "The Cleric of Treason." *New Yorker* 56 (December 8, 1980): 158–95.

Wright, Christopher. *Poussin: Paintings. A Catalogue Raisonné.* London: Chaucer Press, 2007.

Basil Blackwood

Bence-Jones, Mark. "Kipling's Viceroy." *The Viceroys of India.* London: Constable, 1982.

Betjeman, John. *Letters.* 2 volumes. London: Methuen, 1994.

Black, Charles Edward Drummond. *The Life of the Marquess of Dufferin and Ava.* London: Hutchinson, 1903.

Blackwood, Caroline. *Great Granny Webster.* 1977; London: Picador, 1978.

Hillier, Bevis. *Betjeman: New Fame, New Love.* London: John Murray, 2002.

———. *Young Betjeman.* London: John Murray, 1988.

Kirby, Major-General S. Woodburn. *The War against Japan. Volume IV, The Reconquest of Burma.* London: HMSO, 1965.

Mullally, Frederic. *Silver Salver: The Story of the Guinness Family.* London: Granada, 1981.

Nicolson, Harold. *Helen's Tower.* London: Constable, 1937.

Rankin, Nicolas. *Telegram from Guernica: The Extraordinary Life of George Steer, War Correspondent.* London: Faber, 2003.

Schoenberger, Nancy. *Dangerous Muse: The Life of Caroline Blackwood.* New York: Doubleday, 2001.

The Times (London), April 5, 6 and 10, 1945.

Waugh, Evelyn. *Diaries.* Ed. Michael Davis. 1976; London: Penguin, 1979.

———. *Letters.* Ed. Mark Amory. New York: Ticknor & Fields, 1980.

Wilson, A. N. *Betjeman: A Life.* New York: Farrar, Straus and Giroux, 2006.

Derek Jackson

Interview with Janetta Parladé; email messages from Artemis Cooper and Simon Courtauld; Ohio State University, Rugby School and Trinity College, Cambridge.

Bleaney, Brebis. "Derek Ainslie Jackson (1906–1982): Some Recollections of a Great European Spectroscopist." *Notes and Records of the Royal Society* 55 (May 2001): 285–87.

Boyd, Brian. *Vladimir Nabokov: The Russian Years.* Princeton: Princeton UP, 1990.

Churchill, Winston. *The Second World War. Volume 4, The Hinge of Fate.* Boston: Houghton Mifflin, 1950.

Courtauld, Simon. *As I Was Going to St. Ives: A Life of Derek Jackson.* Norwich: Michael Russell, 2007.

Fermor, Patrick Leigh. *Dashing for the Post: The Letters of Patrick Leigh Fermor.* Ed. Adam Sisman. London: John Murray, 2016.

Fermor, Patrick Leigh, and Deborah Devonshire. *In Tearing Haste: Letters between Deborah Devonshire and Patrick Leigh Fermor.* Ed. Charlotte Mosley. London: John Murray, 2008.

Greig, Geordie. *Breakfast with Lucian.* New York: Farrar, Straus and Giroux, 2013.

Hastings, Selina. Review of Courtauld's *As I Was Going to St. Ives. Spectator,* October 27, 2007: 53–54.

Holroyd, Michael. *Augustus John.* London: Penguin, 1976.

Jackson, D. A. "Hyperfine Structure in the Arc Spectrum of Caesium and Nuclear Rotation." *Proceedings of the Royal Society of London* A:121 (1928): 432.

Jones, R. V. *Most Secret War.* London: Hamish Hamilton, 1978.

Kuhn, H. G., and Christopher Hartley. "Derek Ainslie Jackson." *Biographical Memoirs of the Fellows of the Royal Society* 29 (1983): 268–96.

Lewis, Jeremy. *Cyril Connolly: A Life.* London: Cape, 1997.

Lovell, Mary. *The Sisters: The Saga of the Mitford Family.* New York: Norton, 2002.

Morrell, Jack. "Jackson, Derek Ainslie." *The Oxford Dictionary of National Biography.* Ed. H. C. G. Matthew and Brian Harrison. Oxford: Oxford UP, 2004. 29:475–76.

Mosley, Diana. *Loved Ones: Pen Portraits.* London: Sidgwick & Jackson, 1985. Pp. 70–95.

Mosley, Oswald. *My Life.* New Rochelle, N.Y.: Arlington House, 1968.

Mount, Ferdinand. Review of Courtauld's *As I Was Going to St. Ives. London Review of Books,* February 7, 2008.

Partridge, Frances. *Diaries, 1939–1972.* Ed. Rebecca Wilson. London: Phoenix, 2001.

Plomer, William. "[Rugby]." In *The Old School.* Ed. Graham Greene. 1934; Oxford: Oxford UP, 1984. Pp. 111–26.

Price, Alfred. *Instruments of Darkness.* London: William Kimber, 1967.

Reynolds, Paul. "Nancy Mitford Spied on Her Sisters." BBC News online, November 14, 2003.

Skelton, Barbara. *Weep No More.* London: Hamish Hamilton, 1989.

Weidenfeld, George. *Remembering My Good Friends.* London: HarperCollins, 1994.

Zinovieff, Sofka. *The Mad Boy, Lord Berners, My Grandfather and Me.* New York: HarperCollins, 2015.

Nicola Chiaromonte

Abel, Lionel. *The Intellectual Follies.* New York: Norton, 1984.

A.L.T. Review of *The Paradox of History. Journal of European Studies* 3 (1973): 79.

Arendt, Hannah, and Mary McCarthy. *Between Friends: The Correspondence of Hannah Arendt and Mary McCarthy,*

1949–1975. Ed. Carol Brightman. New York: Harcourt Brace
Jovanovich, 1995.

Barrett, William. *The Truants.* Garden City, N.Y.: Anchor, 1983.

Bellow, Saul. *Letters.* Ed. Benjamin Taylor. New York: Viking,
2010.

Bianco, Gino. *Nicola Chiaromonte e il tempo della malafede.*
Manduria (Taranto): P. Lucaita, 1999. Bianco's impersonal
biography does not use sources in English and devotes only
22 pages to Chiaromonte's seven years in New York.

Brightman, Carol. *Writing Dangerously: Mary McCarthy and
Her World.* New York: Clarkson Potter, 1992.

Bromwich, David. Review of *The Paradox of History. Dissent* (Fall
1976): 443–45, 448.

Chiaromonte, Nicola. "In Praise of Florence." *Partisan Review* 27
(Summer 1960): 558–60.

———. Letter to Dwight Macdonald, February 3, 1953.
Beinecke Library, Yale University.

———. *The Paradox of History.* 1970; Philadelphia: University
of Pennsylvania Press, 1985.

———. "Wilson among the Ruins." *Partisan Review* 15 (February 1948): 247.

———. *The Worm of Consciousness.* Ed. Miriam Chiaromonte.
New York: Harcourt Brace Jovanovich, 1976.

Christian, R. F. Review of *The Paradox of History. Modern Language Review* 82 (1987): 430.

Coleman, Peter. *The Liberal Conspiracy: The Congress for Cultural
Freedom and the Struggle for the Mind of Postwar Europe.* New
York: Free Press, 1989.

Frank, Joseph. Foreword to *The Paradox of History.* Pp. xi–xviii.
Expanded as "Nicola Chiaromonte: The Ethic of Politics."
Responses to Modernity. New York: Fordham UP, 2012. Pp.
86–95. I regret that I did not discuss Chiaromonte with my
close friend Joseph Frank before his death.

Gelderman, Carol. *Mary McCarthy: A Life.* New York: St. Martin's, 1988.

Giroud, Vincent. *Nicolas Nabokov: A Life in Freedom and Music.* New York: Oxford UP, 2015.

Howe, Irving. Review of *The Worm of Consciousness. New Republic* 75 (May 1, 1976): 26–27.

Kiernan, Frances. *Seeing Mary Plain: A Life of Mary McCarthy.* New York: Norton, 2000.

Leader, Zachary. *The Life of Saul Bellow.* New York: Knopf, 2015.

Lottman, Herbert. *Albert Camus: A Biography.* London: Weidenfeld and Nicolson, 1975.

Macdonald, Dwight. *A Moral Temper: The Letters of Dwight Macdonald.* Ed. Michael Wreszin. Chicago: Ivan Dee, 2001.

Malraux, André. *Man's Hope.* Trans. Stuart Gilbert and Alistair Macdonald. New York: Random House, 1938.

McCarthy, Mary. *Cast a Cold Eye* and *The Oasis.* New York: Signet, 1953.

———. *Conversations.* Ed. Carol Gelderman. Jackson: UP of Mississippi, 1991.

———. "Nicola Chiaromonte and the Theatre." *New York Review of Books,* February 20, 1975, 25–30.

———. Postface to *The Paradox of History.* Pp. 149–56.

———. Preface to *The Worm of Consciousness.* Pp. xiii–xvi.

Morgan, Sarah. "Nicola Chiaromonte (1905–72)." *The Oxford Companion to Italian Literature.* Oxford: Oxford UP, 2002. P. 125.

Nabokov, Nicolas. *Bagazh: Memoirs of a Russian Cosmopolitan.* New York: Atheneum, 1975.

Pacifici, Sergio. *A Guide to Contemporary Italian Literature.* Cleveland: World, 1962.

———. Review of *La Situazione drammatica. Books Abroad* 35 (1961): 179.

Phillips, William. *A Partisan View.* New York: Stein and Day, 1983.

Pugliese, Stanislao. *Bitter Spring: A Life of Ignazio Silone.* New York: Farrar, Straus and Giroux, 2009.

Saunders, Frances. *The Cultural Cold War.* New York: New Press, 1969.

Stwertka, Eve, and Margo Viscusi, eds. *Twenty-Four Ways of Looking at Mary McCarthy.* Westport, Conn.: Greenwood, 1996.

Sumner, Gregory. *Dwight Macdonald and the "Politics" Circle.* Ithaca: Cornell UP, 1996.

———. Email message, July 15, 2016.

Survey 26 (Spring 1982): 1–49. Tribute to Chiaromonte.

Todd, Olivier. *Albert Camus: A Life.* Trans. Benjamin Ivry. New York: Knopf, 1997.

Tucci, Maria. Interview, July 8, 2016.

Wieseltier, Leon. Review of *The Worm of Consciousness. New York Review of Books,* May 13, 1976: 45–48.

Wilson, Reuel. Email message, July 8, 2016.

Wreszin, Michael. *A Rebel in Defense of Tradition: The Life and Politics of Dwight Macdonald.* New York: Basic Books, 1994.

Young-Bruehl, Elisabeth. *Hannah Arendt: For the Love of the World.* New Haven: Yale UP, 1982.

Xan Fielding

Unpublished material from Charterhouse School; Harrow School; Imperial War Museum; National Archives, Kew; National Library of Scotland; New College, Oxford; Orley Farm School; Southern Illinois University (Durrell Papers); *Times Literary Supplement;* Travellers Club; and University of St. Andrews. Letters from Graham Colville on Cyprus, Robert Messenger and Terry Risk.

Beevor, Anthony. *Crete 1941: The Battle and the Resistance.* 1991; New York: Penguin, 2014.

Boulle, Pierre. *The Bridge over the River Kwai*. Trans. Xan Fielding. New York: Vanguard, 1954.

———. *My Own River Kwai*. Trans. Xan Fielding. New York: Vanguard, 1957.

Brenan, Gerald, and Ralph Partridge. *Best of Friends: The Brenan-Partridge Letters*. Selected and ed. Xan Fielding. London: Chatto and Windus, 1986.

Chatwin, Bruce. *Under the Sun: Letters*. Ed. Elizabeth Chatwin and Nicholas Shakespeare. New York: Viking, 2010.

Cooper, Artemis. *Patrick Leigh Fermor: An Adventure*. New York: New York Review Books, 2012.

Davis, Wes. *The Ariadne Objective: The Underground War to Rescue Crete from the Nazis*. London: Bantam, 2014.

Durrell, Lawrence, and Henry Miller. *A Private Correspondence*. Ed. George Wickes. New York: Dutton, 1964.

Fenwick, Simon. "Shank's Europe." *Times Literary Supplement,* November 16, 2012.

Fermor, Patrick Leigh. *Abducting a General: The Kreipe Operation and SOE in Crete*. London: John Murray, 2014.

———. *Between the Woods and the Water*. 1986; New York: New York Review Books, 2005.

———. Obituary of Xan Fielding, *Daily Telegraph,* August 20, 1991.

———. "Observations on a Marine Vulcan." *Twentieth Century Literature* 33 (1987): 305–7.

———. *A Time of Gifts*. 1977; London: Penguin, 1979.

Fermor, Patrick Leigh, and Deborah Devonshire. *In Tearing Haste: Letters between Deborah Devonshire and Patrick Leigh Fermor*. Ed. Charlotte Mosley. London: John Murray, 2008.

Fielding, Daphne. *The Adonis Garden*. London: Eyre & Spottiswoode, 1961.

———. *Mercury Presides*. New York: Harcourt, Brace, 1955.

————. *The Nearest Way Home.* London: Eyre & Spottiswoode, 1970.

Fielding, Xan. *Aeolus Displayed.* Francestown, N.H.: Typographeum, 1991.

————. "Another Durrell." *Twentieth Century Literature* 33 (1987): 303–4.

————. *Corsair Country: The Diary of a Journey along the Barbary Coast.* London: Secker & Warburg, 1958.

————. *Five Poems.* Rhodes, Greece: privately printed, 1946.

————. *Hide and Seek: The Story of a Wartime Agent.* 1954; Philadelphia: Paul Dry, 2013.

————. *A Hideous Disguise.* Foreword by Patrick Leigh Fermor. Francestown, N.H.: Typographeum, 1994.

————. *Images of Spain.* London: Hamlyn, 1991.

————. *The Money Spinner: Monte Carlo and Its Fabled Casino.* Boston: Little, Brown, 1977.

————. *One Man in His Time: The Life of Lieutenant-Colonel N. L. D. ("Billy") McLean, DSO.* London: Macmillan, 1990.

————. *The Stronghold: An Account of the Four Seasons in the White Mountains of Crete.* London: Secker & Warburg, 1953.

Fleming, Ann. *Letters.* Ed. Mark Amory. London: Collins Harvill, 1985.

Foot, M. R. D. "Fielding, Alexander Wallace." *Oxford Dictionary of National Biography.* Oxford: Oxford UP, 2004. 19:497–98.

Herrera, Hayden. *Arshile Gorky: His Life and Work.* New York: Farrar, Straus and Giroux, 2003.

Lawrence, D. H. *Lady Chatterley's Lover.* 1928; New York: Signet, 1959.

MacNiven, Ian. *Lawrence Durrell: A Biography.* London: Faber and Faber, 1998.

Messenger, Robert. "Xan Fielding: A Brief Life (1918–1991)" and foreword. *Hide and Seek* by Xan Fielding. Philadelphia: Paul Dry, 2013. Pp. ix–xxiii.

————. "Xan Fielding: A Brief Life (1918–1991)" and foreword. *The Stronghold* by Xan Fielding. Philadelphia: Paul Dry, 2013. Pp. ix–xxvi.

Mulley, Clare. *The Spy Who Loved: The Secrets and Lives of Christine Granville.* London: Macmillan, 2012.

Parker, Peter. *Isherwood.* London: Picador, 2004.

Partridge, Frances. *Diaries, 1939–1972.* Ed. Rebecca Wilson. London: Phoenix, 2001.

Psychoundakis, George. *The Cretan Runner: His Story of the German Occupation.* Trans. Patrick Leigh Fermor, annotated by the translator and Xan Fielding. London: John Murray, 1955.

Shakespeare, Nicholas. *Bruce Chatwin: A Biography.* New York: Doubleday, 2000.

Stannard, Martin. *Evelyn Waugh: The Later Years, 1939–1966.* New York: Norton, 1992.

Stroud, Rick. *Kidnap in Crete: The True Story of the Abduction of a Nazi General.* London: Bloomsbury, 2014.

Waugh, Evelyn. *Letters.* Ed. Mark Amory. New York: Ticknor & Fields, 1980.

Waugh, Evelyn, and Diana Cooper. *Letters.* Ed. Artemis Cooper. New York: Ticknor & Fields, 1992.

INDEX